THE
LABOR MARKET DYNAMICS
OF
ECONOMIC RESTRUCTURING

THE
LABOR MARKET DYNAMICS
OF
ECONOMIC RESTRUCTURING

The United States
and Germany in Transition

RONALD SCHETTKAT

PRAEGER

New York
Westport, Connecticut
London

Library of Congress Cataloging-in-Publication Data

Schettkat, Ronald.
    The labor market dynamics of economic restructuring : the United
States and Germany in transition / Ronald Schettkat.
        p.   cm.
    Includes bibliographical references and index.
    ISBN 0–275–93910–3 (alk. paper)
    1. United States—Economic policy—1981–   2. Germany—Economic
policy—1990–   3. Labor market—United States.   4. Labor market—
Germany.   I. Title.
    HC106.8.S34   1992
    331.12′042′0943—dc20   91–23688

British Library Cataloguing in Publication Data is available.

Library of Congress Catalog Card Number: 91–23688
ISBN: 0–275–93910–3

First published in 1992

Praeger Publishers, One Madison Avenue, New York, NY 10010
An imprint of Greenwood Publishing Group, Inc.

Printed in the United States of America

The paper used in this book complies with the
Permanent Paper Standard issued by the National
Information Standards Organization (Z39.48–1984).

10 9 8 7 6 5 4 3 2 1

Contents

Tables and Figures

TABLES

FIGURES

Preface

This study was supported by numerous institutions: A substantial part of the work was done when the author held an American Council of Learned Societies (ACLS) Fellowship (academic year 1988–89) and was located at Stanford University and at the University of California at Berkeley. In Berlin the work was supported by the Wissenschaftszentrum and the manuscript was completed while the author was a Fellow of the Royal Netherlands Academy of Arts and Science at the Netherlands Institute for Advanced Study (NIAS) in Wassenaar during the academic year 1990–91. The stimulating and "workaholic" atmosphere at NIAS made it possible to bring the work to a successful conclusion.

Although institutions are important, the research would not have been possible without the help and advice of numerous colleagues and friends. I would like to thank especially Eileen Appelbaum (Philadelphia and Washington), Peter Kalmbach (Bremen), and Kurt Rothschild (Vienna), as well as Katherine Abraham (Washington), Peter Albin (New York), Peter Auer (Berlin), Hans-Uwe Bach (Nuremberg), Bob Bednarzik (Washington), Christoph Büchtemann (Santa Monica), Rich Burkhauser (Syracuse), Ulrich Cramer (Nuremberg), Philip DeJong (Leiden), Bob Flanagan (Palo Alto), Aldi Hagenaars (Rotterdam), Bent Hansen (Berkeley), Jop Hartog (Amsterdam), Francis Horvath (Washington), Ron Kutscher (Washington), Jonathan Leonard (Berkeley), Ray Marshall (Austin), Egon Matzner (Berlin and Vienna), Hugh Mosley (Berlin), Mel Reder (Palo Alto), Günther Schmid (Berlin), Klaus Semlinger (Munich), David Soskice (Berlin and Oxford), Jules Theeuwes (Leiden), Lloyd Ulman (Berkeley), and Kurt Vogler-Ludwig (Munich). Needless to say, neither the mentioned colleagues nor the institutions are responsible for any remaining errors.

In addition I received support in Berlin from David Antal, Karin Figge, Kirsten Janiesch, Thomas Kirsch, Monika Nowotny, and the Wissenschafts-zentrum's superb library and staff. Finally, I would like to acknowledge the support and guidance of all of the editors at Praeger Publishers. Thanks to all of them.

THE
LABOR MARKET DYNAMICS
OF
ECONOMIC RESTRUCTURING

1

Outline: Economic Progress, Structural Change, and Labor Market Dynamics

1.1 INTRODUCTION

"There is a fact, a big unmistakable unsubtle fact: essentially everywhere in the modern industrial capitalist world, unemployment rates are much higher than they used to be two or three decades ago. Why is that?" (Solow 1986, S23). This question is at the center of this study, which is an investigation of theories and facts that might explain the rising unemployment rates in the United States and Germany. There have been, and still are, differences in the performance of the U.S. and the West German economies. The most obvious difference is the persistently high level of unemployment in West Germany and Europe in general since the mid-1970s accompanied by very modest employment growth. In contrast, the U.S. economy has added a tremendous number of jobs and has experienced decreasing unemployment rates in the 1980s. Other important differences are sectoral developments and the integration of the two economies in the world market.

Numerous explanations for these differences in economic trends have been put forward. The most prominent focus on the assumed differences in the flexibility of the labor market and, hence, on the ability to adjust to changing conditions—an ability demonstrated by the economies that have become better integrated in the world economy. The United States is often regarded as the major example of the job-creating potential of flexibility, whereas Germany is used as an example of an overly regulated labor market that has prevented employment from growing.

Economic theories still do not provide adequate explanations for the increase in unemployment. With great oversimplification, the deficiencies of the two main economic theories—neoclassical and Keynesian—might be characterized as focusing on individual characteristics alone (some neoclassicals) or not at all (some Keynesians). For some neoclassical economists, the aggregate either does not exist or is simply the sum of individual outcomes; for some Keynesian economists, labor markets are irrelevant. This is a description of the very extremes of a continuum. As usual in the real world, the position of most researchers will be found somewhere in between. To be clear from the beginning, the term "labor market" is used in this study as a synonym for a matching system that brings labor supply and demand together. It does not denote a market in the strict economic sense, in which prices are sufficient to direct the market to equilibrium.

In an ideal market model, unemployment could not be a problem. It simply could not exist, since necessary adjustments would have been made immediately. The same is true for a static economy, which does not change at all. The allocational function of the labor market is simply unnecessary. But the matching function of the labor market is of great importance if the assumptions of a static system and of perfect markets are relaxed. Even in an economy on a steady-state growth path; that is, an economy that does not change its structure, the labor market has to fulfill the matching function. This is even more important in a dynamic economy with competition between firms, structural change, and technological progress. A great deal of allocation—and, most importantly, reallocation—must be undertaken, and in non-ideal markets, friction will occur.

L. Pasinetti (1981) has identified three basic sources for economic change: (1) population growth and changes in participation, (2) technological progress causing productivity growth, and (3) demand shifts. These three developments change the structure of the economy continuously and cause friction in the labor market. "Some of the most serious troubles characterizing industrial economies arise precisely from the structural dynamics of employment" (Pasinetti and Scazzieri 1987, 527). The overall growth rate of an economy is the result of the weighted growth rates of the economy's individual industries. Industries can grow at different rates, and some may even shrink. Expanding and declining industries can coexist. Furthermore, recent empirical work shows that even within an industry, expanding and shrinking firms coexist during upswings as well as downturns (Leonard 1987b, Cramer and Koller 1988, König and Weißhuhn 1989). Another possible source of adjustments within industries and firms is technological progress requiring skill adjustments. The typical economy is not static but dynamic. Changes occur constantly, and there is a continuous process of growing and shrinking industries, growing and shrinking (even appearing and disappearing) firms, and changes in the demand for and supply of labor with certain skill characteristics.

There is no doubt in economic theories, whether neoclassical or Keynesian, that the dynamics mentioned are a source of unemployment (see chapter 2), but the amount of unemployment caused by these changes is disputed. Is unemployment cyclical or structural? For neoclassical economists, the ineffectiveness of labor market institutions causes frictional or structural unemployment because prices are not allowed to fulfill their functions. Demand deficiency cannot occur in a functioning market economy in the long run, according to Say's law. Keynesian economists, by contrast, have worked more on macroeconomic relationships, either leaving the "details" to others or simply neglecting them altogether. In mainstream microeconomics, the world after Keynes was as it had been before (Galbraith 1987), although some alternative approaches were developed (e.g., Kalecki 1954).

This situation has given way to the "second revolution in economics" (Tobin). The "menu for politicians" (Samuelson and Solow 1960) that allowed policy-makers to choose between unemployment and inflation through variations of demand lost its importance as a concept for politics during the 1970s, and the sloped Phillips curve became vertical in the long run (Friedman 1968; Phelps 1970a) and even in the short run (rational expectations). The Phillips curve concept (Lipsey 1965), however, was essentially the assumption that the unemployment rate is determined by demand in the economy, with an underlying implicit assumption about the functioning of the labor market. Another stylized description of the labor market that had received much less attention until recently is the Beveridge curve. The Beveridge curve links unemployment and vacancies (or unused labor supply and unsatisfied labor demand). Movements along a Beveridge curve describe variations in overall economic activity, whereas variations in the mismatch between supply and demand are displayed by variations in the curve's location (see chapters 2, 3, 5 and 6).

To what extent are changing dynamics over time or different dynamics in different countries responsible for rising unemployment rates or for different rates in different countries? The labor market can be regarded as being in equilibrium if flows between labor market categories balance, no matter what the level of unemployment is. In other words, equilibrium (balanced) unemployment could exist at high or low rates of unemployment. Within this concept of flow equilibrium (see sections 3.4, 5.5, and 6.5), unemployment is directly determined by labor market dynamics rather than by price variables. It is influenced by institutional arrangements, job and labor turnover, structural change, and other factors. Nevertheless, price variables—such as wage rates and differentials—may influence labor market dynamics. Still, in terms of direct effects, the emphasis is on variables of the economic system—such as stability of employment, job turnover, and skills—which themselves might be explained by price variables as well as by other variables.

Many researchers (e.g., Summers 1986) have concluded that the normal (other terms are equilibrium or natural) rate of unemployment must have risen in the United States as well as in Europe over the last decades. In other words, the full employment ratio that is not accompanied by inflationary pressures has decreased in the Western industrialized countries. But did the equilibrium rate of unemployment shift in Europe more than in the United States?

One answer to the question of why equilibrium unemployment rates have risen in Western industrialized countries might be sought not in the functioning of labor markets as such but in the necessity to adjust to a higher pace of structural change. Janet Yellen (1989, 65) has identified the question of whether cyclical unemployment is caused by sectoral rather than by aggregate shocks as a leading—"perhaps the leading question—in macroeconomics since the publication in 1982 of David Lilien's paper." Lilien (1982) has argued that cyclical unemployment should be interpreted as shifts in the "natural rate of unemployment" that are caused by restructuring rather than by demand deficiency. But Katherine Abraham and Lawrence Katz (1986) have shown that a considerable amount of unemployment can be explained by variations in aggregate demand rather than by sectoral shocks (see discussion in chapter 2). There is no doubt, however, that increasing structural change could be one explanation of rising equilibrium unemployment rates. Whether structural change has in fact increased is an empirical question.

As mentioned above, structural changes are not the only developments that make labor market mobility necessary. Firms grow and decline, which causes job turnover and hence labor turnover (see chapter 3 for the distinction between these concepts), and there is a certain amount of labor turnover that is not related to the job turnover or sectoral restructuring. These dynamic processes in the economy produce continuous flows, and an increase in these dynamics could cause equilibrium unemployment to increase.

The arguments made so far concentrate on the increasing mobility caused by dynamic economic development and are all related to the entry side of unemployment. Variables that focus more on the exit side of unemployment would concentrate on mismatch—that is, the differing skills provided by the unemployed and the skill requirements of jobs. A less intense search activity on the part of the unemployed may be one cause for increasing unemployment duration, and national differences may be explained by different regulations of the unemployment insurance system. It is also argued, however, that employers have become more reluctant to hire (Flanagan 1989), which might be due to various reasons. Uncertainties concerning future demand, employment regulations, and higher costs of firing may together have caused less hiring. In addition, higher skill requirements may have prolonged the matching process (Soskice 1990), or the choosiness of employers may simply have increased. Some of these variables would cause the duration of vacancies to increase, but some (e.g., a reluctance to hire) would cause vacancies not to appear at all.

Until recently, labor market analysis was based mainly on stock data, which are a suitable data source for the investigation of structural and aggregate phenomena; they do not allow for the analysis of processes behind the net changes identified by stock data. It is necessary to identify the dynamics in the labor market with information on flows. The flow data that have become available in recent years show that an enormous amount of labor market mobility is occurring every month. The view that the unemployed are a fixed block is far from reality, although long-term unemployment is increasingly important (see chapter 6).

The use of flow data to analyze questions of the mismatch in the labor market and the underlying labor market dynamics has been suggested (Krelle 1987, 330). These data are used in the analysis presented in this study of labor market dynamics in the United States and Germany. The aim is to develop a framework for the analysis of labor market dynamics based on concepts of flows rather than of stocks. Therefore, this study will link dynamic concepts of labor market adjustment to flow data, which are the only data source that allows for the investigation of processes.

It has also been suggested that a theory of structural unemployment does not exist and would be difficult to develop (Krelle 1987, 330). Some work on this issue has been done already (see chapters 2 and 3), and this study is intended as a contribution to a theory of structural unemployment in a dynamic economy.

1.2 ORGANIZATION OF THE STUDY

First, the various theories that try to explain unemployment are investigated. Chapter 2 begins with descriptions of the very basic competitive labor market model and the Keynesian approach. This step is followed by a discussion of more recent theoretical developments that are generally focused more on the functioning of the labor market. Theories dealing with the adjustment processes in particular are considered. Unemployment is increasingly regarded as a general phenomenon, rather than as one concentrated on specific groups only. High levels and long durations of unemployment, which used to be explained largely in terms of "individualized equilibrium explanations," have in recent years been explained in terms of "disequilibrium," a perspective that either emphasizes the interests of the employees in fixed wages (implicit contracts) or the interests of the employers in fixed wages (efficiency wage models).

Recent work in economic theory has also led to hypotheses that take asymmetrical developments into account. That is, past economic developments have been linked to current economic performance. In the case of unemployment, these theories have become known as "hysteresis." Different channels of hysteresis have been identified in order to explain persistently high levels of unemployment. The insider-outsider version of hysteresis is optimistic insofar as it does not assume that the unemployed are unemployable but rather that insiders keep outsiders out of employment. A more pessimistic version of hysteresis is that the unemployed lose their ability to work after some period of unemployment. Although there is empirical evidence that this is the case, there is also evidence that unemployment itself works as a selection criterion. It signals "lemon" to potential employers, a characteristic that seems to be especially true for the long-term unemployed. The concluding section of chapter 2 summarizes the hypotheses of the various theories and focuses on their dynamic aspects.

The dynamics of labor market analysis are discussed in a more formalized way in chapter 3. Possible ways of adjusting to changes in the labor market are delineated, and various indicators and measures of labor market dynamics are discussed systematically. In the final part of this chapter, the theoretical hypotheses developed from the labor market theories in chapter 2 are linked to the more formalized indicators in order to develop a framework for the empirical investigations. The hypotheses investigated in this study can be summarized under the following headings: (1) the wage structure has destroyed incentives for mobility, (2) the pace of structural change has increased, (3) insiders exclude outsiders from employment, (4) employers are reluctant to hire, (5) mismatch and bottlenecks have occurred, and (6) (long-term) unemployment is self-sustaining (hysteresis).

Before actual labor market dynamics in the United States and Germany are analyzed, chapter 4 gives a survey of the main trends in the two economies from the early 1960s on, including economic growth, productivity growth, the composition of the GDP (gross domestic product), the structure of the economies, and the pace of structural change. This section shows that citing differences in institutions to explain differentials in unemployment and employment trends in the United States and Germany might lead to hasty conclusions. In the 1960s, U.S. unemployment was high compared to that in Germany, and during that time, European institutions were quite often regarded as better able to promote employment growth. Today, the opposite is argued. In the meantime, however, important institutional changes have occurred. If these changes are to provide an explanation for differentials in the performance of the two economies, one has to show that they have had an effect within the countries. Before strong conclusions can be drawn from an international comparative analysis (the cross-sectional perspective), one must determine whether institutional changes have in fact had an impact on the functioning of the labor market within each economy (the longitudinal perspective; see Schettkat 1989b).

In chapters 5 and 6, indicators for labor market dynamics in the United States and Germany are presented and analyzed. Included are measures for the aggregate dynamics in the labor market, the decomposition of unemployment into an inflow and a duration component, and the decomposition of employment and unemployment flows. Labor and job turnover are then analyzed on the industry level, and various mismatch indicators and their trends are investigated. The last sections of chapters 5 and 6 contain an analysis of the "flow equilibrium rate of unemployment," and of the components of change. Chapter 7 summarizes the findings, and contrasts the empirical results with the theoretical hypotheses developed in chapters 2 and 3.

2

Labor Market Dynamics
and Economic Theory:
Explaining Unemployment

The first section of this chapter develops the main differences between alternative approaches to the analysis of labor markets. The following sections investigate specific aspects or approaches that focus on labor market adjustment processes rather than on levels of employment or unemployment. Discussion of the levels of employment or unemployment, however, cannot be omitted for they are closely related to these adjustment processes. In the last section, the discussion is summarized and conclusions are drawn for the analysis of adjustment processes in the labor market.

2.1 THEORETICAL CONCEPTS OF THE LABOR MARKET:
THE BASIC COMPETITIVE LABOR MARKET MODEL
AND KEYNESIAN APPROACHES

Two principal approaches to labor market analysis can be distinguished in economics—those based on the neoclassical model and those in the Keynesian tradition. These labels are used throughout this study to cover a broad variety of models. Other, perhaps better, labels would be equilibrium and disequilibrium models. Neoclassical models have become increasingly sophisticated in recent decades, but they are nevertheless still based on strong assumptions about human behavior. The theoretical developments in this line of research might be described as ''normal'' science (Rothschild 1984), because the emphasis has been on the advancement of the theory within the same scientific paradigm (Kuhn 1970). This does not mean that the specifics of labor markets are not taken into account, but rather that they are integrated in the equilibrium model in a way that allows one to make use of the traditional instruments. As Eli Ginzberg (1976) has put it, the neoclassical model can be classified as a "commodity approach," since labor markets are in principle analyzed in the same way as other markets.

On the other hand, economists in the Keynesian (and post-Keynesian) school of thought have developed somewhat different approaches based on less strict assumptions about human behavior. This school, although dominated by macroanalysis, emphasizes the interrelationship of the individual and institutions within the society (Appelbaum 1982). This line of theory suggests the distinctiveness of labor markets from other markets and has been characterized as the "human resources approach" (Ginzberg 1976).

2.1.1 The Basic Competitive Labor Market Model

The basic neoclassical labor market (textbook) model, which still defines the preferred framework for many economic labor market analyses, is based on several well-known assumptions: All workers are identical in terms of their skills (homogeneous labor); all jobs have the same skill requirements; every economic actor has information about market trends (prices, wages) at little or no cost; adjustments are made immediately; workers are lazy and do not enjoy working; workers do not have preferences for specific employers and employers do not have preferences for specific workers; marginal productivity is a decreasing function of labor input; and technology is constant. Prices of goods are determined in competitive markets and are equal to their marginal costs. Every production factor is paid for according to the value of its marginal productivity; in other words, wages are equal to the value of the marginal product of labor. This basic model leads to equilibrium (full employment) with one wage rate for every (identical) worker. Variations in demand across firms or sectors will be adjusted rapidly by a high mobility of labor between companies and across sectors.

The equilibrium wage is the only wage rate at which full employment occurs. Lower or higher wage rates can be achieved only if the demand or supply curves shift as a result of external shocks or institutional changes. For example, a shift of the demand curve toward the origin will result in a lower wage and a lower level of employment if the supply curve is not completely inelastic. Despite this shift, however, the labor market remains in equilibrium because lower wages will cause some workers to prefer leisure instead of income (work). If the market wage is below their reservation wage, they adjust their supply of labor either by shortening their working time or withdrawing from the labor market. In this system, disequilibrium or involuntary unemployment (section 2.2.2) cannot be deduced from within (Ostleitner 1978, 89). Only transitory wage differentials can occur in this basic model since it tends toward equilibrium immediately. Disequilibrium or involuntary unemployment cannot persist because workers will move from firms with lower wages to firms with higher wages, accept wage cuts, or withdraw from the market. The whole market will switch back to equilibrium, and wage equality will be the result (see Meidner and Hedborg 1984).

In fact, labor markets are obviously not a "one commodity" market but are instead distinct markets (Phelps 1970a). Working conditions, skill requirements of jobs, skills of workers, motivation of workers, and wages, for example, are not equal; they vary. Adjustments are not easy to make and take time. There is no auctioneer who transmits information on current wages and brings demand and supply into equilibrium. Most importantly, labor contracts are distinct from sales contracts (Simon 1959). Capital can be used without restrictions but not labor. "However, having hired a laborer, management faces considerable restriction on how it can use its labor. Not only are there legal restrictions, but the willing cooperation of labor itself must usually be obtained for the firm to make best use of the labor service" (Akerlof 1982, 545). Periods with zero or near zero unemployment seldom occur in economic history, and for about fifteen years, highly industrialized Western countries have suffered from high rates of unemployment.

These facts have been recognized by neoclassical theory. Indeed, neoclassical economics has integrated many real world phenomena in recent analyses. Alfred Marshall (1890, 465) himself, unlike many of his successors, was eager to mention the specifics of labor markets. Many of the theoretical attempts to explain the "non-clearing" of labor markets can be grouped according to the definition or interpretation of equilibrium that they employ.

First, it is argued that some unemployment is consistent with equilibrium (full employment) in the labor market; this is true for both Keynesian and neoclassical arguments (section 2.2). Friction causes unemployment to be positive even with full employment. In neoclassical economics, however, unemployment is regarded as mainly voluntary, as the consequence of optimizing behavior or of wage rigidities. This school of thought, therefore, attempts to explain real unemployment largely by factors related to the individual's decision making, "search theories" (section 2.2.2) being a case in point. Market imperfections or rigidities are also seen as a factor causing unemployment. There is some "natural rate" of unemployment in the economy that can be reduced only by measures that improve the matching process but not by expansionary policies.

Recently, the level of the "natural rate of unemployment" has been linked to the pace of technological and structural change in the economy and, hence, to the necessity for labor mobility (Lilien 1982, section 2.5.3). Demand deficiency in the economy is not regarded as relevant for the explanation of unemployment. It is supply that matters in these lines of argumentation. In principle, the labor market tends toward full employment equilibrium.

In the real world, equality of wages has never been observed, and (money) wages are sticky in case of a decreasing demand for labor or rising unemployment. Instead, persistent wage differentials between sectors have been observed. These wage differentials still exist even if occupations are controlled for statistically, nor is there evidence that persistent wage differentials between sectors can be explained by variations of working conditions (section 2.3). If empirical evidence is not in line with theory, Karl Popper's criteria would suggest falsification. In practice, however, theories are extended or the empirical evidence is declared to be insufficient (Kalmbach 1989b, 162–63). The stickiness of wages is considered in implicit contrast models, insider-outsider approaches, and efficiency wage theories (section 2.3).

As will be shown here and has been shown in other work, the neoclassical development of theory still rests on the central assumptions of "rational behavior" and of the market as a mechanism that tends toward equilibrium in principle. Concepts of "super rationality" (Nelson and Winter 1982) or the "real equilibrium" have been introduced. Referring to the attempts of some neoclassical economists—"search theorists" specifically—Kurt Rothschild (1978, 27) has stated: "Their research seems to be oriented less to a better and better theoretical understanding of labor market reality but rather to a search for more and more refined methods which shall bring undeniable unemployment in line with the premises of the general market and equilibrium theory" (author's translation). Lester Thurow (1983, 173) has commented on these attempts: "The basic thrust of labor economics in the 1950s, 1960s, and 1970s has been to erase the distinction between labor and other factors of production." As for approaches trying to integrate the role of unions, Lloyd Ulman (1989, 1) has written that some models "make unorganized labor markets behave, in some important respects, as if they were unionized," and, conversely, some models make labor markets with unions behave, in some important respects, as "if they were not."

2.1.2 Keynes's Explanation of Unemployment

Although John Maynard Keynes, post-Keynesians, and new-Keynesians do not deny that a higher pace of structural change can increase friction in the labor market (Pasinetti 1981), they are reluctant to declare unemployment "natural." For them, the market system is not stable but rather unstable, and demand is the most important factor in explaining unemployment, which is assumed to be involuntary.

"Keynesian unemployment" has become the label for unemployment caused by deficient demand in the economy. Lagging effective demand was classified by Keynes as the main cause for involuntary unemployment, although he also regarded frictional unemployment and voluntary unemployment as possible categories of unemployment. The Keynesian "revolution" brought the distinction between "micro" and "macro" economics. According to this view, demand for labor depends on effective demand, which determines the equilibrium level of employment (Davidson 1983, 106). It is indirectly linked to demand in goods markets (hierarchy of markets). Thus, wages are a cost and a demand factor at the same time; the microrelationship between wages and costs, on the one hand, and demand, on the other, cannot be generalized (Keynes 1936, 259–60; the fallacy of composition, Galbraith 1987, 234). It is therefore sufficient to relax the assumption that there is an auctioneer who brings demand and supply into equilibrium and thus introduce historical time. "To be a Keynesian, one need only realize the difficulties of finding the market clearing vector" (Leijonhufvud 1967, 404).

In his *General Theory,* Keynes showed that a persistent unemployment equilibrium could exist in the economy. He did not use the term "equilibrium" in the classical or neoclassical sense to describe a situation where all factors of production are fully utilized but rather to characterize situations that persist over some time. Keynes criticized Say's theorem, which states that supply and demand will balance. Keynes allowed for savings not being spent, and unspent revenues reduce aggregate demand for goods and services and thus for output and employment. Keynes emphasized uncertainty as a reason for fluctuations in investment, but this aspect was lost in the interpretation of Keynes's theory by John Hicks (1937). The IS-LM diagram in which Hicks showed an equilibrium between goods and money markets omitted Keynes's concept of uncertainty and paved the way for the neoclassical interpretation of the Keynesian theory in the "neoclassical synthesis" (Kromphardt 1987, 64). In the "neoclassical synthesis," an unemployment equilibrium is just a special case of the neoclassical theory called wage rigidity.

Keynesian analysis was reproached by its critics on two main counts: the inconsistency between Keynesian macroanalysis with neoclassical microanalysis and the lack of microfoundations for Keynesian analysis (Rothschild 1988a, 111–12). Keynes invited some of the criticism when he used the traditional concept of decreasing marginal rates of output in his general theory. The maximum real wage that can be paid decreases, as a function of the marginal product, with increasing labor input. Thus, increasing levels of employment are accompanied by decreasing real wages.

It is not clear, however, that the marginal product of labor decreases with increasing inputs. Later (1939), Keynes became convinced by some of his critics (Dunlop 1938; Tarshis 1939) that real wages and employment could be positively correlated. Something other than the assumed production function with decreasing rates of return could apply (decreasing or constant marginal costs); in the case of underutilized capacity (Kalmbach 1989, 165), there is no reason to assume decreasing marginal productivity. It is assumed that the negative relation between the maximum real wage and labor input does not hold below this maximum. Up to this point, the labor demand curves are vertical (Davidson and Smolensky 1964). Furthermore, empirical trends, such as those for Germany, show that labor input and productivity growth are positively linked (Kromphardt 1987, 67). In post-Keynesian economics, marginal productivity of labor and real wages on the one side and the demand for labor on the other side are linked only very weakly, if at all (Appelbaum 1982, 130).

Keynes argued in his general theory that the real wage is not directly determined in wage negotiations and that labor supply does not respond to real wage changes but that workers are instead more interested in their money wages, which determine their position in the income hierarchy of society (Tobin 1972, 3). "Whilst workers usually resist a reduction in money-wages, it is not their practice to withdraw their labor whenever there is a rise in the price of wage-goods" (Keynes 1936, 9). Money wage cuts can affect workers very unevenly, whereas an increase in the price level affects all workers (more or less) in the same way and hence does not change the relative wage. The individual is nested in the society. This fact distinguishes the labor economics of Keynes and the post-Keynesians from neoclassical economics. In Keynes and post-Keynesian economics, labor supply decisions are thus influenced mainly by societal, institutional factors (Rothschild 1978, 25; Appelbaum 1982), the individual is influenced by other individuals (Duesenberry 1949), and therefore, preferences are not fixed (Schettkat 1987, 1989b).

The resistance of workers to cuts in nominal wages, although explicitly linked to social factors and the fact that the individual is embedded in society (Keynes 1936, 14; Hagemann 1988), was labeled as money illusion or simply irrationality by neoclassical economics. This view stems to some extent from Keynes's failure to spell out in sufficient detail the underlying causes of the downward inflexibility of money wages (Trevithick 1976, 328). Nominal wage stickiness was integrated into the neoclassical framework as wage rigidity in the neoclassical synthesis (Piore 1979a, xiii), and Keynes's general theory became a special case of classical and neoclassical economics.

Keynes also made an argument against the assumption in neoclassical economics that the real wage is directly determined in the bargaining process. "There may exist no expedient by which labour as a whole can reduce its real wage to a given figure by making revised money bargains with the entrepreneur" (Keynes 1936, 13). In full competitive markets, nominal wage reductions would be followed by price reductions, which in turn might increase the real value of nominally reduced wages (Keynes 1936, 269). Bargaining is about money wages, and the real wage is determined later by price variations.

Most important in the context of labor market dynamics is frictional unemployment. Keynes expected frictional unemployment always to be positive in a nonstationary economy. Frictional unemployment could be caused by (1) shifts in demand across products and a false anticipation of these changes, (2) a lag in the response to shifts, and (3) the time needed for adjustments. Keynes obviously did not expect zero unemployment when the economy works at full employment. Richard Kahn (1976, 27) has reported that in Keynes's view, an unemployment rate of 6.5 percent was "normal" (in September 1930). When Keynes defined an unemployment rate of 6.5 percent as normal, the actual unemployment rate was about 20 percent in the United Kingdom, and, of course, his "target" has to be seen in light of experience. "Full employment" is the great ideological label in the general theory, as Joan Robinson (1962, 109) has written, but Keynes used labels like a "satisfactory level of employment" or "high and stable employment" when he was writing on practical politics.

Robinson (1973, 182) herself defined "full employment" in her early writings in a manner very similar to "natural" rate approaches (see section 2.2), but with the emphasis on money wages: "The point of full employment is the point at which every impediment on the side of labour to a rise in money wages finally gives way." In a later comment on this statement, she wrote that a situation representing almost full employment had never been experienced when she made that statement. She corrected her view, denying the assumption that a certain rate of unemployment would yield constant wages (Robinson 1973, 175). She also doubted that the distinction between frictional and demand deficient unemployment is a useful one in practical analysis: "It seems preferable to say that full employment, in a precise sense, can never be attained so long as friction exists, rather than to use 'full employment' in an imprecise sense in which it can be said to be attainable, such unemployment as remains being vaguely attributed to frictions" (Robinson 1937, 42).

Still, the theoretical definitions that Keynes gave of normal or frictional unemployment are partly comparable to Milton Friedman's definition of "natural" unemployment (see section 2.2). This might be the reason that the basic concept of the "natural rate of unemployment" is widely accepted in economics, although there is, of course, substantial disagreement about its level and trend. But it is accepted that the frictional rate of unemployment is influenced by changes in the economy and the functioning of the matching process. Economists in the tradition of thought developed by Keynes have concentrated their work, as Keynes himself did, on the macroeconomic aspects of economics. Little work has been done on a "Keynesian micro foundation" of economics. "In microeconomics the market was, as before, also the business firm and the entrepreneur" (Galbraith 1987, 235). In macroeconomics, new relations were developed, but at the microlevel, the neoclassical system remained largely intact. Keynes did provide hints for a different theory of individuals' and firms' behavior, although some alternative approaches (e.g., Kalecki 1954) were developed. A separation between micro- and macroeconomics developed. "This separation was important; it was at the very heart of the great compromise of Keynes with the classical traditions, the compromise which presented the market nexus" (Galbraith 1987, 268).

Not many articles from a Keynesian or post-Keynesian perspective can be found if one is interested in structural change and the adjustment processes that follow in the labor market. Approaches in the neoclassical tradition clearly dominate this area.

2.1.3 Involuntary Unemployment and the Quality of Jobs

A continuous concern in economics is the question of whether unemployment is voluntary or involuntary. Of course, the answer has important political implications for whether or not the society should fight unemployment and whether unemployment is an individual or a societal problem (see Brown 1983). Important also is the question of whether unemployment is individually voluntary or individually involuntary but collectively voluntary. At least in current scientific discussions among economists, the view of individually voluntary unemployment has become very rare. Rather, institutions in a broad sense have become an important explanation for collectively "chosen" unemployment. This, however, is a very broad definition that could apply to arguments relying on wage rigidities in some sense as well as to arguments relying on demand deficiency.

From the very beginning, however, the dispute about voluntary or involuntary unemployment showed that the answer depends heavily on the political and societal context. This is true for those who argue that unemployment is mainly voluntary as well as for those who argue that it is mainly involuntary. Some definitions of involuntary unemployment and its societal context are given in the following paragraphs. Although the concepts are based substantially on the specification of the labor supply function, these aspects cannot be elaborated here and are touched upon only occasionally (for details, see Schettkat 1987).

In the basic neoclassical labor market framework, unemployment is voluntary since it is assumed that low wages could always bring people into jobs. If unemployment exists, wages are too high. People choose unemployment because their reservation wage exceeds the market wage. By contrast, Keynes (1936, 15) regarded unemployment mainly as involuntary, and he defined it as follows: "Men are involuntary unemployed if in the event of a small rise in the price of wage-goods relatively to the money-wage, both the aggregate supply of labour willing to work for the current money-wage and the aggregate demand for it at that wage would be greater than the existing volume of employment." This somewhat complicated definition was later "translated" into simpler words by Richard Kahn (1976, 21): "There is involuntary unemployment to the extent that, at the current money wage and with the current price level, the number of men desiring to work exceeds the number of men for whose labour there is a demand."

Obviously, labor markets are seldom in equilibrium in the sense of little or no unemployment. In the neoclassical synthesis, it is wage rigidity that prevents employment expansions. In recent decades, more of the real world "rigidities" have been integrated into these models. The fact that individual workers, although qualified for jobs, could not price themselves into employment was explained by group or social optimalization (e.g., implicit contracts, hiring and firing costs, insider-outsider approaches, and efficiency wage models).

Martin Feldstein (1976) has distinguished between individual involuntary unemployment and collectively chosen voluntary unemployment since, in the case of implicit contracts, the collective has voluntarily chosen this "wage package." Efficiency wage models (section 2.3.3.2) provide an economic rationale for firms paying wages higher than the market clearing wage and, hence, for the existence of involuntary unemployment. It could be argued, however, that paying a wage above the market clearing wage is a reaction by firms to (voluntary) shirking that might occur otherwise (Spahn 1986). In this sense, unemployment could be classified as collectively voluntary.

Arthur Lindbeck and Dennis Snower (1985, 49) have given two independent definitions of situations of involuntary unemployment: (1) those in which unemployed workers unsuccessfully seek jobs for which they are just as qualified as the current job holders at the prevailing real wage (for a more precise definition, see Lindbeck and Snower 1986, 236), and (2) those in which unemployed workers seek jobs at real wages that fall short of their potential contribution to society. Lindbeck and Snower regard the "involuntariness" as a private phenomenon in the first case and as a social one in the second case (Lindbeck and Snower 1985, 49). Thus, only workers who require a wage higher than their potential contribution to the economy should be regarded as the "voluntary" unemployed. Unemployment caused by demand deficiency is, by definition (2) of Lindbeck and Snower, social voluntary unemployment since it could be prevented by appropriate policies. In this view, all unemployment can be classified as socially "voluntary" because it is always influenced by structures or political power in society (Schmid 1980). But it is involuntary from the individual's viewpoint. It is important that modern neoclassical economists no longer blame the individual for high levels of unemployment, as they had when following the main view in the 1970s, when individually optimizing searching was put forward as the main reason for unemployment.

Skill differentials and different qualifications are not taken into account in Keynes's original definition of involuntary unemployment, but they are, of course, important in labor markets with nonhomogeneous labor. George Akerlof and Janet Yellen (1986a, 11) have defined involuntary unemployment against the background of dual labor markets: "And although it is true that every unemployed worker might be able to get a secondary job (so that in one sense there is no involuntary unemployment), it is also true that unemployed workers would be more than willing to work in primary sector jobs at prevailing wage rates. In that sense such workers are involuntary unemployed." This definition of involuntary unemployment is broader than that usually applied in statistics since people currently working at jobs below their skill potentials are also included. It brings the quality of work into the discussion and points to social (opportunity) costs that result from the fact that part of the work force is forced into jobs that allow workers to produce only a part of their contribution to society. In this sense, the U.S. job expansion was paid for by slow growth in real wages and productivity. Some additional employment reflects a worsening, not an improvement, in economic well-being (Freeman 1988b, 299).

Commenting about the possibility that skilled workers could accept lower-skilled, lower-paid jobs than they used to have and about the conclusion that their unemployment should be classified as voluntary, Bob Solow (1985, S33) has written: "I think I once pointed out that, by this standard, all American soldiers who were killed in Vietnam could be counted as suicides since they could have deserted, emigrated to Canada or shot themselves in the foot, but did not." He, therefore, has suggested a definition of involuntary unemployment from the "economist's point of view," whereby involuntary unemployment exists whenever "the marginal (consumption) value of leisure is less than the going real wage in occupations for which they are qualified. That definition covers underemployment as well as total unemployment, and it covers both the skilled mechanic who does not take work as a sweeper and the one who does" (Solow 1985, S33).

This last definition of involuntary unemployment—not included in unemployment statistics—is particularly relevant if the quality of job growth is discussed. Are workers in jobs with wages substantially below the average employed or unemployed? These low paid jobs are often accepted as long as the economy has an excess supply of labor, but workers would switch to other jobs if they were to become available (Akerlof, Rose, and Yellen 1989). Recent work seems increasingly to accept the basic fact that theories must take into account that labor markets are distinct from goods markets and that the assumptions of a stylized market theory cannot be applied (Rothschild 1978, 31). Individuals cannot be blamed for acting under current laws and institutional arrangements (Rothschild 1978, 31).

2.2 UNEMPLOYMENT AND INFLATION: THE PHILLIPS CURVE AND THE "NATURAL RATE OF UNEMPLOYMENT"

2.2.1 The Phillips Curve

The Phillips curve (Phillips 1958) depicts the inverse relationship between wage rises (inflation) and unemployment. With the modification made by Paul Samuelson and Bob Solow (1960) and the theoretical foundation provided by Richard Lipsey (1965), the Phillips curve became one of the most influential economic concepts of the 1960s and 1970s (Tobin 1972). The shape of the Phillips curve suggested a conflicting relationship between wage and price stability on the one hand and low unemployment on the other. It was regarded as the "menu of choice" (Samuelson and Solow 1960) for policy-makers, as can be illustrated by the famous statement by West Germany's former chancellor Helmut Schmid, who in the mid-1970s declared that he preferred 5 percent inflation to 5 percent unemployment.

The Phillips curve posed theoretical problems for both Keynesians and neoclassical economists. Keynesians assumed that inflation would not occur before unemployment was reduced to a minimum, while neoclassical economists regarded the level of the real wage as important for the determination of unemployment (Rothschild 1988b, 97). Wage changes (inflation) should theoretically bring the labor market either into or out of equilibrium, but the Phillips relation suggested that zero inflation (wage increase) exists with positive unemployment (disequilibrium) in the labor market.

For both schools of thought, the crucial question is how much unemployment is caused by structural factors and how much is caused by demand deficiency (e.g., Council of Economic Advisers 1962). According to Lipsey (1965, 214), the amount of structural and frictional unemployment (for definitions, see Standing 1983) and of demand deficient unemployment is defined politically. That is, unemployment that can be reduced by demand expansion until the acceptable rate of inflation is reached is due to demand deficiency. Lipsey has maintained that the remaining amount is structural/frictional and can be reduced only by shifts of the Phillips curve, implying the improved functioning of the matching process. (For a discussion of such measures, see Holt 1970b; Meidner and Hedborg 1984; Jackman, Layard, Nickell, and Wadhwani 1990; Carlin and Soskice 1990.) Frictional unemployment was regarded as permanent or removable only at unacceptable costs (Lipsey 1965, 214), so this point might define full employment. At zero excess demand (zero inflation) within one specific labor market, the resulting unemployment is caused only by frictions in this specific market. For the aggregate labor market, the corresponding situation is determined by the distribution of unemployment and vacancies across industries.

Keynesians or "policy choice theorists" have regarded unemployment as caused mainly by deficient demand, whereas "structuralists" have believed that the matching process is most important. Still, Keynesians have never denied that unemployment is caused to some extent by friction (within a specific labor market) and by structural factors (depending on the distribution of unemployment and vacancies across different labor markets).

In the late 1970s, however, when stagflation (rising inflation and persistent unemployment) occurred, the structuralists' view became the dominant paradigm in economic policy. The Phillips trade-off between inflation and unemployment was heavily criticized by economists who argued that unemployment was either voluntary or structural; hence, it could not be reduced by an increase in aggregate demand, at least not in the long run.

2.2.2 The "Natural Rate of Unemployment": The New Microeconomics

The trade-off between unemployment and inflation and the concomitant options for government policies were questioned first of all by Milton Friedman and Edmund Phelps. They argued that the Phillips relation was valid only in the short run but that, after a time of expansionary demand policies, the curve shifts upward. According to them, deficit spending could increase inflation but it could not reduce unemployment in the long run. An unemployment rate below the "natural rate" would require continuously increasing inflation (Sawyer [1987, 10] has also mentioned a "natural concept" requiring general equilibrium). As Friedman (1968, 8) asserted, the locus of the long-run (augmented) Phillips curve was a vertical line at the "natural rate of unemployment." In his view, there was no policy choice between inflation and unemployment in the long run, because unemployment could not be made to fall below the "natural rate" permanently by demand policies. He maintained that only structural cures could reduce the "natural rate of unemployment." Other labels, although sometimes used with slightly different meanings, include non-accelerating inflation rate of unemployment (NAIRU), steady-state unemployment rate, full employment rate of unemployment, and equilibrium rate.

The "natural rate of unemployment" was defined as the rate of unemployment that is consistent with equilibrium in the economy. It does not represent unused labor and cannot be equated with demand deficiency in the economy. As the trade-off between inflation and unemployment had been the dominant economic policy paradigm during the 1960s and early 1970s, the concept of the "natural rate of unemployment" was one of the most powerful and influential in economics during the late 1970s and 1980s, drawing its strength from the "microfoundations" of the economic process.

Friedman (1968, 8) defined the "natural rate of unemployment" as the level that would come out of the Walrasian system of general equilibrium, provided that the actual structural characteristics of the labor and commodity markets are imbedded in the model, including market imperfections, stochastic variability in demand and supplies, the cost of gathering information about job vacancies and labor availabilities, the cost of mobility, and so on. Accordingly, the "natural rate" is not natural in the sense that it cannot be changed at all—by nature—but instead is imbedded in the social and institutional structure of society. Contrary to the common view, economists from this school of thought therefore regard institutions as an important variable for the explanation of unemployment, although they think about institutions mainly in terms of impediments to the otherwise well-functioning markets. Consequently, their policy proposals are attempts to shape the institutional framework to achieve a higher degree of congruence with the ideal market model, which is in principle regarded as the most efficient institution for the clearance of labor markets.

Even expectations are important in this line of analysis. Adaptive expectations are a key variable for the explanation of a vertical long-run Phillips curve because a permanent reduction of the unemployment rate requires increasing rates of inflation. A more radical version is even based on the assumption of a vertical Phillips curve in the short run. "Rational expectations" theorists (Sargent 1973) have claimed that supposedly rational economic agents will foresee the above-postulated development and that a trade-off between inflation and unemployment does not exist even in the short run; the short-run "Phillips curve" is also a vertical line. Only unforeseen shocks can lead the actual unemployment rate to fluctuate around the "natural rate."

Still, it has to be explained why the "natural rate of unemployment" is positive. The "new microeconomics," as developed by various researchers

(Phelps 1970a), provided a detailed theoretical foundation for the "natural rate of unemployment." The main problem was to find an explanation for a positive rate of unemployment in the general neoclassical framework. The Walrasian system's postulate of complete information was removed, and the notion of expectations and adaptive expectations was introduced (Phelps 1970a, 4). In other words, one of the two conditions that yield an economic equilibrium in the Walrasian system—(1) no surprise or full information and (2) no rationing (prices clear markets)—was relaxed, but it was still assumed that prices can, in principle, clear labor markets. With the removal of "complete information," some disequilibrium in the form of "search unemployment" is allowed for. In short, the "auctioneer" who collects demand and supply information and sets the equilibrium price does not exist in the new microeconomics. That auctioneer's function was replaced by the production of information (Stigler 1962) in the form of search unemployment. Consequently, search unemployment is regarded as a productive activity.

Phelps has used the analogy of islands to describe the labor market as a system split up into informational subunits. "To learn the wage on an adjacent island, the worker must spend the day travelling to that island to sample its wage instead of spending the day at work" (Phelps 1970a, 6). It was assumed that searching is done more easily if workers are unemployed rather than if they are searching while on the job (Phelps 1970b, 133). In this view, collecting information (the task of the auctioneer in the Walrasian model) needs time that would otherwise be spent at work. Search unemployment is therefore comparable to a productive activity because it results in a more optimal allocation of labor in the economy. It benefits the searcher who is therefore voluntarily unemployed.

Besides search unemployment, the new microeconomics defined two additional forms of unemployment: wait unemployment, which is voluntary unemployment as well but is caused by stochastic short-term demand variations and fixed wages, and queue unemployment, which is involuntary unemployment caused by an excess supply of labor or wage stickiness.

Wait unemployment is voluntary unemployment. Workers choose to be unemployed temporarily rather than to adjust their wages according to stochastic demand variations. The wage is set at a level that meets average demand, but workers do not accept wage reductions in times of slack demand. Examples of people working in this kind of labor market are professionals like lawyers, architects, or consultants, who set their wages according to an average demand and do not vary their wage/prices with stochastic fluctuations in demand but choose leisure instead. The concept behind this form of wait unemployment is that demand would be higher at lower prices and vice versa but that such workers prefer income variations instead of wage variations. This conception underlies models of implicit contracts as well (see section 2.3.3.1).

The professionals mentioned by Phelps are distinguished from ordinary employees since professionals can vary their working hours freely and are thus only partially "unemployed." A similar concept has been used in a life-cycle context. It is argued that during low-wage periods, people withdraw from employment because leisure during such times entails fewer opportunity costs; therefore, "choosing" unemployment during these periods is rational and maximizes lifetime wealth (Brunner, Cuikerman, and Meltzer 1980). Rothschild (1988b, 34) has considered these explanations absurd since they try to keep the theory's standard under any circumstances.

Queue unemployment is involuntary and is caused by job rationing, a link that is difficult to explain in the framework of neoclassical economics in general. " 'Job rationing' occurs when a worker is unable to find work at a firm despite his willingness to work for less than some already employed worker who is broadly like him in ability and skill" (Phelps 1970b, 133). A simple explanation is the "monopoly power" of unions, setting wages too high for a clearance of the labor market (see the section on wages, 2.3). But why does unemployment exist in countries with weak unions? Why are wages sticky in nonunion companies? And why do employers not simply hire non-union labor at a lower wage? How can it happen, and what possible economic rationale is behind it?

In the new microeconomics, sticky wages and thus job rationing were explained by the positive marginal recruitment costs of labor. Firms may pay wages to a buffer stock of idle or near idle workers to ensure their ability to meet randomly high demands for their products (Phelps 1970a, 13–14). Moreover, the risk of losing workers if the wage rate is too low has also been mentioned in the new microeconomics (Phelps 1970a, 14). These principal arguments are further developed under labels like "efficiency wage models" and "insider-outsider theories" (see sections 2.3.3.2, 2.5.2).

With respect to dynamics in the labor market and, hence, to inflows into employment and unemployment and outflows from these categories, the new microeconomics is based on the assumption that the "natural rate" is influenced—under the condition of imperfect information—by (1) unexpected wage variations, (2) higher productivity growth caused by higher labor mobility and higher skill flexibility (Phelps 1970b, 158–59), (3) higher growth of the labor supply, assuming that the new entrants' unemployment is caused by imperfect information (Phelps 1970b, 149), and (4) product-demand shifts and nonuniform technological progress (Phelps 1970b, 132).

The first argument is central to the new microeconomics since it establishes the main reason for job searching, but it is a short-run phenomenon. Arguments 2, 3, and 4, by contrast, determine the level of the "natural rate of unemployment" in the longer run. In neoclassical theory, they are linked to argument 1, since the wage rate is the signal in the market. They are set apart here, however, because variations of wages can be the result of stochastic demand shocks, for instance, and are not necessarily linked to arguments 2, 3, and 4, which emphasize more the long-run changes in the economy. In any case, the above-mentioned changes result in labor market mobility. That is, the higher the stochastic wage variations, the greater the flows between employment and unemployment and vice versa. The higher the pace of structural and technological change, the higher the labor market flows.

The relationship between quits and the level of economic activity is not clear in the new microeconomics. A positive relation (Phelps 1970b; Alchian 1970) as well as a negative one (Holt 1970a) has been assumed. Edmund Phelps (1970a, 10) has noted that the assumption of a negative association between quit rates and the unemployment rate involves the phenomenon of job rationing in the labor market. For Armen Alchian, a negative relation is inexplicable as well. He has argued that the same unexpected wage rise that shortens the search process of the unemployed should cause some employees to stay on because they experience an unexpected wage rise in their current jobs.

A positive correlation between quits and unemployment (or a negative correlation between quits and economic activity) has become identified with the new microeconomics and the search theories of unemployment (Mortensen 1986), although some of Charles Holt's arguments seem to diverge from this view. According to Phelps (1970b) and Alchian (1970), unemployment is explained by quits (into unemployment) that are caused by a decrease in wages or by an increase that is less than the expected one. Imperfect information poses the problem that the individual employee initially does not know whether changes in wages are affecting him or the company solely or whether such changes are a general phenomenon. A decrease in wages or an increase less than the expected one therefore increases quits. Workers start to search for another job, and this search is done while they are unemployed. It follows that stagnation of the economy and unemployment are positively linked, a view that no one would contest, but such unemployment is voluntary since it is caused by voluntary action of the employees. It is search unemployment.

To summarize, the new microeconomics has provided a detailed theoretical foundation for a positive equilibrium rate of unemployment, "the natural rate," but unemployment is still classified as mainly voluntary. A lack of effective demand in the economy cannot be a reason for unemployment if prices are set at the proper level: "macroeconomic theory does not explain why demand decreases cause unemployment rather than immediate wage and price adjustments in labor and non-human resources" (Alchian 1970, 27). Explanations of unemployment in the new microeconomics or, more generally in neoclassical economics, are based on the assumption that unemployment can be reduced by wage reductions. The price mechanism is in principle able to direct the labor market to equilibrium. There is always sufficient demand for labor if wages are low enough (see section 2.3 on wages). The explanations for unemployment are therefore individualistic. In principle, every individual can, by variations of his or her wage, reduce the risk of becoming unemployed and, hence, can secure employment or easily find employment if the reservation wage is adjusted.

Compared with previous neoclassical models, the new microeconomics integrates some real-world "imperfections" into analyses and relaxes the assumption of an auctioneer who sets equilibrium prices. Instead, the search process has to be used to ascertain prices. The costs for searching (unemployment opportunity costs) substitute the auctioneer's costs. Only market imperfection (e.g., imperfect information or institutional constraints) and unsystematic, stochastic variations, which have to be included in more realistic models, cause the equilibrium unemployment rate to be positive. The models of search unemployment classify unemployment as voluntary. Such models are, therefore, a complement to older neoclassical theories (Mortensen 1986, 850) rather than a concurrence with them. The integration of imperfect information into the analysis is the new component in the new microeconomics.

Meanwhile, several empirical studies have shown that the positive relationship between quits and unemployment as assumed in search theories cannot be found in reality (Murphy and Topel 1986; Hall 1980; Rothschild 1978). It has also become clear that most workers search for other jobs while still employed (Akerlof, Rose, and Yellen 1989; Noll 1984). If the new microeconomics postulate of voluntary search unemployment is correct, then we would expect unemployment to be caused primarily by inflows from employment rather than by a long duration of unemployment. At least for Germany, the opposite has been true for the 1980s (see chapter 6). The construction of the "natural rate of unemployment" on the basis of voluntary labor market flows might be plausible for low levels of unemployment, but it is implausible for high levels of unemployment and for rising "natural rates."

Serious doubts about the validity of the "natural rate" concept have also been raised by the great variations in the estimated rates between countries and within countries. Bob Solow (1985, S32) has mentioned that "natural rate" estimates for Germany increased from 1.6 percent to 8 percent in ten years; he asked: "Can the dramatic changes be rationalized in a satisfactory way?" Solow has noted further that the "natural rate" might depend on the actual rate (hysteresis; see section 2.5). He then concluded: "A natural rate that hops around from one triennium to another under the influence of unspecified forces, including past unemployment rates, is not 'natural' at all. 'Epiphenomenal' would be a better adjective; look it up" (Solow 1985, S33). Consequently, much recent work has dealt with explanations of why the "natural rate" might have shifted (section 2.6).

2.3 THE FUNCTION OF WAGES

Besides the fact that wages are the most important source of income for most people, one might distinguish three general functions of wages: (1) the allocation (signaling) function, (2) the employment-preserving and employment-creating function, and (3) the productivity promotion function. The first function relates to the allocation of labor across industries, firms, and jobs. It refers to the necessity of labor mobility in a dynamic economy. Prices (wages) are regarded as the guiding indicator and should direct labor to those jobs where it can be used most efficiently. The second function relates to the level of employment in the overall economy as well as in specific industries or firms and the potential impacts of wages on that level. The last function refers to the fact that employment contracts are incomplete and the productivity (effort) of workers is endogenous; that is, productivity depends on wages themselves instead of the opposite situation of wages being set according to (external) given productivity. These models have been discussed recently under the heading of efficiency wages.

We begin the discussion with the first function, and distinguish between developments that begin in labor market equilibrium and those that start in labor market disequilibrium. In the following discussion of the employment-preserving and creating functions, several channels through which wages may affect employment are distinguished: (1) the effect of wages on prices and the demand for goods and services in the overall economy as well as in particular industries, (2) the possible effect of wages on the pace of technological progress, and (3) the influence that the function of creating and preserving employment has on the marketability of certain low-productivity goods and services. This analysis is followed by a discussion of two groups of models—implicit contract models and efficiency wages models—that attempt to provide explanations for the rigidity of wages. The section concludes with the results of recent empirical studies on the flexibility of wages, especially in the United States and in Germany.

2.3.1 The Signal Function

In the competitive labor market model, price signals are regarded as a means to achieve equilibrium. The price—the wage—is assumed to be an information device that reduces complexity to one indicator. In competitive labor markets, wages should set signals to direct workers to jobs where they are most needed. One of the criticisms that the new microeconomics leveled at earlier theories, however, was that an auctioneer does not exist in labor markets; friction (temporary disequilibrium) thus occurs, caused, for example, by searching. The incompleteness of information is also important since prices (wages) cannot transmit all information on jobs and workers. There is a substantial portion of important factors that cannot be easily observed, if at all (Reder 1964, 309–10).

Nonetheless, it is argued that all wages would be identical in equilibrium, except for those differences related to personal factors or job specifics. Differentials in observed wages would represent nonpecuniary job benefits or disamenities, respectively. In the "fundamental (long-run) market equilibrium" (Rosen 1986, 641), monetary and nonmonetary wage differentials would equalize or, in other words, would be compensated. "The actual wage paid is therefore the sum of two conceptually distinct transactions, one for labor services and worker characteristics, and another for job attributes'' (Rosen 1986, 643). But Rosen has noted that the theory of equalizing wage differentials or compensating differentials is valid only in markets with perfect information. Recent empirical work on the importance of compensating differentials is presented in section 2.3.4.

The direction of labor mobility and the way it would influence the average wage paid in an economy are described by Holt (1970a). Starting from the assumption that the labor market is in equilibrium, he has theorized that new sectors with a higher productivity would attract workers from other sectors and from unemployment since the unemployed are assumed to have reservation wages higher than the current market wage. This is the situation that Holt (1970a) referred to when he argued that labor mobility causes wage increases. Unlike other authors of the new microeconomics (see Phelps 1970b; Archibald 1970; section 2.2), he has assumed a negative relationship between the unemployment rate and quits, arguing that if demand for labor is high, more workers quit their jobs for higher-paid jobs. This leads to the increasing growth of the average wage rate and shortens the duration of unemployment, especially search unemployment, because more workers accept job offers at higher wages. Movements to sectors with higher wages are the reason for quits, which result in interfirm mobility rather than in unemployment.

In labor market equilibrium, as used in the sense of neoclassical economics, unemployment is mainly ''reservation wage unemployment.'' Structural change and mobility thus lead to a higher average productivity in the economy because only higher wages can attract workers to the expanding sectors. The situation is different, however, if there is a shift to less productive sectors—some service sectors, for example. From the ''equilibrium viewpoint,'' there could be no such development. Disequilibrium, perhaps caused by shocks, is a necessary condition for the expansion of low-pay sectors. Since these jobs are lower paid (and often have less attractive working conditions) than others, they can, under the assumption of sufficient labor mobility, survive only as long as ''disequilibrium'' persists. Such disequilibrium, of course, is then not only indicated by unemployment but also by underemployment; that is, by workers who are involuntarily employed in jobs below their skill ability (Solow 1985, S33).

Vacancies seem to be an important factor for voluntary labor mobility (quits). It is meanwhile an established fact that quits and unemployment are negatively correlated (e.g., Murphy and Topel 1987; Hall 1980, 119). Christopher Pissarides has shown that price signals, although important, are less important than quantity signals. Relative wages in Great Britain have been more rigid than vacancies or unemployment, ''so 'job availability' has been an important factor by which labour was encouraged to move to expanding sectors'' (Pissarides 1978, 453). Similar results have been obtained in a recent study by George Akerlof, Andrew Rose, and Janet Yellen (1989).

It has also been argued that wage differentials should set signals for ''investments in human capital'' and should direct potential labor to those qualifications most urgently needed. Education and training, however, require a long time horizon, so uncertainty is extremely high for the individual. "Many human investment decisions also have to be made at an age when the investor himself is not making his own decisions" (Thurow 1983, 178). Society at large and parents provide opportunities and influence the individual's decision on education.

Against the assumed positive effect of wage flexibility on employment it is argued that more wage variation would increase the level of uncertainty. More uncertainty might reduce investment and thereby shift the aggregate demand curve to the left. "The effect of this is to increase the level of unemployment in the economy" (Dutt 1986, 288). In Germany, representatives of the employers' association have argued against a completely flexible and individually negotiated wage because they favor competition on the product market but not on the labor market. The latter would destroy the equal starting condition for competition (Erdmann 1985).

2.3.2 The Employment-Preserving and Employment-Creating Function of Wages

2.3.2.1 Effects on Demand

The argument that wage variations can prevent quantity reactions relates to the employment-preserving function of wages. If wages are becoming rigid, it is argued, the economy responds to demand variations with changing levels of employment, and thus unemployment, instead of with variations of wages at constant employment. The argument has a global component—the variations of the wage level according to macroeconomic demand conditions. It also has a microcomponent—the dispersion of wages across sectors to reflect industry-specific conditions or demand variations. Wages can affect employment through different channels. One channel is the influence of wages on prices and the demand for goods and services. Another is the impact of relative factor prices on factor input ratios. In the following discussion, the general wage argument is analyzed with respect to (1) the effects of wages on prices of goods and the subsequent demand reactions and (2) the effects of wages on factor input relations. The theoretical arguments are then confronted with results from empirical research on Germany and the United States.

The argument that excessively high wages prevent the growth of employment or the creation of additional employment is an "evergreen" (Kalmbach 1985) of economic and public debates. In the United States, the impact of a minimum wage rise has long been under intense discussion (Adams 1987), and in Germany, the Council of Economic Advisers (Sachverständigenrat) has argued that wages should increase less or even shrink to promote employment growth. With respect to the longitudinal development of real wages in Germany (Kalmbach 1985), it has been argued that there is no evidence that real wages have caused Germany's unemployment. This position is supported by international comparative studies using different approaches as well (Bell 1986; Appelbaum and Schettkat 1990a). Robert Gordon (1987a, 116) has noted that during the period when the unemployment problem emerged, the wage gap was lower than the values of more prosperous periods (before 1972). Even an analysis based on a survey of firms, which one would expect to be extremely sensitive to labor cost issues, has concluded that excessively high wages are a comparatively unimportant source of employment reductions (König and Zimmermann 1986).

At least since the publication of Keynes's general theory, it has been known in economics that wages are a cost component but that they are relevant for demand in the economy as well. In a closed economy, the effect of a wage reduction on employment, even in real terms, thus depends on its impact on effective demand in the economy. One of the most important changes in recent decades has been the increasing integration of the national economies in the world market. This trend has shuffled the cards for the supporters of a low-wage policy (Kalmbach 1985, 374), because the world market represents an almost infinite and highly price-elastic demand. The German Council of Economic Advisers (Sachverständigenrat 1988–1989, TZ 153) has argued that in the state of global markets, demand considerations are relevant for only a few sectors (e.g., construction) but that the important variable for economic growth in an open economy is the size of the labor force. (For other relevant factors, see chapter 4). In other words, only supply factors are relevant.

While this statement might be true in pure theory, the lists of "unfair trading partners" announced by the Bush administration in 1989 show that the world is not as open as one might think. Someone must buy, and countries build barriers against excessively high levels of imports from other countries (Blazejczak 1989). An international comparative study shows that exports are already the driving force of German economic development, and there seems to be a great need for increasing domestic demand, at least compared with the United States (Appelbaum and Schettkat 1990a). Even in an "open" economy, domestic demand matters.

It is also unclear whether a nominal wage reduction or a slower increase in nominal wages necessarily translates into similar real wage trends (Keynes 1936, 269). A comparative study by Linda Bell of wage trends in the United States and Germany (1986, 15, Table 2), for example, shows that Germany's lower increase in nominal wages in manufacturing from 1980 to 1985 translated into a much higher real wage growth there. Nevertheless, the growth in unit labor costs in Germany's manufacturing industries was only three-quarters of that in the United States (Bell 1986, 15, Table 3).

The process of wage setting is identified as one cause for hysteresis (Blanchard and Summers 1986; Lindbeck and Snower 1986). Insiders set wages to maximize their income and secure their employment. A reduction of employment reduces the number of insiders who set wages to fit the new situation.

For several reasons, unemployed persons do not exert downward pressure on wages (see section 2.5). The assumption about causation is that the wage rate determines employment, and this mechanism would make any level of employment self-sustaining.

In recent years, the main argument about the impact of wages on employment has shifted from the importance of the overall wage level and its flexibility to the effect of an overly rigid wage structure across industries and occupations. U.S. employment growth has been related both to more flexible labor markets and especially to more flexible wages found there as a result of the more decentralized bargaining structure. The relationship between wage flexibility and employment, however, is not as clear-cut as it is often suggested to be. Bell and Freeman (1985) have argued that flexible wages can affect employment positively during periods of contraction, in which a downward shift in wages prevents a decrease in demand and, hence, in employment. Still, it may well be that during periods of expansion, the corresponding upward shifts in wages prevent employment growth or adversely affect its rate of growth. Thus, "flexible wages" are not favorable for employment developments in general but, according to Bell and Freeman, only under specific circumstances.

If wages change according to demand variations in industries, this alteration can improve the employment situation. In sectors with decreasing demand, lower wages might sustain demand and thereby prevent employment from falling, whereas in sectors with growing demand, wage increases might attract labor (the competitive flexibility case, Bell and Freeman 1985; see also the allocation function of wages). If, however, labor costs were to rise less in the expanding sectors, it clearly would lead to higher employment growth, given demand and given the attractiveness of this sector for labor. If wages respond to productivity developments instead of to short-run demand variations, low wages could prevent employment from declining in low-productivity industries. By the same token, rising wages in high productivity industries would prevent employment from growing or would at least reduce the rate of expansion (the productivity flexibility case, Bell and Freeman 1985). The overall effect depends on the distribution of positive and negative shocks and on the responsiveness of wages. Bell and Freeman have concluded that the flexibility of wages in the United States in the 1970s did not contribute to employment growth: "If anything, the disaggregate data suggest that the flexibility of industry wages to industry value productivity has been harmful to employment" (1985, 25).

2.3.2.2 Effects on Technological Progress

Numerous arguments relating wages, productivity growth, and employment have been put forward. It has often been argued that wage increases should be oriented to overall productivity trends in order to prevent inflation. (For an analysis of this line of argument, see Kalmbach 1989a.) By contrast, it has also been suggested that wage changes should be linked to the productivity growth of individual firms or industries. Still other mechanisms underlie the idea of employment promotion via a lower productivity rise in the economy. It has sometimes been argued that the outcome of collective bargaining is a "distorted" wage structure (that is, one in which wages for unskilled labor are too high) that causes the substitution of capital for unskilled labor and thus spurs productivity growth. On the other hand, excessively high wages, and thus overly high costs, push low-productivity services out of the market. With lower wages, these services could provide employment opportunities.

Based on the idea that each factor is used in the production process to the extent that the value of its marginal product equals its marginal cost, it has been deduced that high wages, especially for unskilled labor, promote the substitution of capital for labor. Furthermore, "wrong" factor price ratios cause technological progress itself to be biased in the direction of labor-saving. Unskilled labor is pushed out of the market, by excessively high minimum wages, for example, with machinery being substituted for such labor. The minimum wage policy thus has an adverse effect. It increases low wages, but it reduces the demand for low-wage (unskilled) labor. In this way higher wages cause "technological unemployment of a third degree" (Giersch 1983). Since this argument of the relationship between relative factor prices and capital input has some plausibility, one is surprised to find that some low-wage sectors are highly capital intensive. The most prominent examples of such a low-wage sector are "McDonald jobs," and they clearly show that the relationship is a more complex one. "McDonald jobs" are capital intensive everywhere, although labor is paid mostly at a low or the minimum wage. An empirical analysis based on an equilibrium approach (Kugler, Müller, and Sheldon 1989) for Germany's manufacturing industries shows a significant labor-saving bias of technological progress, but a positive effect of factor prices on the pace of the technological progress has not been found (Kugler, Müller, and Sheldon 1989, 221). In principle, the question still remains whether low-skill jobs are rationalized because labor costs are too high or because these jobs involve simple tasks that allow for mechanization.

Assuming that lower wages would reduce the incentive for further rationalization or might even lead to a resubstitution of labor for capital (Wicksell 1934; for a critique, see Pasinetti 1981), thereby slowing down the pace of technological progress, the question is whether reducing wages would be an efficient policy for society. The situation can be seen differently in the case of low-productivity industries (see 2.3.2.3) but is it a favorable outcome to reduce productivity growth and produce essentially the same quality and quantity of output? This would amount to inefficient production, since, with technological progress, the same output could be produced with less input of labor. Assuming that the substitution mechanisms are effective, making allowance for low wages is thus not an effective allocation policy but rather a distribution policy. Distributional problems would be solved by less efficient production, but from a societal viewpoint, this solution is suboptimal.

2.3.2.3 Effects on Low-Productivity Industries

Arguments relying on the wage structure and lower average productivity growth in the economy should be regarded differently when it comes to the promotion of employment in low-productivity services. An expansion of these services decreases the overall level of productivity (or its growth rate), but in this case the outcome is caused by low productivity in the production of additional output and not by inefficiencies in the production of essentially the same quality and quantity of output. Still, low-productivity, low-wage sectors can survive only in a noncompetitive labor market or in a competitive labor market with a continuous excess supply of labor. If a competitive labor market were to reach equilibrium, there would be no wage differentials between sectors, except those related to personal factors like education, skills, and certain working conditions. In equilibrium, everybody would get the same wage (Meidner and Hedborg 1984). This is a situation analyzed by William Baumol (1967) in his seminal article on unbalanced growth.

High wage differentials would survive only in an economy with a continuous excess supply of labor, even if a competitive labor market is assumed. This may be the case in the labor markets of the highly industrialized countries, which seem to be markets with a continuous excess supply of labor; at least they have been for the last one-and-a-half decades. Institutional arrangements can also shape the labor market in one direction or another (Scharpf 1990). Since services, especially personal services, depend overwhelmingly on domestic demand, employment in low-productivity, consumption-oriented private services could increase if wages in these sectors were low compared to the average wage. These services can expand on a private-market basis, however, only if there is demand from high-income groups at the same time.

Does the decision come down to a choice between "bad jobs" and "no jobs" (Ginzberg 1979), or is there another alternative? Obviously, services can also be financed publicly and provided by either the public sector itself or by private institutions. Public financing and provision is quite common in education, for example, where comparatively high wages attract skilled workers and where it would be suboptimal, from society's viewpoint, if the educational decision were to rely on private incomes only. Besides the direct public provision of services, other arrangements are also possible. Low-productivity services, for instance, can be financed by subsidies to consumers or to producers.

Persistent low wages, which may be necessary to make certain services marketable, are a specific form of subsidy: a subsidy from the worker to the consumer of this service (Appelbaum 1990, 94). If demand for this service exists only at low costs connected with very low wages, then one can argue that this service is obviously not of high enough value for the consumer. It will disappear as soon as other work opportunities—with higher wages—become available. It is difficult, however, to decide what defines a "bad job" and which wage to regard as the minimum one. In the end, this decision has to be a normative one, but unquestionably, a wage level that does not allow for an income high enough for reproduction is certainly too low.

2.3.3 Explanations for Rigid Wages

2.3.3.1 Implicit Contracts

Implicit-contract models try to provide an explanation for why wages are sticky; that is, why they do not fall when there is an excess supply of labor. Implicit-contract theories emphasize different degrees of risk aversion on the side of employers and employees. Since employees have invested mainly in human capital (themselves) and have not diversified their risks, as capital owners have done, they try to reduce their risk and seek long-term contracts with stable wages. The wage thus contains one component related to marginal productivity and another component related to the insurance against income instability (Azaridis 1979, 223). This insurance-wage package is cost-minimizing for firms in the long run.

The resulting rigidity of wages leads to nonclearance of labor markets within the basic neoclassical labor market model. Instead of varying wages, one will observe varying employment through reduced working time or layoffs (Feldstein 1976). This inherent consequence of the model is very difficult to understand if it is argued that the actual wage is partly defined by an insurance against income variations. The wage is assumed to be fixed across business cycles, which means that it is above the market wage during recessions and below the market wage during periods of excess demand for labor. In the neoclassical labor supply model, it is assumed that workers would adjust their labor supply (in hours) according to wages: "Thus, the firms' employment adjusts to demand changes via the effect of wage changes on labor supply" (Killingsworth 1983, 61). In implicit-contract models, however, workers have a risk aversion against such varying wages and therefore prefer a fixed wage.

The unemployment insurance is an important component in implicit contracts between employers and employees since unemployment benefits and leisure ("unemployment holidays," as they are termed by Feldstein 1976, 939) are an attractive alternative to low-wage employment. Christopher Pissarides (1981, 68) has argued that Feldstein's argument is no expansion of the basic neoclassical labor market model since it only modifies opportunity costs.

It remains unclear why employees should shy away from the risk of wage variations but remain open to periods of unemployment and consequently income variations. More plausible seems to be an interest in a permanent employment contract and a fixed income on the employees' part (Schettkat 1987, 56). "For one thing, although wage stability may be good for morale, presumably instability of employment is not" (Solow 1979, 81).

Almost every job is idiosyncratic because certain firm-specific knowledge and skills are necessary to some extent in every task. To the extent that jobs are unique, they lack an external labor market. According to theories of idiosyncratic exchange, this circumstance gives monopoly power to employees but simultaneously to employers as well because employees cannot make use of the firm-specific skills in the external labor market. Some labor theories (e.g., Braverman 1977) have suggested that the capitalistic employer would try to reduce employees' power by an ever-higher degree of the division of labor.

In the Taylorist or Fordist way of thinking, such minute divisions of labor would result in very standardized tasks. Tacit knowledge on the part of employees would be reduced as far as possible, and the employer would easily be able to exchange a specific employee for another worker hired on the external labor market (Krupp according to Brödner 1986, 39). Much of the knowledge in Fordist production regimes was embodied in machinery, and this process, together with the Taylorist (vertical) division of labor, increased the power of management.

In recent years, it has been argued that the Fordist production regime has become counterproductive because more flexible, quality production is required instead of mass production (Piore and Sabel 1984; Boyer 1987, 1989). Indeed, the negative effects of Fordism were already being experienced in the production of the Model T (Raff and Summers 1987, 363). Flexible specialization (Piore and Sabel 1984) and intelligent quality production (Sorge and Streeck 1987) are the new watchwords for a changed production regime that requires flexible machinery and flexible, highly skilled workers. We are possibly on a new wave of a Kondratieff cycle, a wave driven by specialized rather than mass production of consumer goods (Blackburn, Coombs, and Green 1985, 193). The integration of tasks (Kern and Schumann 1984) rather than a further division of labor is necessary to fulfill the new requirements (for a more comprehensive discussion, see Schettkat 1989a). These developments, however, would cause internal labor markets to gain importance, thereby increasing the importance of idiosyncratic exchange. At the same time, the external labor market would lose importance. Indeed, there has recently been a revival of the segmented labor market theory (Rosenberg 1989; Dickens and Lang 1988; Ostermann 1984).

2.3.3.2 Efficiency Wage Models

Whereas implicit-contract models explain wage rigidity in terms of employee interests, efficiency wage theories—although this term covers a variety of approaches (see Ruerup 1989; Gerlach and Huebler 1989a)—explain wages above the market clearing level in terms of the firm's own interest. In all efficiency wage models, workers' productivity depends on the wage, so that a cut in the wage could cause productivity to decline and costs to rise.

Four broad classes of efficiency wage models can be distinguished (Akerlof and Yellen 1986a, 2–9), each differing substantially in the foundation of its argument. In some models, the argument is rooted very much in traditional economic assumptions (e.g., the shirking model of Shapiro and Stiglitz 1984), but other models are more complex and take not only "economic factors" but also "sociological factors" into account. The latter, therefore, offer a deeper explanation of economic outcomes. George Akerlof's model (1982), for example, includes such notions as fairness, obviously an explanation that relates efficiency wages to norms and social interaction. The alternative efficiency wage models can be summarized under four headings: (1) shirking, (2) labor turnover, (3) adverse selection, and (4) sociological models. In the following paragraphs, a short overview of these models and related criticism of them will be presented.

Shirking models (Shapiro and Stiglitz 1984) start from the fact that no specification of workers' effort can be fixed in employment contracts. Furthermore, it is difficult or impossible to monitor workers' behavior on the job. Together with the basic assumption that employees try to avoid work if they can, the argument in these models is that it is rational for employers to raise the risk that employees face if they lose their jobs. The part of the wage above the market clearing wage is a disciplinary device or an incentive to work harder rather than to shirk. Rising unemployment increases the risk of job loss and thus increases the risk of income losses.

In the *labor turnover model,* it is argued that firms pay more than the market clearing wage in order to reduce turnover (Schlicht 1978; Holt and David 1966). The higher the relative wage and the higher unemployment, the more reluctant the employees would be to quit their jobs. Turnover costs increase with skills, and this could establish dual labor markets if employers pay a premium to skilled workers but not to unskilled workers. In their study "Did Henry Ford Pay Efficiency Wages?" D.M.G. Raff and Lawrence Summers have shown that Ford's introduction of the $5.00 workday was certainly not motivated by the two standard arguments for raising wages (to attract either more labor or better qualified labor; 1987, S64–S65). Instead, the dramatic increase in the wage rate paid by Ford increased productivity through reduced turnover, less absenteeism, and improved morale, which had suffered from the high degree of labor division. It is rational—cost-minimizing or efficient—from the employers' viewpoint to pay wages above the market clearing wage if this raises the employees' productivity.

The *adverse selection model* suggests that if a worker's ability and his reservation wage are positively correlated, a higher wage will attract more able employees. A worker who offers to work for wages that are too low will be identified as a lemon (Akerlof and Yellen 1986a, 7). This argument implies that there is no way to measure effort and performance of workers on the job. It is argued, however, that pay schemes have been designed to induce potential workers to reveal their true characteristics. Neglected here is the notion that even workers may not know how they will perform in a certain environment. Furthermore, workers' productivity depends on the social context, on teams, in a production process based on the division of labor (Thurow 1983; Lindbeck and Snower 1986).

Models classified as *sociological models* by Akerlof and Yellen (1986a, 8) do not rely on the assumption of individual and independent utility maximization of all agents. Social conventions, norms, labor market power, and other factors are taken into account. Akerlof (1982) has argued that the efficiency wage is partly a gift—to the extent that it is above the market clearing wage—and that this gift increases employees' effort. Having received a gift, workers do not shirk. Here, social norms (see also Akerlof and Yellen 1988 and 1990) are a major variable for the explanation of the relationship between wages and effort. "The fair wage received by the worker depends on the effort he expends in excess of the work rules, the work rules themselves, the wage of other workers, the benefits of unemployed workers, as well as the number of such worker's wages received in previous periods" (Akerlof 1982, 556). Support for the so-called sociological model comes also from research done on the innovation process. "Learning by using" (Rosenberg 1982) requires "voice" instead of "exit" (Hirschman 1970) and, as has been shown by Nina Shapiro (1990), very few innovations could occur in a pure competitive model. Numerical flexibility, connected to the "invisible hand" of unfettered market forces in the neoclassical model (Leithäuser 1988, 187), might then produce inflexibilities with respect to cooperation, skills, and the ability to create new products. Innovations require some stability and a model of exchange that is not based on market prices alone, that requires a longer time horizon, and that might be described as "reciprocity" (Polanyi 1944).

Efficiency wage models, together with insider-outsider models and a nonhiring explanation of unemployment, have become the most discussed in labor economics. Efficiency wage models gain their importance by offering an explanation of nonclearing labor markets within the rational paradigm. Since it has become obvious to most analysts that persistently high unemployment cannot plausibly be classified as voluntary, it has been necessary to find another explanation. In the traditional line of analysis, unemployment could be avoided if prices were flexible enough. Efficiency wage models therefore give an economic rationale for sticky wages from the employers' perspective. It is no longer the monopoly power of unions or the risk aversion of employees (see implicit contracts, 2.3.3.1) that leads to nonclearing labor markets (although these reasons are not necessarily excluded) but rather the tendency of productivity to depend on wages, regardless of what causes that dependence.

With efficiency wage models, however, it is not necessarily assumed that employers pay wages above the marginal value of the last labor unit. The traditional labor demand function is still assumed, but it is shifted because a higher wage reduces direct or indirect labor costs, which should be a more important variable than wages. In shirking models, it is assumed that monitoring costs, which would otherwise be necessary, are reduced. In turnover models, it is assumed that hiring and firing costs are saved. In selection models, the reduction of searching and testing costs is assumed. Sociological models might be regarded differently because they are based on the assumption that effort depends on a "fair share." In efficiency wage models, it is not necessarily the case that the resulting wage is equal to marginal values of labor units; in fact it is more likely that it is not.

Jonathan Leonard has tested the shirking and the turnover models with firm-specific data from one U.S. state. He hypothesized from these models that there is a trade-off between wage premiums and turnover and supervisory costs. He was able to control for detailed occupational groups (290 classifications), and he concluded that "there is little evidence that considerable differences in occupational wages paid across industries can be accounted for by the shirking model" (1987a, 150). The turnover model seems to be more in line with the data. Higher wages reduce turnover, but "the reductions in turnover achieved are not sufficient to establish the profitability of wage bonuses" (Leonard 1987a, 150).

The "sociological model" draws its strength from allowing for wage determinants broader than just marginal costs or values. It is the only model that could explain persistent interindustry wage differentials (Thaler 1989). Some empirical evidence supporting this view can be found in a longitudinal analysis of technological progress, profits, and wages in German manufacturing industries (Erber and Horn 1989). The other models could explain only interindustry wage differentials that are controlled for occupations and skills (ability) if the risks of shirking, turnover costs, and selection vary systematically across industries. It is plausible that these costs do vary with occupations, but the idea that they vary by industry and thus similarly affect all jobs is less convincing. Assuming a competitive framework, however, it is hard to explain why some industries are able to achieve higher profits over a long period.

2.3.4 Recent Empirical Results

It is a theoretical question whether a more flexible wage structure can result in higher levels of employment, but it is an empirical question whether a wage structure is stable or not. Recent as well as older studies (e.g., Salter 1960; Ulman 1965) on wage differentials between industries in the United States and Germany (Krueger and Summers 1987; Dickens and Katz 1987; Vogler-Ludwig 1985) have shown that the industrial wage structure is very stable over time. Furthermore, wage differentials across industries occur in every occupation and cannot be explained by differences in working conditions even if they are controlled for (Krueger and Summers 1987). Similar results were obtained by Knut Gerlach and Olaf Hübler (1989b) for Germany; education and occupations are an important determinant for wages (Helberger 1980) but industries matter. The analysis by Kurt Vogler-Ludwig (1985) has reported stable industrial wage structures for both economies. The wage structures of 1970 correlated with those of 1982, with a coefficient of 0.92 in the United States and 0.94 in Germany, respectively. However, a stable wage structure is not necessarily a fixed wage structure and industries with small wage increases were those that were stagnating, whereas the wage was rising at a higher rate in the expanding sectors (Vogler-Ludwig 1985, 25). Moreover, Linda Bell (1986) has found that long-run industry wage movements from 1970 to 1980 were related to long-run industry productivity movements.

Stable industry wage structures may be due to unmeasured quality differences (Murphy and Topel 1987), so the wage differentials actually compensate for those differences. In that case, they are fully compatible with the competitive labor market model. The empirical evidence of Alan Krueger and Lawrence Summers, however, gives little support for the assumption of unmeasured quality, if one does not assume that the unmeasured variables are more important than education and occupation; unmeasured quality might be positively correlated with measured skills (Krueger and Summers 1987, 19). Furthermore, they found industry effects also for workers who had been dismissed, clearly not the group in which one would expect unmeasured quality variables to be extraordinarily good. Therefore, the persistent industrial wage structure that could not occur in fully competitive (labor) markets must rely on labor immobility or other noncompetitive factors in goods markets as well. We cannot go into the competitiveness of goods markets here, but wage models linking profits and wages have been put forward.

Although wage bargaining is much more centralized in Germany than in the United States, empirical analysis has clearly refuted the view that a uniform wage structure exists in Germany (Franz and König 1986). In manufacturing, the ratio between the highest and the lowest wage was 1.78 for 1978 (Friderichs 1985), and increases in wages were not uniform either. In the collective bargaining agreements of 1984, for example, the average increase of monthly incomes ranged from 2.1 percent in public services to 3.4 percent in trade, banks, insurance, energy, water supply, and mining (Wagner 1985).

Bell and Freeman (1985) have reported a ratio of 2.82 between the highest and lowest wage at the two-digit industry level for the United States in 1982. In a comparative study, Bell (1986) has reported that ratios for relative wage levels (the manufacturing wage divided by the industry-specific wage) ranged from 90 percent to 180 percent in the United States in 1985 and from 110 percent to 150 percent in Germany (see Table 2.1). The ratios for sector-specific gross earnings per employee in the particular sector to the average for all sectors in 1983 were 72 percent in the United States and 80 percent for trade and restaurants in Germany; for services, the ratios were 85 percent and 88 percent respectively (Appelbaum and Schettkat 1990a). A further disaggregation of "services" in the United States produced a ratio of 43 percent for personal services (Wohlers and Weinert 1986). Wage differentials are still higher in the United States than in Germany. U.S. wage dispersion over 10 sectors of the economy is roughly 160 percent of the wage dispersion in Germany (Ap-

Table 2.1
Relative Wage Levels in the United States and Germany

	manufacturing wage levels divided by industry wage levels							
	US				Germany			
	1971-73	1974-79	1980-85	1985	1971-73	1974-79	1980-85	1985
wholesale trade	0.9	0.9	1.0	1.0	1.3	1.3	1.3	1.3
retail trade	1.4	1.5	1.7	1.8	1.4	1.4	1.5	1.5
banking	1.2	1.2	1.2	1.2	1.1	1.2	1.2	1.2
insurance	0.8	0.9	0.9	0.9	1.2	1.1	1.1	1.1

Source: Bell 1986: Table 4.

	effective wage per hour as a ratio to the average wage in 1982[°]			
	US		Germany	
	ratio	industry	ratio	industry
highest ratio	1.62	oil	1.31	oil
lowest ratio	0.68	clothing	0.70	leather
standard deviation	25.90		13.00	

[°] private enterprises, excluding agriculture
Source: Vogler-Ludwig 1985: Table 3.

	standard deviation of compensation per employee					
	US		Germany		US value / German value	
	1979	1985	1979	1985	1979	1985
standard deviation/ mean	0.40	0.38	0.25	0.24	1.60	1.58

Source: Appelbaum and Schettkat 1990: Table 6.

pelbaum and Schettkat 1990a). Using hourly wages, Vogler-Ludwig (1985) has arrived at an even higher dispersion for 27 sectors in the United States, where dispersion is almost double that in Germany (see Table 2.1).

In their empirical study, Dickens and Katz (1987, 53) have found that industry wage differentials are highly correlated across occupations. Since working conditions are most likely to be linked to occupations rather than to industries, their result does not support the "compensating differentials theory." Furthermore, industry wage differentials are persistent over long periods (Krueger and Summers 1987, 22–24). It also seems that the correlation between positive nonpecuniary "wage elements" (job satisfaction and status, for example) and pay levels is highly positive (Scitovsky 1976, 103; see also section 5.3), not negative as the "compensating theory" would suggest.

2.4 MATCH AND MISMATCH:
BOTTLENECKS AND THE BEVERIDGE CURVE

2.4.1 The Bottleneck Model

One explanation for structural unemployment is the scarcity of labor with specific qualifications, a scarcity that constitutes a bottleneck. The labor market does not adjust quickly enough to avoid unemployment caused by such a bottleneck, and the economy could grow (or could grow faster) if this bottleneck did not exist. The idea behind this explanation of structural unemployment is that there is a specific production function and an expansion path of the economy, with well-defined ratios between different categories of labor (skilled and unskilled). For the simple case with only two categories of labor, this situation is displayed in Figure 2.1. The economy can expand along the "employment expansion path" (Berman 1965, 258) defined by the ratio of the two categories of labor.

At point B (in Figure 2.1), skilled labor is exhausted, and M'B', unskilled labor, is unemployed. Structural unemployment exists, caused by the structural relationship between the two labor categories and the scarcity of skilled labor. The economy could expand along the "employment expansion path" (P_0) if enough skilled labor were available. The scarcity of skilled labor creates a restriction for the employment growth of unskilled labor. To overcome the situation represented by point B in a closed system, some unskilled labor has to undertake training in order to become skilled labor and to open the bottleneck. Given the employment expansion path (P_0), full employment, in the sense of no unemployment, would exist at point C, where all labor is employed (MM' equals NN'). Some unskilled labor (F, E) has to be trained in order to enable the economy to reach the full-employment labor market equilibrium. In this simplified model, higher levels of employment could be achieved only if a structural adjustment process (training of unskilled labor) takes place.

The bottleneck conception of the labor market has serious consequences for economic policy. It means, for example, that full employment (no unemployment) in the economy cannot be achieved so long as bottlenecks exist. An expansionary fiscal policy would thus fail to increase employment and to clear the slack labor market. Instead, it would lead to inflation (wage increases) in the labor markets experiencing scarcities (the labor markets for skilled labor). These considerations were the basis for Gösta Rehn's suggestion that the demand level of the economy should be held below the level of "full employment" and that training programs should be provided for workers in industries with excess labor (Meidner and Hedborg 1984). The bottleneck concept of structural unemployment is quite clearly also the underlying rationale for the

Figure 2.1
The Bottleneck Model

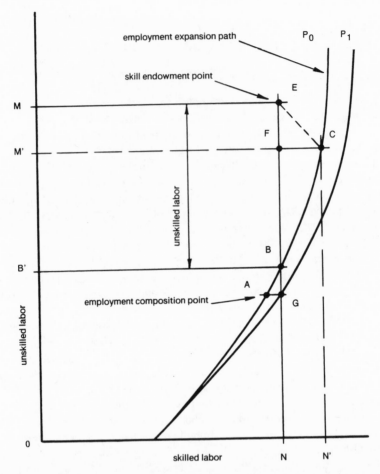

"Qualifizierungsoffensive" in Germany. In fact, many of the arguments against the positive employment effect of shorter working hours are based on this conception as well. It is therefore important to investigate the skill flexibility of the labor force and hence the ability of the economy to overcome bottlenecks from this side.

In the short run, the skill requirements of the production process, with respect to different categories of labor, might be limited or fixed, but in the long run, it is possible not only to train unskilled labor, but to adjust the skill requirements as well, as shown in international comparisons (Lutz 1976). This would result, for example, in a shift of the employment expansion path to a higher ratio of skilled to unskilled labor (from P_0 to P_1 in Figure 2.1). Technological progress can, of course, also change the shape of the employment expansion path. The debate on deskilling versus upgrading, or polarization versus reprofessionalization (see Auer and Riegler 1990; OTA 1986; Kern and Schumann 1985; Braverman 1977; for a short overview, see Schettkat 1989a) can be summarized in the terms presented here as whether the path shifts leftward (deskilling; that is, more use is made of unskilled labor) or whether it shifts rightward (upgrading; that is, more use is made of skilled labor). The expansion path of the whole economy is influenced as well by the structural composition of the economy. A shift to industries with higher skill requirements would move the overall employment expansion path in Figure 2.1 rightwards, and vice versa.

Indeed, many highly industrialized economies have shifted their employment expansion path to the right; that is, they are making more and more use of skilled labor (for the United States, see Kutscher 1990; for France, Petit 1990; for Germany, Warnken and Ronning 1989; Baethge 1988). Although there has been discussion in the United States that the changing structure of industry is shifting the economy to low-wage, less skilled labor, especially in service industries (Harrison and Bluestone 1988; Appelbaum and Albin 1990; Davidson and Reich 1989), overall developments still indicate a trend toward the use of more skilled labor (Kutscher 1990; Dickens and Lang 1987). For Germany, it has been argued that high wages combined with insufficient downward flexibility have caused the economy to follow an employment expansion path that makes too much use of skilled labor and thus creates insufficient employment opportunities for unskilled labor. The result has been "technological unemployment of the third degree," as Giersch (1983) has labeled this idea.

2.4.2 The Beveridge Curve: Unemployment and Vacancies

In 1958, Dow and Dicks-Mireaux published an analysis of the "Excess Demand For Labour," in which they argued that some unemployment (and often unfilled vacancies) is due to a maladjustment of demand and the supply of labor. Even at very high levels of demand, there would remain some unemployment; beyond a certain point, the decrease of unemployment would be less and less sensitive to increases in demand. The reverse is true for unfilled vacancies. That is, even with low demand in the labor market, some vacancies will remain (Dow and Dicks-Mireaux 1958, 4). This argument is summarized in Figure 2.2. The straight line C-C' represents a situation in which full employment, in the sense of no unemployment, can be achieved in principle. If there is no mismatch in the labor market, vacancies could be used directly as a measure of excess demand (line C-C' in quadrant I). If there is maladjustment in the labor market, however, the unemployment rate and the vacancy rate could not come down to zero simultaneously but would be positive, as indicated by curves 1-1 and points A_u and A_v in Figure 2.2. These points represent a situation in which the qualification requirements of the vacancies and the qualifications of the unemployed do not fit. Vacancies do not simply

Figure 2.2
The Relationship between Unemployment and Vacancies according to Dow/Dicks-Mireaux

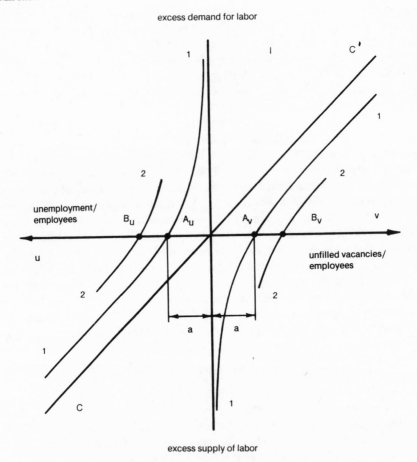

at points A and B: maladjustment (u = v), zero excess supply of labor

represent excess demand for labor but rather are demands for labor of different types. Unemployment could decrease only at the expense of higher demand creating scarcities in other areas and most likely inflation. In modern terms, this unemployment rate connected to points A_u and A_v would be called the "natural rate of unemployment." The curves 2-2 represent a labor market with a more serious mismatch, in which the unemployment and the vacancy rate are equal at a higher level.

The relationship developed by Dow and Dicks-Mireaux (1958) is the same one that underlies the concept of the Beveridge curve (Figure 2.3). The 45° line in the Beveridge curve diagram represents situations in which the unem-

Figure 2.3
The Beveridge Curve

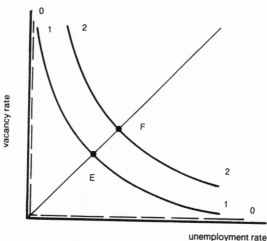

ployment rate equals the vacancy rate, such as at points A_u, A_v, B_u, and B_v, in Figure 2.2. Above the 45° line in Figure 2.3, there is high demand, and below the 45° line, there is low demand for labor. Successive points on the 45° line give different degrees of maladjustment. The further the point is from the origin, the higher the degree of maladjustment. For any given maladjustment, there are different combinations of vacancy and unemployment rates (iso-mismatch curves, 1-1 or 2-2 in Figure 2.3), depending on demand in the economy.

In the case of homogeneous labor, the unemployment-vacancy curve would be right-angled through the origin (curve 0-0 in Figure 2.3). In the absence of excess demand vacancies would never exist if perfect information and the immediate filling of positions (no friction) are assumed. Demand deficiency would be the only cause of unemployment. If different sectors are considered, the described vertical relation would occur if no barriers to labor mobility between industries existed. If, on the other hand, "perfect maladjustment" existed in an industry, a horizontal (respectively a vertical) unemployment-vacancy curve would result. Demand variations could not affect unemployment and supply variations would leave vacancies unaffected. In the case of the "perfect immobility" of labor, this curve would also occur if demand expanded in a sector other than the actual one. These two situations are extremes, however, and reality would be in the middle, represented by the conventional convex unemployment-vacancy curves. The two extremes are nevertheless useful to characterize mismatch in industries and economies.

Cyclical changes in the rate of excess demand correspond with movements along the unemployment-vacancy curve, while shifts in the position of the curve correspond with shifts in the degree of structural maladjustment in the labor market (Flanagan 1973, 115). These basic relationships also underlie the arguments concerning the Phillips curve and the natural rate of unemployment. Increasing maladjustment in the labor market leads to an outward shift of the curves in the Dow and Dicks-Mireaux diagram (Figure 2.2) as well as to an outward shift of the Beveridge curves in Figure 2.3.

An outward shift of the unemployment-vacancy curve could also occur if sectors grew at different rates and to an even greater extent if some sectors grew and others shrank at the same time. Furthermore, upswings and downturns could cause the ratio of unemployment-vacancy rates to circle counterclockwise around the median level. In this ratio, downturns take place at lower levels than upswings because, in a downturn, vacancies are reduced before unemployment rises; in upswings, vacancies change before employment if rigidities are allowed for (Hansen 1970, 17–18). This situation causes difficulties in the interpretation of small movements of the unemployment-vacancy curve because cyclical movements might be misinterpreted as a permanent outward shift of the curve.

Structural change accompanied by slow or no employment growth poses the most difficulties for adjustments in the economy (section 2.5.3; Pasinetti 1981). Abraham (1987) has used an example in which all sectors initially have both equal vacancy and unemployment rates (points v_o and u_o in Figure 2.4) and the same underlying unemployment-vacancy curve and in which labor demand is increasing in some sectors while decreasing at the same magnitude in other sectors. With immobile labor and without any further shocks to the system, this pattern of structural change would result in higher vacancies and lower unemployment in the growing sectors (point B in Figure 2.4), while sectors in which labor demand has fallen would move to lower vacancies and higher unemployment (point C in Figure 2.4). Although total labor demand would not have changed, the aggregate vacancy rate and unemployment rate would have risen from v_o to v_1 and from u_o to u_1, respectively. The overall Beveridge curve would have shifted outward, indicating increasing mismatch in the economy.

This movement is caused by the convexity of the unemployment-vacancy curves. If the position of the unemployment-vacancy relation is similar on identical curves across sectors, "any increase in the dispersion of demand across sectors with relatively impermeable boundaries—whether defined along geographic, industrial, or other lines—could increase the aggregate unemployment rate" (Abraham 1987, 235). If, on the other hand, the expanding sectors are those with initially high unemployment and low vacancies (starting at point C in Figure 2.4) and the shrinking ones are those with low unemployment and high vacancies (point B), overall unemployment and vacancies can move to lower values. This is a situation in which an economy with labor immobility between sectors can move to a more nearly equal development of the industries.

Complication arises if the unemployment-vacancy curves are different in individual industries. A sector employing mainly high-skilled labor could, for example, have both higher vacancies and unemployment, that is, an unemploy-

Figure 2.4
Sectoral Dispersion and the Beveridge Curve

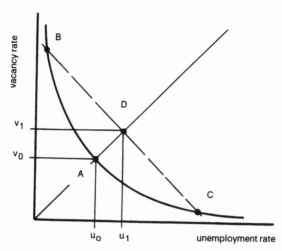

ment-vacancy curve farther away from the origin. This sector might also be slower in adjusting to increased labor demand and would have a greater mismatch, although this circumstance would not necessarily indicate an unfavorable development of the economy (Soskice 1990).

A substantial part of the economic debate in the last decades has been about whether to classify unemployment as structural or demand deficient. Support for arguments that the "natural rate of unemployment" is rising would include an outshifting unemployment-vacancy curve, and indeed some support has been found in empirical studies (e.g., Abraham 1987; Franz 1987a and 1987b; for an overview, see Johnson and Layard 1986). Recent studies and arguments are discussed in section 2.5.3, and in chapter 3, various mismatch indicators and their underlying assumptions are discussed. Since labor market flows between various labor market categories affect the evaluation of the question of whether the labor market's ability to adjust has improved or worsened, approaches based on flows are developed in chapter 3.

2.5 STRUCTURAL FACTORS AND DEMAND DEFICIENCY: RECENT THEORETICAL AND EMPIRICAL DEVELOPMENTS

2.5.1 Hysteresis

Recent theoretical developments in the explanation of unemployment have focused on structural and technological change as a source of varying "natural rates of unemployment" instead of demand variations (see section 2.5.2). Others have tried to explain Europe's persistently high unemployment by hysteresis

(Blanchard and Summers 1986; Lindbeck and Snower 1986). Hysteresis in unemployment arises if the actual rate of unemployment depends entirely or partly on past rates of unemployment. The three dominant theoretical explanations of hysteresis are based on (1) the disappearance of physical capital, (2) the decay of human capital, and (3) insider-outsider models (Gordon 1988, 296).

The wage-setting mechanism has been discussed primarily in terms of "membership groups" (Blanchard and Summers 1986) or insiders (Lindbeck and Snower 1986). These explanations were discussed briefly in section 2.3 and are treated together with nonhiring models in the following section. As an explanation of persistently high unemployment, the disappearance of physical capital holds that, with decreasing employment, the capital stock is reduced and the remaining physical capital is simply inadequate to employ the existing labor force. Blanchard and Summers (1986, 27) have been sceptical of this argument because of historical evidence. Substantial disinvestment during the 1930s did not preclude the rapid recovery of employment that was associated with rearmament in a number of countries. Similarly, the very substantial reduction in the size of the civilian capital stock that occurred during World War II did not prevent the attainment of full employment after the war in many countries. It is hard to support the argument that reduced capital accumulation has an important effect on the level of unemployment with historical examples. In chapter 4, trends in capital stock since the 1960s are discussed briefly.

The human-capital argument of hysteresis works through different channels. First, it is argued that the unemployed are disconnected from the learning process (learning by doing) and thus are disadvantaged after suffering a period of unemployment, during which their human capital deteriorates as well. This is essentially the same reason that women who have left the labor market for a period face difficulties in returning to work (Mahoney 1961; Cottman-Job 1979). Second, unemployment status might stigmatize and create negative signals for employers. In this situation, it might be important whether dismissal was selective or whether all groups were dismissed, as might happen with plant closure (Gonäs 1990). In the latter case, unemployment would be regarded as an accident and not linked to individual abilities. Third, long-term unemployment might lead to a loss of working abilities. It has been found that long-term unemployment has a diminishing effect not only on work ability but also on activity levels in general (Miles 1983). All these approaches suggest that unemployment might have long-lasting effects, and some of the labor market training programs are obviously designed to compensate for the damages mentioned. It also follows that periods of high unemployment will have long-term costs for society.

2.5.2 Unemployment as a Hiring Problem—
Insiders versus Outsiders

According to Robert Flanagan (1987, 1989) persistent and increased European unemployment might be caused by employers' reluctance to hire additional employees because the associated risks have increased. In this view, the growth of European unemployment is less the result of job loss than the result of the failure to be hired (Flanagan 1987, 192)—that is, of a failure to create employment (see chapter 4). In his empirical analysis, Flanagan (1987, 184) has concluded that almost the entire increase in secular unemployment is due to a decline in the likelihood of leaving unemployment (the flow from unemployment to employment, divided by unemployment). Although vacancies have increased, the chance of leaving unemployment has decreased (Flanagan 1987, 185).

Flanagan (1989) has focused on three groups of variables that may have caused employers to be more reluctant to hire new employees: (1) fixed employment costs, (2) uncertainty about employees' qualifications, and (3) uncertainty about future demand.

Fixed employment costs are sometimes confused with nonwage labor costs. Nonwage labor costs have grown relative to wages in almost all countries belonging to the Organization for Economic Cooperation and Development (OECD). This trend provides an incentive to achieve a given labor input with fewer workers and more hours on average. Rising average wage costs also provide an incentive to substitute capital for labor. Furthermore, a fixed increase in nonwage labor costs raises the wage of unskilled labor relative to skilled labor, thereby providing an incentive to favor existing employment (insiders) at the expense of job seekers (outsiders). It is unclear what the difference between wage costs and nonwage labor costs is from the employer's perspective. The arguments above refer to different incentives set by wage or nonwage costs that vary with the wage rate (or with hours worked) and those that are entirely independent of the wage rate (or hours worked). Therefore, it is appropriate to distinguish, as Flanagan did, between variable labor costs—wages and nonwage labor costs—and fixed labor costs.

Part of the fixed (and nonwage) labor costs are hiring and firing costs. These are prominent in insider-outsider theories because they can establish a rent that can be captured fully or partially by the existing employees (insiders). Lindbeck and Snower (1986, 236) have developed from this assumption the argument that the new entrants' wage is less than or equal to the insiders' wage minus the firing costs and that the entrants' wage will not exceed the outsiders' reservation wage by more than the marginal hiring costs. Insiders can thus claim a wage above the market clearing wage and capture the "firing rent," thus preventing the labor market from clearing. These considerations are obviously related to a situation of stagnating employment when the question comes down to the pure exchange of insiders by outsiders.

Fixed wage labor costs depend to a substantial degree on ceilings for social security contributions. Since these ceilings are very high in Germany (but comparatively low in the United States), this part of fixed nonwage labor costs is relevant only for high-income white-collar male employees in Germany. In all other income groups, the social security contributions do not establish fixed nonwage labor costs (Schettkat 1984). The U.S. ceilings are much lower, so the proportion of employees whose social security contributions establish fixed nonwage labor costs is higher in the United States than in Germany. For 1978, Flanagan (1989) has reported fixed nonwage labor costs of 11 percent in the United States and 5.3 percent in Germany. According to these figures, "non-hiring" arguments based on the amount of fixed labor costs should be less important in Germany than in the United States.

Uncertainty about the prospective employees' qualifications is one of the most important hiring problems and complicates hiring in general (Semlinger 1989). Uncertainty can be reduced by trial and error; that is, newly hired employees are tested during a certain period and are replaced if they do not fulfill the requirements. Uncertainty can also be reduced by self-selection strategies, such as a compensation system that will be accepted only by stable, high-performance employees. Lastly, pre-employment screening is a suitable measure to reduce uncertainty. Still, uncertainties concerning qualifications remain a permanent issue in a changing world where firms need employees with high skill flexibility.

Whereas Flanagan's arguments concentrate on uncertainty in the hiring process, Lindbeck and Snower have emphasized the power of insiders to choose whether to be cooperative with entrants and whether to have good relations with them. Refusing cooperation would reduce productivity, and rejection of entrants would increase their work disutility and thus their reservation wage (Lindbeck and Snower 1986, 237). Thus, insiders can protect themselves from underbidding by outsiders and can create an economic rent. Based on the necessity for insiders to cooperate in the training or introduction of outsiders into the firm's production process, others have formulated similar arguments (Thurow 1983; Marshall and Briggs 1989).

Another reason that firms do not replace high-wage insiders' labor by low-wage outsiders' labor is that the implied labor turnover would have an adverse effect on the morale and work effort, and, hence, on the productivity of their employees (Lindbeck and Snower 1984; Lindbeck and Snower 1986, 238). Unions are able to increase insiders' power by (a) the threat of strike (a rent-seeking tool, according to Lindbeck and Snower 1986, 238), (b) increasing hiring and firing costs (e.g., by severance payments), and (c) increasing the effectiveness of harassment and noncooperation. While unions are clearly capable of acting as Lindbeck and Snower have described, the question is whether they actually have acted in this way (Flanagan, Soskice, and Ulman 1983). Furthermore, unions may have positive effects as well. They may increase the willingness of workers to cooperate and thereby produce efficient outcomes (Sorge and Streeck 1987).

Uncertainty about future demand leads firms to restrain their hiring and opt for overtime hours if they are faced with expansions that they do not believe will last. Such uncertainty also leads firms to restrain their firing and opt for labor hoarding during a recession that they believe to be transitory. "Given adjustment costs, firms have always favoured greater utilisation of insiders at the expense of outsiders as a way of coping with uncertainty'' (Flanagan 1989, 10). Increasing uncertainty about future demand ends in a growing preference for insiders and an increasing reluctance toward hiring. According to Flanagan (1989, 10–11), increasing uncertainty can be handled analytically as an increasing tax on employment adjustments and has the same effects as a tax.

Empirical studies (Sengenberger 1987; Abraham and Houseman 1988) have shown that firms in the German economy respond relatively slowly to demand variations with respect to persons employed but not with respect to hours worked. In the United States, the reaction with respect to hours worked is almost the same as in Germany, but it is achieved by a reduction of persons employed in the United States whereas average hours worked vary in Germany. For the comparison of the U.S. and German economies, two institutional variables have to be taken into account. In the United States, temporary layoffs seem to favor ''external'' adjustments and, hence, the flow from employment to unemployment (see chapter 5). In Germany by contrast, the measure of ''short-time work'' reduces the flows.

Uncertainty has been distinguished from risk in the economic literature (Knight 1921; Rothschild 1981). With respect to future demand, two distinct variations should be analyzed. First, it may be that there are variations in the level of demand but not in its structure. In this case, uncertainty might be reduced to a risk; Keynesian-style demand policies were designed to reduce this form of uncertainty or risk. The second source of uncertainty is variation in the structure of demand. This is the widely discussed case of higher risks in goods markets, a situation that forces firms to be flexible.

2.5.3 Structural and Technological Change: Variations of the "Natural Rate" or Demand Deficiency?

Lilien (1982) has argued that the cyclical behavior of unemployment is not caused by the actual unemployment rate fluctuating around the ''natural rate'' but by variations of the ''natural rate'' itself. Like Pasinetti (1981), he has argued that two economies, in both of which employment is growing at a rate of 2 percent, could be very different when it comes to the generation of unemployment. If, in one economy, every sector and firm is growing proportionately at 2 percent, the effort required for the economy to adjust is far less than that required in another economy in which employment is growing at a rate of 8 percent in half of the sectors while firms are shrinking at a rate of 6 percent in the other half (Lilien 1982; 780). The reallocation of employment is a significant source of (''natural'') unemployment.

Within the model presented by Lucas and Prescott (1974), stable aggregate demand but stochastic demand shocks for individual firms lead to equilibrium unemployment that varies with the quantity of reallocation of employment in the economy. During the 1970s, exogenous demand shocks unevenly distributed over the sectors, together with a slow adjustment of labor, led to rising unemployment. Lilien has used a flow model of labor to demonstrate the significance of his argument for rising unemployment. The unemployment rate is influenced by two factors—the risk of becoming unemployed (layoff rate) and the possibility of finding a new job (duration of unemployment, see chapter 3). Therefore, higher displacement and job growth will both influence unemployment. It is not high turnover as such that causes unemployment, however: it is the duration of unemployment (see critique of Oi 1962 in Reder 1964, 316).

Finding a new job is regarded as particularly difficult when workers have a strong firm-specific or sectoral-specific attachment, associated with wage premiums, that leads them to be reluctant about accepting employment in other sectors at a lower wage. Indeed, studies of the job-search process of displaced workers in the United States show that those who remain in the same sector have smaller wage losses than those who switch sectors (Podgursky 1988; Podgursky and Swaim 1987a and 1987b; Bednarzik and Sabelhaus 1985). Similar results have been obtained in a recent study of the German economy (Gerlach and Schasse 1990; Blüchel and Weißhuhn 1989). Therefore, unemployment will rise if the pace of structural change increases, especially if it leads to growing and shrinking sectors at the same time and if the overall growth of employment is low.

According to Lilien, the "natural rate" of unemployment itself has fluctuated. He has concluded that the unemployment in the United States in the 1970s was mainly "natural" and could not have been lowered by demand policies. "Here, however, the term 'natural rate' must be given a somewhat different interpretation, that is, the level of unemployment associated with the average or typical quantity of labor reallocation required within the economy" (Lilien 1982, 791). This is a proposition common to economists relying on the natural rate argument (see section 2.2), but it has become stronger since cyclical variations of the unemployment rate can also be considered "natural." This definition of a varying "natural rate of unemployment" caused by sectoral shifts and the at least partial rejection of explanations of business cycles dependent on variations of aggregate demand were heavily criticized, and the shift hypothesis stimulated many discussions.

Abraham and Katz (1986) have argued that aggregate demand shocks could result in a greater dispersion of sectoral growth rates if sectors (a) have different trends in growth and (b) differ in their sensitivity to aggregate demand fluctuations. If Lilien's view is correct that a varying unemployment rate is caused by variations of the pace of structural change, then the result should be a positive relationship between the unemployment rate and a dispersion index representing structural change (see chapters 3 and 4). Increasing unemployment caused by shrinking sectors should occur simultaneously with vacancies in the expanding sectors. The unemployment-vacancy curve should shift outward (see section 2.4).

If, conversely, the aggregate demand scenario is correct, a positive correlation between the dispersion index and unemployment can still occur because sectors might be affected unevenly by demand shocks. In contrast to Lilien's case, the relationship between the unemployment rate and the vacancy rate should be negative. A downward shift in demand would affect all sectors, although at different rates. From their empirical work, Abraham and Katz (1986) have found that the unemployment rate and the dispersion index move in the same direction but that vacancies and unemployment move in opposite directions. Therefore, they have concluded that business cycles are caused mainly by aggregate demand fluctuations and not by sectoral shifts.

Abraham (1983) has investigated whether unemployment in the United States can be classified mainly as structural-frictional unemployment or whether demand deficiency might be the reason. She found that unemployment rates and vacancy rates are negatively correlated; there are, however, serious problems with vacancy statistics in the United States (Abraham 1983, 709–14; Abraham 1987; for Germany, Kuehl 1970, sections E4, F4). In other words, high unemployment occurs simultaneously with low vacancies. Ratios of unemployment rates to vacancy rates in various periods (during the 1960s and 1970s) yielded values well above 1, although the Beveridge curve seems to have shifted outwards in the United States in the 1970s (Abraham 1987, 210, 226). Although Abraham's study (1983) was criticized by Schwartz, Cohen, and Grimes (1986) on statistical grounds (they objected to Abraham's steady-state assumption in the computation of the duration of vacancies and her argument that new hires are a better indicator than vacancies), their critique did not reject the conclusion that unemployment in the United States had been caused mainly by demand deficiency (Abraham 1986, 275).

Nevertheless, the pace of structural change can clearly influence unemployment since frictions are increasing. It seems clear, however, that aggregate demand remains a substantial explanation for unemployment.

2.6 SUMMARY: THE IMPORTANCE OF ADJUSTMENTS AND MOBILITY

The developments in economic labor market theory have been strongly influenced by new empirical research that forced neoclassical economics to modify the basic competitive labor market model and to take more and more real-world facts into account. Long-term employment relationships, rather than pure market exchanges, are now recognized; a negative rather than a positive relationship between voluntary labor mobility (quits) and unemployment is an established fact; unemployment is no longer seen as merely a status chosen voluntarily by the individual but rather as a societal problem; wage rigidities have become part of the rational world rather than simple external irrationalities. Not much seems to be left of the stylized competitive labor market of the basic neoclassical model, although it still often seems to be the reference model.

That some positive rate of unemployment is consistent with full employment is a widely accepted fact in economics of all schools of thought, but the interpretation and the value of the positive equilibrium rate of unemployment are heavily debated. Some interpret the positive full employment rate of unemployment as the real labor market equilibrium, in the sense that it represents the utility maxima. The unemployed are voluntarily unemployed, at least concerning a job in the secondary labor market segment, because their reservation wage is above the current market wage. Institutional arrangements are shaped in a way that maximizes individual or group utility. It is solely, or at least mainly, the interests of employees that establish these arrangements (implicit-contract models).

More recent models have emphasized firms' own interest in fixed and above market clearing wages (efficiency wage models). Productivity is not externally defined but is itself a function of wages. The models discussed under this heading all share the view that productivity is partly determined endogenously, but they vary widely concerning the explanation of this relation. Efficiency wage models provide an explanation for the noncleaning of labor markets. Nevertheless, there is a lack of explanations for why unemployment has increased in nearly all Western countries and why a new equilibrium rate of unemployment seems to have appeared.

Economic growth still makes an important difference for the employment trends in the United States and Germany, and demand in the economy, although somewhat out of fashion in economics, plays an important role. Blanchard and Summers (1986), however, have written that the "demand story" cannot tell the whole story for Europe, since inflation did not come down as it should have in the 1980s. The negative relation between unemployment and inflation seems to have broken down in the 1980s (Blanchard and Summers 1986). Although Europe is seen by some analysts as one region (Gordon 1988), Germany seems to fall into the traditional regime in which a trade-off between inflation and unemployment was assumed. The inflation rate came down to zero when unemployment reached record levels in the mid-1980s (see chapter 4). Although deficient demand still seems to be an important cause for unemployment, changes in the functioning of labor markets seem to be important as well, and there might be a relation between initially deficient demand unemployment and labor market dynamics (hysteresis).

Little or no empirical evidence has been found for the hypothesis that a less intense job search on the part of the unemployed is caused by either the increasing participation of "marginal" labor market groups or overly generous unemployment benefits (Burtless 1983; Summers 1986). Nevertheless, Beveridge curves do seem to have shifted outwards. In other words, at each level of vacancies (an indicator of unsatisfied labor demand), the unemployment rate is higher than it used to be. Abraham (1983 and 1987) has found this shift for the United States. For Germany, results from Wolfgang Franz (1987b) have pointed in the same direction. Recently, approaches that focus on the functioning of labor market dynamics with respect to matching, hiring, and structuring have been put forward: insider-outsider models, unemployment as a hiring problem, hysteresis, and varying natural rates.

An outward shift of the unemployment-vacancy curve is not in itself an indicator for the decreasing efficiency of the matching process. It could be caused simply by the increased necessity for matching. For example, it could be due to a higher pace of structural change, less stable employment, and higher labor turnover, or to more competition. Even if the matching process itself is as efficient as before, increased turnover in the economy can cause increased matching problems. In other words, frictional unemployment may have increased. This mechanism can be regarded as a structural factor.

Changes in the dynamics of labor markets are at the center of the following chapters. Needless to say, it is of great importance for economic policies whether the matching process has become less efficient, whether matching necessities have increased, or whether unemployment is caused by demand deficiency. In chapter 3, different indicators for labor market dynamics are developed, and the principal adjustment mechanisms are discussed. The relation between the equilibrium rate of unemployment and labor market dynamics is developed formally, and the matching process is investigated. Chapter 3 will close with a subsection that links theoretical hypotheses with more formal indicators of changing labor market dynamics.

3

Analyzing Labor Market Dynamics: A Conceptual Framework

3.1 FLOWS IN THE LABOR MARKET

Conventional labor market analysis is based on stock data, such as the number of persons employed or unemployed during a certain period, on a specific day or week. Although data on the number of persons within particular labor market categories are ideally suited to the analysis of changes in the levels of these aggregates and their respective structures (Neubourg 1987), such stock data are not well suited to the analysis of labor market processes. Stock information is not sufficient for the analysis of dynamic processes in labor markets because the gross flows are hidden. Changes in stocks are only the net results of large flows in and out of the categories.

In the early 1970s, research on the dynamic aspects of unemployment was undertaken at the Brookings Institution (Hall 1970, 1972a; Perry 1972; for earlier work, see Wolfbein 1960), and in the middle of the 1970s, contributions investigating the different components of unemployment were published (Cramer and Egle 1976; Freiburghaus 1978; Clark and Summers 1979; Akerlof and Main 1981). Research on the dynamics of unemployment has shown that a constant figure for the average annual level of unemployment or for the unemployment rate can conceal a wide range of different situations (Freiburghaus 1978). Equal annual average levels of unemployment can be composed of a given number of people who remain unemployed for the entire year but also of a far greater number of persons who each experience a short spell of unemployment. Situations with an equally high level of unemployment can differ substantially both in the number of people experiencing unemployment and in the average duration of unemployment. The overall unemployment risk can therefore be divided into two components: a risk of becoming unemployed, that is, of entering unemployment; and a risk of remaining unemployed, that is, of not finding other employment or an alternative to unemployment. An indicator for the risk of remaining unemployed is given by the duration of unemployment, whereas the risk of becoming unemployed is given by the number of persons entering unemployment relative to the number of persons who can potentially be affected by unemployment (usually the employed).

The same general qualifications that apply in the unemployment process apply in employment dynamics. Even if the number of persons employed remains constant, it does not necessarily mean that employment at different times (the stock) is composed of identical persons. Most likely, it is not. For example, the number of persons employed in Germany increased by 200,000 in 1985. This employment growth was the result of larger flows in and out of employment. Including multiple movements of individuals, 5.2 million inflows and 5 million outflows were counted during the twelve-month period (Reyher and Bach 1988). In every time period, there are substantial flows in the labor market from employment to unemployment and nonparticipation, or in the opposite direction. As with unemployment, every stock (e.g., employment, vacancies) can be decomposed into a component representing stability (duration) and another component representing mobility (inflow or outflow).

Another dynamic aspect of economic development is the growth and decline of firms and establishments. Within an industry, growth and decline in the subunits coexist (König and Weißhuhn 1989; Cramer and Koller 1988; Leonard 1987b; Bluestone and Harrison 1982). In recent years, important research efforts have been made to investigate the process of intra-industry gross job growth and decline. It has been shown that even in shrinking industries some firms grow and that in expanding industries some firms decline, although the proportion of growing and shrinking firms varies with the business cycle (Leonard 1987b).

These studies concentrate on job turnover, which is distinct from labor turnover because the latter can occur even without any job turnover. Job turnover is the gross change of the number of jobs within an industry or in the economy. One example is job destruction in one firm and job creation in another firm at the same time. This process can be the result of "creative destruction" or, more generally, of competition within an industry.

In the extreme, it could well be that all new products are produced in newly established plants and that old plants, producing the old products, will disappear from the market. Therefore, the amount of job turnover depends on the degree to which some establishments grow at the cost of others. Empirical work for Germany suggests that product innovation and process innovation, which are highly correlated (Schettkat 1989a), are a substantial part of interfirm competition that results in the expansion of production by the innovative firms and a decrease of production by the noninnovative firms (Scholz et al. 1989).

Interfirm and interindustry job turnover that is caused by economic change

Figure 3.1
Flows in the Labor Market

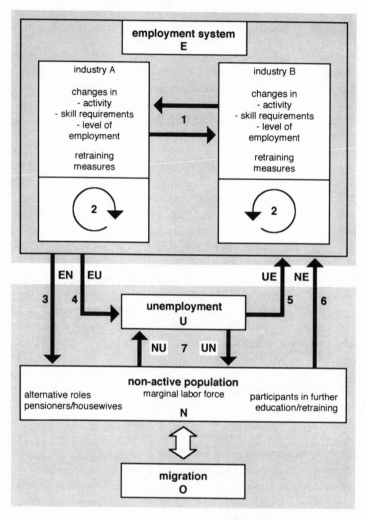

For abbreviations see text

is also the underlying idea of the so-called Swedish model of industrial and labor market policies developed by Gösta Rehn and Rudolf Meidner (Meidner and Hedborg 1984). The solidaristic wage policy in Sweden, with its strong emphasis on low wage dispersion, was designed to enable progressive (in the sense of the ability to pay high wages) firms to expand rapidly and to force less progressive firms either to improve or to disappear from the market.

Individual worker's moves can be (a) from one occupation to another, (b) from one employer to another (see flow 2 in Figure 3.1), (c) from one industry to another (flow 1), (d) from one area to another, (e) between employment and unemployment (flows 4 and 5), and (f) into and out of the labor force (flows 3, 6, and 7) (Kerr 1954, 310). Furthermore, the population can vary, and flows into every labor market category can come from outside the analyzed economy, through migration or natural demographic change (birth and death), for example. Instead of movements between industries (flow 1), one can also think of movements between the primary and secondary labor market segments, which might coincide with industries (Davidson and Reich 1989).

Particularly relevant for labor market and employment policies are changes in the flows over the business cycle and secular trends. Are the unemployed mainly displaced workers, or are they new entrants in the labor market who cannot find initial employment? In other words, is the inflow rate into unemployment from employment constant, thereby making the flow out of unemployment the only thing that varies over the business cycle (Burda and Wyplosz 1990)? How sensitive are these flows with respect to employment variations? Flows into and out of employment partly reflect variations in the number of persons employed. With growing employment, a higher inflow rate into employment is expected; at the same time, the outflow rate is expected to decline, and vice versa. But there is also turnover that is not caused by variations in the level of employment. How is structural change reflected in labor market flows? Are there direct flows from the shrinking into the growing sectors (Parnes and Spitz 1969, 58)? Or does the economy adjust mainly by intergenerational exchange of workers and skills?

Most labor market theories are implicitly or explicitly related to adjustment processes. Discouraged and additional worker theories argue that a high elasticity of labor supply with respect to the business cycle (Hansen 1970) yields flows into and out of the labor force. Search theories focus on labor market adjustments to changing conditions (wage expectations). And even the basic market model is a model of a (finished) adjustment process governed by price or wage signals.

In the following subsection, a more formal accounting framework for labor market processes is developed, and the relationships between different measures are analyzed systematically. Measurement problems and definitions that influence the values of the mobility indicators are examined in the third subsection. The discussion there draws on the data sources used in chapters 5 and 6, although the issues raised are more general in the present section. In the fourth subsection, mobility indicators are combined and a classification scheme for industries is produced. The relation between various labor mobility indicators in labor market equilibrium (the steady state) will be developed. Furthermore, the relation between variations of unemployment, vacancies, and mismatch is analyzed. This background provides the analytical basis for the empirical analysis. Lastly, the theoretical arguments made in chapter 2 are linked to indicators for labor dynamics.

3.2 ACCOUNTING FOR LABOR MARKET DYNAMICS: FLOW MATRIX AND MOBILITY INDICATORS

With the three labor market categories from Figure 3.1—employment, unemployment and nonparticipation, and an additional category that includes those individuals who are outside the population—one arrives at the matrix in Figure 3.2. The main diagonal (EE, UU, NN) of the matrix contains all individuals who did not change their labor market status in the relevant period. EU and EN are formerly employed persons who are currently unemployed or nonparticipating, respectively. UE and NE are movers into employment from unemployment and nonparticipation. These abbreviations correspond with those in Figure 3.1. To account for more than two steps, that is, in the panel data, the dimensions of the matrix in Figure 3.2 could be expanded (see Riese, Hutter, and Bruckbauer 1989, 74–75). For the actual measurement of the flows, it is important to know whether moves are counted continuously or whether the labor market statuses at two points of time are compared (see section 3.3.3).

In addition to flows between the labor market categories within the population already in the area of investigation (in the specific economy), there are flows into and out of the population that are caused either by migration or by natural change of the population (birth and death). Persons outside the population are of specific importance in the case of surveys or panels (see chapter 5) because the definition of the population can substantially affect measurement. From the matrix in Figure 3.2, the principal labor market flows and their relationship to the changes in the level of the categories can be written directly. Changes in the level of employment:

$$E_t - E_{t-1} = (U_{t-1}E_t + N_{t-1}E_t + O_{t-1}E_t) - (E_{t-1}U_t + E_{t-1}N_t + E_{t-1}O_t) \tag{3.1}$$

In this study, flows are always written as flows from $t-1$ to t, and time subscripts will be dropped in the following formulas for flows. They are used if misunderstandings might occur otherwise or if stocks are used.
Changes in the level of unemployment:

$$U_t - U_{t-1} = (EU + NU + OU) - (UE + UN + UO) \tag{3.2}$$

Changes in the level of nonparticipation:

$$N_t - N_{t-1} = (EN + UN + ON) - (NE + NU + NO) \tag{3.3}$$

Absolute flows are difficult to compare over time, between countries, and between industries since they depend on the size of the related aggregates. Therefore, ratios or probabilities are a more appropriate measure. Flows also depend on the length of the period (see section 3.3.3), so it is necessary to

Figure 3.2
Matrix of Labor Market Flows

labor market status in t

labor market status in t-1	employment (E)	un-employment (U)	non-participation (N)	outside the population (O)
employment (E)	EE	EU	EN	EO
unemployment (U)	UE	UU	UN	UO
non-participation (N)	NE	NU	NN	NO
outside the population (O)	OE	OU	ON	OO

The meanings of the abbreviations include:
EE = employed in both periods
EU = movers from employment to unemployment
EN = movers from employment to nonparticipation
EO = movers who are leaving the population of investigation

standardize the time frame (usually a year) as well. In the following passages, ratios related to employment and changes in this category are discussed mainly, but similar rates can be computed for other categories as well.

The *accession rate* or *hiring rate* (a) is the number of persons entering employment during a certain period divided by initial employment (alternatively, the denominator could be average employment during the period). It is defined by this formula:

$$a = \frac{UE + NE + OE}{E_{t-1}} = ue + ne + oe \tag{3.4}$$

If mobility between industries is taken into account, one arrives at:

$$a_j = \frac{UE_j + NE_j + OE_j + E_iE_j}{E_{j,t-1}} = ue_j + ne_j + oe_j + e_ie_j \tag{3.4a}$$

for all $i \neq j$

with: i,j = indices for industries

The accession rate (or the hiring rate) is distinct from the job-finding rate (f, which is the ratio of formerly unemployed persons who found a job divided by initial unemployment; see formula 3.16) because the two rates have different denominators.

The *separation rate* for employment (s) or, in the case of time-discrete data (see section 3.3) the *instability rate* as well, is defined by those who leave employment as a ratio to initial employment:

$$s = \frac{EU + EN + EO}{E_{t-1}} = eu + en + eo \qquad (3.5)$$

and with mobility between industries:

$$s_j = \frac{E_jU + E_jN + E_jO + E_jE_i}{E_{j,t-1}} = e_ju + e_jn + e_jo + e_je_i \qquad (3.5a)$$

for all $i \neq j$

Of particular relevance for labor market dynamics is the amount of labor flow that is not related to changes in the level of the categories. It is given by the *substitution rate* (subr), which is the lower value of either the separation rate (s) or the accession rate (a) and which gives the magnitude of turnover not caused by variations of employment levels (see also section 3.3.2):

$$subr_e = a \mid a < s$$
$$subr_e = s \mid a > s \qquad (3.6)$$

or

$$subr_e = \frac{1}{2} (a + s - |a - s|) \qquad (3.6a)$$

with: subr = substitution rate
    e = subscript for employment

The employed person's risk of becoming unemployed is described by ''rue,'' the ratio computed by the flow from employment to unemployment divided by employment:

$$rue = \frac{EU}{E_{t-1}} = eu \qquad (3.7)$$

The ratio of persons who remain employed during the period to the number of persons initially employed produces the *stability rate* or *continuation rate* (ee) (Perry 1972):

$$ee = \frac{EE}{E_{t-1}} \tag{3.8}$$

If one distinguishes old members from new members, that is, from those who were employed during a certain period, a cohort, one can compute the *survival rate* (sr) or *wastage rate* (wr):

$$sr = \frac{E_{k,t}}{E_{k,t-1}} \tag{3.9}$$

$$wr = \frac{E_{k,t-1} - E_{k,t}}{E_{k,t-1}} \tag{3.10}$$

with: k = index for the cohort

The survival rate of formula 3.9 defines survivors as those persons who remained in the population (here, in employment) during the period from $t-1$ to t. The denominator is the total population of the cohort; that is, the number of persons who were employed at $t-1$. The wastage rate, on the other hand, gives the ratio of those who left the cohort. Since cohort data are difficult to gather, survivors are sometimes defined as those persons who have been members of the population for a certain period at the time t. For example, persons are asked when they first entered the population. Because the initial size of the cohort to which these survivors belong is unknown, the actual population is used as a denominator, producing a biased survivor rate.

From the analysis of unemployment spells and unemployment duration, one knows the difference of the unemployment duration of those currently unemployed (uncompleted duration) and the average duration of an unemployment spell (completed duration). If the stock of the unemployed always consists of 2 persons, with person 1 unemployed the whole year and person 2 always having a one-week spell of unemployment—that is, the second unemployed person alternates—then there are 53 persons who experience some unemployment over the year. The average duration of unemployment is thus a little less than 2 weeks (52 weeks + 52 weeks divided by 53 persons = 1.96 weeks). If, on the other hand, the duration of those currently unemployed is computed, one finds one person in the pool who has a very short duration of unemployment (1 week at maximum), whereas the other person in the pool has a very long duration of unemployment. At the end of the year, the average duration of unemployment of those currently unemployed will be roughly 26 weeks (52 weeks + 1 week divided by 2 persons). Long-term unemployment counts for half of total unemployment, but short-term unemployment affects many more persons (Johnson and Layard 1986).

Again, the same qualifications apply for employment and vacancies as for unemployment. For employment, measures of duration are developed, and the duration of vacancies, for example, is used for the analysis of mismatch problems (Abraham 1987). It makes a difference how duration is actually measured, but the available information leaves little choice of how to compute durations. Under the assumption of a steady-state process, that is, a process in which the inflows and outflows are equally distributed over the period and balance each other (constant levels), the average duration can be computed with the following formula:

$$\text{duration} = \frac{\text{stock}}{\text{flow}} \qquad\qquad (3.11)$$

This is, however, only a very crude formula for an empirical analysis, since the assumption of a steady state is almost never fulfilled (see also section 3.4.2). Nevertheless, a lack of data often prevents more precise computations, which are more complicated. Still, the duration according to formula 3.11 seems to give a rough approximation to more sophisticated measures (Freiburghaus 1978). Before the various measures are put into a more analytical context of labor market dynamics (section 3.4), some problems with the definitions and measurements that are important in this context will be addressed.

3.3 DEFINITION AND MEASUREMENT ISSUES

Definitions of jobs, occupations, and industries can have important effects on measured labor market flows, which may also be influenced by the specific measurement methods used. It makes a tremendous difference whether one counts movements of persons or movements in and out of a labor market category. The former measure is of interest mainly if one wants to investigate the relation between the characteristics of individuals and mobility. The latter measure relates mainly to the characteristics of the category—an industry, for example. Without doubt, the greatest amount of information is collected if a combination of both measures is available. Such combinations are relatively rare, however, and only very seldom can both characteristics be combined. The social sciences urgently need to develop data sets that allow one to combine individual characteristics with the economically relevant variables of companies and industries. As described in sections 5.1 and 6.1, the data used in this study are concerned mainly with categories since the focus is on the restructuring of economies.

3.3.1 Jobs and Occupations

Job turnover is a central indicator when it comes to the dynamics of the demand side of the labor market, but it is not very clear what a "job" is. A job can be defined by (1) its physical location, (2) its legal location, (3) the equipment used, (4) the task performed, or (5) the skills required. If a job is defined as a working place connected to a specific firm (legal location), then competition within an industry could result in intra-industry gross job growth and decline. The net change in the industry might be zero, and the job as defined by the machinery used, the necessary tasks and skills, and even its physical location (the establishment) might remain identical. In the extreme, even the worker might be the same, but, by using the legal criteria, the job would be counted as gross job creation. At the same time, a pure change in the ownership, causing the birth of a "new" firm, is, of course, irrelevant when it comes to the question of labor market dynamics (see also the concrete statistical data problems described in chapters 5 and 6).

At the other extreme, the job could change completely in terms of the machinery used, the tasks and skills involved, its position in the organization, or the person performing the job, even if it remains in the same legal location or firm. It is, therefore, important to discuss the statistics that are the basis for indicators of job turnover. Usually job turnover, or gross job growth and decline, is based on changes in the level of employment in a specific establishment or company.

Obviously, the definition and actual measurement of jobs is very vague and can focus on very different aspects. The same can be said of other economic and social variables, like occupations (see Schettkat 1989a, 39–40), and even for such standard measures as the GDP. Clearly, it is impossible to cover every aspect of a certain job. Empirical and theoretical concepts of jobs, occupations, skills, and other economic and social variables will always be vague as long as they are claimed to have general relevance. The very detailed analysis of job changes found in case studies or in specific analysis (see, e.g., BIBB and IAB 1981, 1987) is without doubt of enormous value, but it is not applicable to studies intended to describe and explain general phenomena and trends. Here the compromise between specificity and generality has to be made or has in practice already been made because of the statistics available.

3.3.2 Turnover Rates

Concerning the adjustment processes in the labor market, it is more appropriate to focus on labor turnover than on job turnover. Nevertheless, these indicators of labor market dynamics are linked. Changes in the level of employment cause some job turnover, which will in turn cause labor turnover. But even without any job turnover, there could still be labor turnover. The following hierarchy exists for changes in the level of employment, job turnover (excluding "job creation" caused by shifts of the owner), and labor turnover:

net change ≤ job turnover ≤ labor turnover   (3.12)

Because of intra-industry gross job creation and destruction, job turnover will usually be higher than net changes of employment. Likewise, since workers can switch between employers and industries and can move to unemployment and nonparticipation, labor turnover will be higher than job turnover.

One indicator that measures how much of the job turnover is necessary for adjustments in the economy is interindustry job turnover (IIJ), which is defined by (OECD 1989):

$$IIJ = 1 - \frac{\sum\limits_{j=1}^{n} |E_{j,t} - E_{j,t-1}|}{\sum\limits_{j=1}^{n} JT_j} \tag{3.13}$$

with: E = employment
        JT = job turnover (gross job creation + gross job destruction)
        j = indicator for industries

The indicator of formula 3.13 takes its lowest value of zero if there is no intra-industry job turnover, that is, if all job growth and decline takes place between industries and thus is necessary to adjust to structural change. IIJ equals 1 if there is no structural change and no net employment growth in the economy but there is intra-industry job turnover. This measure thus indicates how much of the job turnover in the economy is caused by the changing structure or size of the economy and how much is caused by intra-industry developments, such as competition between firms.

An industry-specific indicator for the relation between job turnover and changes in employment (D) is:

$$D_j = \frac{JT_j - |E_{j,t} - E_{j,t-1}|}{JT_j} \tag{3.14}$$

In sectors with little or no competition between firms, one expects D to be low; in sectors with high intra-industry competition, one expects D to be high. The more homogeneous the firm-specific employment trends in an industry, the lower D will be and vice versa.

3.3.3 Flow Measurement

The measured magnitude of the gross flows depends not only on the underlying dynamics but also on the length of the time period and the number of categories. The longer the time period, the higher the flows, since changes are more likely to occur if flows are measured continuously. If, on the other hand, flows are measured by a comparison of an individual's positions at two points of time (time-discrete), then measured flows can decrease with the length of the period because temporary transitions are not counted.

It thus makes a tremendous difference whether one counts every movement between categories during a certain period (continuous flows) or whether one computes flows from the comparison of the labor market status at two different times (time-discrete flows). With the latter method, the magnitude of the flows is influenced by the length of the time interval between the actual dates of measurement. Steve Davis and John Haltiwanger (1988, 1) have reported, for example, that the job turnover (defined in their study as establishment job growth) rate in manufacturing industries ranged from 13 percent to 20 percent per year from 1979 to 1983 if measured on a year-to-year basis. Based on quarterly data, however, their calculations showed that an annual job turnover rate of 31 percent to 57 percent would result.

With data related to persons, one can distinguish between those who change their labor market status permanently and those who move only temporarily. Obviously, the continuous observation of movements would count both with the same probability. In the case of time-discrete observations, however, the number of counted movements depends on the length of the time period. For very short periods, the number of actual and observed movements is equal, but for longer time periods, the number of actual movements and counted movements will differ. The latter will be lower than the former, and the difference depends on the number of temporary movements.

To illustrate this relation, those persons who are leaving employment temporarily and those who are leaving permanently are distinguished:

$$EX = EX_{perm} + EX_{temp} \tag{3.15}$$

with: E = employment
           X = every nonemployment status (unemployment [U], nonparticipation [N], out of the population [O])
           perm = permanently
           temp = temporarily

With the time-discrete method, the number of movements missed increases with the number of temporary leavers and the length of time between the observations. For example, if the period between the two observations is one year, then all movements caused by seasonal variations will not be counted. If the period is a month, most of the temporary movements will be observed.

There is obviously an inverse relation between the number of measured movements and the length of the period if time-discrete data are used. The reason for this negative correlation is that transitory movements are underrepresented at any given time. The more stable individual positions are, the higher the probability that they will be included in the sample and the smaller the pool of temporary movers (Bruni 1988, 6–8). Both methods—continuous and time-discrete counts of movements—are applied in the investigation of labor market flows (chapters 5 and 6). All other things being equal, the magnitude of the flows increases with the number of categories that one distinguishes. If, for example, employment is disaggregated by sectors, then measured flows in the labor market will be higher since interindustry mobility would be counted as well.

3.4 CHANGES IN THE ECONOMY AND LABOR MARKET DYNAMICS

3.4.1 Stability and Turnover: Industry Characteristics

Before discussing the relation between unemployment and various flows in the labor market in a more systematic framework, the relation between employment stability and the substitution rate will be discussed. The combination of these two rates provides one systematic criterion for distinguishing between the primary and secondary labor markets. Intuitively, one would expect sectors with low substitution rates to have high employment stability. Sectors with lower turnover rates, however, are not necessarily sectors with high stability of employment from the employees' perspective, since it could well be that with the same substitution rate, the number of affected persons varies. A substitution rate of 100 percent, for example, could mean that all persons initially employed have left employment, that half of the persons initially employed have left twice, or that a fifth of the persons initially employed have changed five times. In the first case, employment in the whole industry or firm is unstable, while the second and third cases reflect a combination of unstable and stable employment.

In one sector, turnover may be high because of the multiple movements of a few persons in and out of employment, whereas, in other sectors, turnover might be more evenly distributed over a greater population. Whole industries may be part of the secondary labor market, or only parts of an industry may belong to this segment. The substitution rate measures turnover not caused by changes in the level of employment, whereas the stability rate gives the proportion of employees who remain with their establishments or sectors during a certain period. Substitution and stability rates thus have different denominators and different ranges of values. Stability rates can range from 0 percent to 100 percent, whereas the substitution rate can take values that range from zero to infinitely large. The two rates cannot be compared directly, but their combination provides valuable information.

As always, other measures based on flow data also have their advantages and disadvantages (for a comprehensive discussion, see Price 1977). A disadvantage of the separation rate (formula 3.5) is that one has no information about how this rate relates to the number of persons actually moving among categories. Combined with the stability rate, the crude (Price 1977) turnover rates of formulas 3.4 (the accession rate) and 3.5 (the separation rate) are extremely good indicators for describing the segmentation of labor markets. An industry without any segmentation of its labor force would have a low value for the separation rate (formula 3.5) and a high value for the stability rate; conversely, highly segmented industries would have a high turnover rate and a high stability rate. At the same time, when a high value of the separation rate and a low value of the stability rate coexist in an industry, this indicates that the whole industry is part of the secondary labor market.

3.4.2 Labor Market Equilibrium and Flows

Both types of mobility (accessions and separations) can cause frictions and thus unemployment. Equilibrium in the labor market can be interpreted as balancing flows. Using a model developed by Robert Hall, Robert Barro (1988) has defined the steady-state rate of unemployment as equal to the "natural rate of unemployment," or the unemployment rate caused solely by frictions in the labor market. Under the assumption of a constant labor force, the difference between unemployment rates in different time periods can be expressed by:

$$u_t - u_{t-1} = s\,(1 - u_{t-1}) - f\,u_{t-1} \qquad (3.16)$$

with: $u = U/L$
$L = $ labor force (employment plus unemployment)
$s = $ separation rate (EU/E_{t-1})
$f = $ job-finding rate (UE/U_{t-1})
$t = $ time subscript

By definition, the rate of unemployment cannot change in a steady-state situation, and 3.16 becomes:

$$u^* = \frac{s}{(s+f)} = \frac{1}{\left(1 + \dfrac{f}{s}\right)} \qquad (3.17)$$

To show that the steady state of unemployment depends on separations and the duration of unemployment only, formula 3.17 can be written by making use of these terms and the definition of the duration of unemployment from formula 3.11:

$$u^* = \frac{1}{\left(1 + \dfrac{1}{s\,\text{durue}}\right)} \qquad (3.17a)$$

with: $\text{durue} = $ average duration of unemployment in the steady state

Under the assumption of a constant labor force (composed of identical persons), the ratio of the job-finding rate (f) to the job-separation rate (s) determines the "natural rate of unemployment" because flows can occur only between employment and unemployment—either (EU) or (UE). In this model, a rise in the job-separation rate would increase u* only if the job-finding rate (f) were to rise less than proportionally. Frictions in the labor market, expressed by the duration of unemployment, are the only cause for the "natural rate of unemployment." Without frictions, that is, with instantaneous adjustments, the "natural rate of unemployment" would be zero.

The actual unemployment rate can fluctuate around the steady-state rate. An exogenous negative demand shock, for example, could increase the job-separation rate. This would produce a drop in the job-finding rate rather than a proportional rise because fewer vacancies (labor demand) would be available. A negative demand shock, however, would be offset in the next periods, and the economy would return to its "natural rate of unemployment," the steady-state rate.

Without any demand shocks, a higher pace of structural change in the economy ("internal shocks") can increase the job-separation rate and decrease the job-finding rate, caused, for instance, by an increasing mismatch and hence a longer duration of unemployment. The "natural rate of unemployment," the rate caused only by frictions, would thus rise. But even without an increase in mismatch, as reflected in the duration of unemployment, a higher pace of structural change (i.e., greater separation and accession rates) leads to a higher unemployment rate in the assumed model even if the unemployment duration remains constant, simply because frictions have become more common. Increasing restructuring will most likely also require a higher skill flexibility, so mismatch or the duration of unemployment could be expected to increase.

The arguments made above are based on a constant labor force and assume a labor force composed of identical persons. In this case, a higher pace of structural change together with changing skill requirements is bound to cause additional frictions. In real economies, however, mobility occurs not only between employment and unemployment—flows cross labor market borders as well. This situation leaves more options for the balance of flows into and out of unemployment and employment, and it opens additional channels for adjustments. It might make a difference, therefore, whether one investigates a labor market with high or low external mobility (across the borders), although the size of the labor force might be constant in both cases. With high external mobility, the steady-state rate of unemployment might be lower than otherwise. To include flows across the labor market borders, formula 3.16 requires additional terms like the share of separations which end in unemployment (z) and flows between unemployment and nonparticipation (UN, NU):

$$u_t - u_{t-1} = z \ s \ (1 - u_{t-1}) - f \ u_{t-1} + (nu_u - un_u) \ u_{t-1} \qquad (3.18)$$

with: $z = EU/EX$, i.e., the proportion of the overall outflow out of employment which ends in unemployment

$$nu_u = NU/U_{t-1}$$
$$un_u = UN/U_{t-1}$$

(The subscript [u] indicates the denominator of the flow ratio.)

Although flows between unemployment and nonparticipation balance ($nu_u - un_u = 0$), they might be an important source of skill adjustments. The share of the separations that end in unemployment relative to overall separations (z) influences the impact of separations on unemployment as well. A formula similar to 3.18 can be written for changes of the employment rate:

$$e_t - e_{t-1} = f\, u_{t-1} - s\,(1 - u_{t-1}) + (ne_e - en_e)\, e_{t-1} \qquad (3.19)$$

with: $e_{t-1} = E_{t-1}/L_{t-1}$
$$ne_e = NE/E_{t-1}$$
$$en_e = EN/E_{t-1}$$

A growing labor force itself would not necessarily affect the employment or unemployment rates. These remain constant if both categories are growing at the same percentage rate and if the average duration of unemployment remains constant as well (steady-state growth). In a steady-state growth situation, all categories would grow at the same rate, and labor force internal flows would still balance. The magnitude of the flows would increase but the ratios of flows to the size of the categories would remain constant. With a higher level of employment, for example, we would expect the flows into and out of employment to be higher as well, but the flow ratios remain constant if the behavior of employers and employees stays unchanged.

Flows across the labor force borders—in other words, from employment or unemployment into nonparticipation or in the other direction—would not balance in case the size of the labor force changes. Under the assumption of steady-state growth, the terms "$nu_u - un_u$" in formula 3.18 and "$ne_e - en_e$" in 3.19 are no longer equal to zero but are instead positive or negative. The differences of the flow ratios would diverge from zero by the change in the labor force (dL). Formula 3.18 can thus be expanded to:

$$u_t - u_{t-1} = z\, s\,(1 - u_{t-1}) - f\, u_{t-1} + [(nu_u - un_u) - dL]\, u_{t-1} \qquad (3.20)$$

The steady-state growth condition requires that "$nu_u - un_u$" is equal to dL, the growth rate of the labor force. Similar to formula 3.17, the more general expression for the steady-state rate of unemployment in a situation of labor force growth can be written as:

$$u^* = \cfrac{1}{\left(1 + \left(\cfrac{f}{s\,z} - \cfrac{nu_u - un_u - dL}{s\,z}\right)\right)} \qquad (3.21)$$

$$u^* = \cfrac{1}{\left(1 + \cfrac{f - nu_u - un_u - dL}{s \; z}\right)}$$

Under the steady-state condition, however, the term "$nu_u - un_u - dL$" is zero and formula 3.21 is equal to formula 3.17, except that now only part of the separations end in unemployment (expressed by z). In other words, the steady-state rate of unemployment depends on the ratio of the hiring rate and the separation rate if all labor market categories grow proportionally. An important assumption that has to be made, however, is that the hiring rate and the separation rate are independent of the growth of the labor force and of employment. This underlying assumption is most likely not fulfilled in reality (see section 2.2). It is important for empirical research whether steady-state growth processes are a reliable assumption or whether there are important deviations from such a smooth growth process.

If the focus is on variations in the unemployment rate that are caused by changes in the underlying labor market dynamics and if one assumes that labor market dynamics depend mainly on employment dynamics, then the employment substitution rate, rather than the actual flow ratios, might be used in the formulas above. Making use of the substitution rate for employment rather than of the actual flows, formula 3.17 can be rewritten:

$$u^* = \cfrac{1}{\left(1 + \cfrac{subr_e \; y \; \cfrac{E_t}{U_t}}{subr_e \; z}\right)} \qquad (3.22)$$

$$u^* = \cfrac{1}{\left(1 + \cfrac{y}{z} \cfrac{1}{subr_e \; z \; durue}\right)}$$

with: $subr_e$ = substitution rate for employment (either the separation rate [s] or the accession rate [a], see formula 3.6)

$y = UE \, / \, XE$, i.e., the share of accessions that originated in unemployment in relation to overall accessions

In the steady state, the values for the share of hiring from unemployment (y) and the share of separations that end in unemployment (z), as well as the substitution rate (subr) and duration of unemployment (durue), will be constant. In the real world, however, the variables will not be constant, and formula 3.22 can be used to identify the variables that contribute to the differences between actual unemployment rate and the "natural rate of unemployment."

A long duration of unemployment itself is not necessarily an indicator of a deterioration of the functioning of the labor market. If allowance is made for disequilibrium in the labor market, a long duration of unemployment can be caused by demand deficiency as well. In addition, some political measures, such as a dependence of early retirement benefits on a certain duration of unemployment, might influence unemployment duration as well. It is therefore necessary to evaluate increasing durations of unemployment, and hence increasing "normal" rates of unemployment, against the background of the matching process, overall economic trends, and political measures.

The evaluation of labor market flows also depends on the source of "shocks." With external shocks, it is true that the labor market will regain equilibrium more quickly if flows are higher (see Barro 1988). This is why many economists believe that high flows (external adjustments) are essential for the smooth functioning of labor markets. This situation might be different with respect to "internal shocks," that is, technological progress. In the latter case, one might additionally distinguish between transition periods during which the economy shifts into a more progressive mode of production, and a situation in which the economy has reached this stage of production already. In the latter case, it might well be that more skilled labor is employed and that employment is more stable, a situation that has been found for Germany's manufacturing sectors (Schettkat 1989). Still, explanations of rising "normal" unemployment rates (Summers 1986) either relate to higher mobility (turnover) in the labor market with essentially the same matching function or are based on the assumption that the matching function itself has deteriorated. These two developments are not mutually exclusive, of course. The analysis of the matching process will be developed in the following section.

3.5 THE MATCHING PROCESS

Important for the explanation of trends in labor market dynamics are changes in the skills required by jobs and the skills supplied by workers. The matching process describes how both sides of the labor market come together. "Mismatch" is the economist's catch word for a situation in which the skill requirements of vacancies and the skills of the labor force do not fit. Structural unemployment is a situation in which unemployment and labor demand (vacancies) are both high but appear in different labor markets. A situation of demand deficiency, on the other hand, is expected to show low vacancies and high unemployment in the same market. As mentioned above, skills and qualifications have manifold aspects that are difficult to measure. In economics, however, mismatch is usually measured by an index constructed with vacancies (labor demand) and unemployment (labor supply). In this section, several match and mismatch indicators are discussed, and the matching process as well as the most important variables for this process—vacancies and unemployment—are investigated. Indicators are discussed first.

3.5.1 Matching and Nonmatching

Matching refers to the complex process of bringing jobs and workers together. This process is not limited to what is conventionally called the labor market, that is, an allocation system external to the firm. Matching—the allocation and reallocation of jobs and workers—is undertaken within firms as well (internal labor markets; Doeringer and Piore 1971; Osterman 1984). Of course, the way in which jobs and tasks are structured within the internal labor market has impacts on what one can see happening in the external labor market. Although the allocation and reallocation of jobs and workers may be more intense in the internal labor market, it is less of a problem for more macroeconomically oriented approaches to labor markets, because it is rather a matter of the firm's organization. For this study, it is more important to investigate the matching processes in the external labor market, for it is there that sources of unemployment are identified in economic theory.

The external labor market is still a very important component of the allocation process, a fact reflected in the enormous amount of hiring that takes place during a year. For the employers as well as the employees, the decision on a specific employment contract is dichotomous. In this regard, hiring is no different from many other social phenomena. But, from the macroeconomic viewpoint, hiring also is a continuous process in an advanced economy. "Thus, successful recruiting in the labor market is important to the firm, just as finding a job is important to the worker" (Holt and David 1966, 80).

The indicators most used for labor demand are vacancies or vacancy rates. Since labor turnover is very frequent (for empirical evidence, see chapters 5 and 6), vacancies represent not only additional labor demand but also labor demand that compensates for employees who quit their jobs, who are dismissed, or who retire. Because hiring is always a difficult decision (Semlinger 1989), it needs some time to fill vacant jobs. Therefore, there is a varying time lag between the announcement of the vacancy and actual hiring. "Consequently, new vacancies need to be created in anticipation of future needs, both to compensate for expected losses of the work force through quits, retirements, and termination during the lead time, and to build up the work force for higher production that may be desired in the future" (Holt and David 1966, 82-83).

Overall vacancies thus can be broken down into one component that represents the difference between actual and desired employment and another component that represents labor demand that substitutes for leavers during a certain period:

$$V = \hat{E} + (EU + EN + EO) \tag{3.23}$$

with: V = vacancies
           $\hat{E}$ = anticipated change in employment
           EU, EN, EO represent the flows out of employment (see section 3.2).

Using substitution rates (i.e., the lower value of the flow ratios) instead of the outflows and assuming that these rates represent turnover that is unaffected by the business cycle (normal or natural to the system), formula 3.23 can be rewritten:

$$V = \hat{E} + E_t \, subr_e \qquad\qquad\qquad (3.24)$$

with: $subr_e$ = substitution rate, that is, the lower value of the accession or the separation rate (see section 3.2)

The lead time for vacancies—in other words, the time span between announcing a vacancy and actual hiring—either clearly influences the uncertainties for vacancies or obscures the estimate of the number of vacancies to be announced. Depending on the "announcing mode," this effect might cause the announced vacancies to be higher than they would be otherwise. Where announcing vacancies is a free good, one would expect vacancy figures to be higher than otherwise—one problem for the international comparison of absolute vacancy figures.

One might expect that skilled labor is more difficult to hire (Semlinger 1989) than unskilled labor and that this difference results in a longer lead time (Soskice 1990). More skilled labor has a much lower turnover rate, however. Thus, the duration of hiring, the lead time, might increase, but the necessity for hiring might decrease as well. This relationship has not been worked out very well so far, perhaps because of a lack of data, but work has been done on the relation between the likelihood of filling a vacancy and the number of unemployed persons.

Assuming that the matching process is purely stochastic, that is, that workers are randomly allocated to jobs, then the chance of finding a job will increase with the number of vacancies and the chance of filling a vacancy will increase with the number of unemployed persons. Without assuming any mismatch, the chance of finding a job or filling a vacancy will vary with the business cycle.

Richard Jackman, Richard Layard, and Christopher Pissarides (1989) and Olivier Blanchard and Peter Diamond (1989) have argued that the proportions of vacancies that are filled during a certain period are a function of the ratio of job seekers to vacancies. Thus, the number of engagements during a certain period is the probability of a match multiplied by the number of potential matches (vacancies):

$$e = p \; v = c \; \frac{u}{v} \; v$$

(3.25)

with:
- p = probability of a match
- e = engagements (hirings)
- c = proportion of effective job seekers
- u = unemployment
- v = vacancies

The distinction between effective and noneffective job seekers could mean either that some of the unemployed are no longer regarded as employable from the employer's viewpoint or that the unemployed are not all really searching for employment. The ratio of hiring to vacancies is a good indicator for either of these explanations.

Employers and employees start the search and matching process from different ends. Employers define minimal wages and maximal skill requirements; workers start with maximal wage and minimal skill expectations. This process, however, is flexible with respect to both wage and skill requirements. Workers may accept less favorable working conditions (including wages), while employers may accept less skilled workers at a higher wage.

If skills (in terms of both supply and demand) are less flexible than wages, then unemployment will be concentrated among the unskilled. This process was discussed by Melvin Reder (1964) in the early 1960s. According to him, explaining high unemployment concentrated among unskilled workers in terms of the differences in turnover costs—Walter Oi's (1962) human capital argument—is not plausible because high turnover in itself does not give enough reason for higher unemployment. Duration of unemployment is the intermediating variable (Reder 1964, 316). Whether it is because of the "minimum wage" or simple "natural minimum wage levels," Reder has argued that in recessions, the wages of skilled workers are more flexible than those of the unskilled. As long as there is an excess supply of skilled labor, unskilled labor will suffer unemployment (Buttler 1987, 27).

This conclusion seems very much in line with reality, but other theories, such as insider-outsider and efficiency wage models, would provide an explanation as well. Why are insiders skilled and outsiders unskilled? Do minimum wages not protect the less skilled but act instead as an impediment for wage competition that protects the skilled? Do differentials in hiring and firing costs explain unemployment differentials? The lower hiring costs of unskilled labor should lead to higher turnover but not necessarily to higher unemployment. As long as there is some degree of substitution between skilled and unskilled workers (and there is the possibility of substituting skilled for unskilled labor) and as long as wages are not completely flexible, however, the skill requirements of vacant jobs will depend on the labor market situation.

3.5.2 Indicators for Mismatch

In recent articles (Blanchard and Diamond 1989; Jackman, Layard, and Pissarides 1989; Franz 1987a and 1987b; Abraham 1987), the conventional measure of the functioning of labor markets that has gained prominence is the Beveridge curve, or the unemployment-vacancy relationship. Since unemployment and vacancies are the outcome of movements into and out of these two categories, both can be broken down into an inflow and a duration component. This decomposition provides information on the dynamics behind specific situations. Labor market situations can be composed very differently with respect to these components. Unemployment and vacancies may increase through higher inflows or through a longer duration. The first possibility represents the situation that one expects with business cycles that are caused by aggregate shocks. Conversely, an increase in unemployment and vacancies that is caused by longer durations is more a sign of the malfunctioning of labor markets.

The two parts of Figure 3.3 illustrate the analysis of the functioning of labor markets in terms of vacancies and unemployment. They complement the conventional Beveridge curve presented in section 2.4 because they investigate the dynamic components. The relationship between flow and duration is analyzed first, on the assumption of a smoothly functioning labor market—that is, a relationship of vacancies (changes and duration) that depend solely on aggregate shocks. No mismatch occurs. In the conventional Beveridge curve diagram, the result is a movement along a stable curve with the qualifications mentioned in section 2.4, that is, a counter-clockwise loop around this curve. A low vacancy rate will occur with a high unemployment rate and vice versa.

Starting in a recession (point 1 in the vacancies diagram of Figure 3.3) and moving into an expansionary period, vacancies will rise. With increasing vacancies, one expects the duration to rise as a function of the pool of unemployed. As long as unemployment exists and no mismatch occurs (the curve between points 1 and 2), duration will not change much with rising vacancies because vacancies can be filled immediately. But at some point (2), it will become more difficult to recruit, and duration will increase. In the "ideal" labor market (homogeneous labor), this will occur at zero unemployment, but in a realistic labor market, this point will occur before unemployment disappears completely. If vacancies increases diminish (after point 3), however, then the duration will continue to increase until demand genuinely shrinks (after point 4).

The vacancy duration would remain at more or less the "full employment level" (curve between points 4 and 5) since a shrinking number of vacancies does not necessarily affect employment and unemployment. Employment could in theory remain constant with no vacancies at all. At some point (5), however, decreasing vacancies will most likely be accompanied by decreasing employment and rising unemployment. The result will be an expansion of the pool of unemployed, a change that makes recruiting easier. Assuming the same func-

Figure 3.3
The Relationship between Changes of Duration of Vacancies and Unemployment in the Business Cycle: Change-Duration Curves

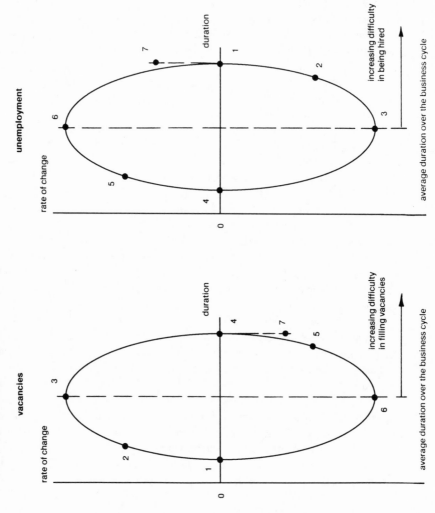

tioning of the labor market, the curve will end at its initial starting point (1). This would be the figure produced by a pure business cycle. The average duration of vacancies over a complete business cycle would shift outwards, however, if malfunctioning of the labor market increases.

In a labor market with a given labor force, the change-duration curve in the vacancies diagram of Figure 3.3 could end up at point 7. In other words, a longer duration of vacancies may establish independently from the level of vacancies simply because the labor supply is exhausted and employment remains constant. For the economy as a whole, of course, such a development is very unlikely, but it might occur in specific labor markets, that is, in particular industries or occupations.

Still, continued unemployment and persistently long periods of vacancy combine to indicate a mismatch in the labor market. If European labor markets are malfunctioning more and more, as has been asserted, then there should be longer durations at all levels of vacancies. In other words, the average duration over the business cycle (the vertical line in the diagram) should shift outwards, a change that would indicate recruiting problems.

An illustration of the relation between changes in unemployment and unemployment duration resembles that for vacancies. Starting with the same situation (point 1 in the second part of Figure 3.3) as with vacancies, one expects unemployment to cease increasing and duration to decline. With increasing labor demand, unemployment will shrink and duration will shorten until expansion levels off (after point 3) to the extent that expansion in labor demand ends. Assuming that employment decreases, unemployment will rise in both components of level and duration. In a functioning labor market, the curve should end at 1 again after a business cycle. If employment remains at high levels, however, one would expect the unemployment curve to remain at point 4. This situation is the equivalent to the line between points 4 and 7 in the illustration of the vacancies diagram. A malfunctioning of the labor market would be indicated if the axis of the "unemployment circle" in Figure 3.3 were to shift outward.

To summarize, the dynamics of vacancies are not independent of supply dynamics. Increasing vacancies with a constant duration (vertical lines) are an indicator of sufficient labor supply, whereas horizontal trends to the right indicate recruiting problems that might be caused by mismatch or simply by exhausted labor supply. An increasing mismatch or an impaired functioning of the labor market is indicated by shifts of the curves in both parts of Figure 3.3. The principal shape of the curves should not be affected, however.

Allowing for flows across labor force borders and an increasing labor force, both the vacancy and the unemployment curves can shift in different directions. It might be possible, for example, that vacancies will be filled by new labor market entrants, and there might be no recruiting problem at all. Nevertheless, the unemployed might be regarded as unemployable, and unemployment would shift outwards to longer durations. This situation is described as hysteresis.

Those who have already been unemployed for a long time have little or no chance to return to employment. Unemployment would start at a higher level when the next cycle begins (point 7 of the unemployment diagram).

The relationship between changes in the level and duration of unemployment and vacancies is one way to describe mismatch in the labor market. Another is the computation of indices. A mismatch indicator commonly used (Franz 1987a; Jackman, Layard, and Pissarides 1989) is constructed in the following formula:

$$mm_1 = \sum_{j=1}^{n} |\frac{v_j}{v} - \frac{u_j}{u}| \tag{3.26}$$

with: v = vacancies or vacancy rate
          u = unemployment or unemployment rate
          j = subscript for industries

This indicator is lowest (0) if all industries have identical vacancy and unemployment rates or proportional shares of vacancies and unemployment. The higher the variation between the rates of individual industries, the higher the value of mm1 (mismatch). Movements of labor from industries (occupations) with excess supply to industries (occupations) with excess demand for labor would reduce the mismatch and unemployment. The latter is not caused by demand deficiency but by the nonfitting of demand and supply, by mismatch. This conclusion, however, is based on the assumption that demand for labor within the categories is homogeneous, an assumption that is more reasonable for occupations than for industries.

Mismatch can also occur within sectors (nonhomogeneous labor within industries). In this case, the values for v_j/v minus u_j/u could be low, or even zero, although the level of both unemployment and vacancies could be very high. Thus, this indicator should be used only if high unemployment and vacancies cannot both occur in one industry at the same time. In other words, formula 3.26 is a useful indicator for mismatch if one assumes that demand shifts across industries are causing discrepancies between labor demand and supply, that barriers to labor mobility between industries are high, and that labor within industries (occupations) is essentially homogeneous. Similar remarks apply to another often used indicator, which is computed by the sum of the absolute differences of industry-specific or occupation-specific vacancies and unemployment.

If, however, technological change causes skill changes and discrepancies between labor demand and supply within an industry, then the measure computed with formula 3.26 could indicate low mismatch, although this is not true for individual industries. Whenever there is a general trend in the economy of specific skills gaining importance in every industry, as with white-collar work (Warnken and Ronning 1989 and Baethge 1988 for Germany; Kutscher 1990 for the United States), mismatch can exist in individual industries but can be evenly distributed across industries. In this case, the indicator computed by formula 3.26 would display little or no mismatch, although the contrary is actually true: Discrepancies between the skill requirements of jobs and the skills of the unemployed are particularly important.

Recently, similar criticism has been voiced by Giorgio Brunello (CEPR 1990), who has argued that conventional mismatch indicators do not capture more or less permanent regional differences in the unemployment-vacancy relation. He has favored another indicator developed by Jackman, Layard, and Savoury (1990), which makes use of the variance of relative unemployment rates across sectors. This, in their view, is the best mismatch indicator:

$$mm_2 = \frac{1}{n} \sum_{j=1}^{n} (u_j - u)^2 \tag{3.27}$$

with: u = unemployment rate
        j = index for industries or occupations

This indicator does not take actual labor demand within industries or occupations into account. The variance of mm_2 could be low, but unemployment could still be at a very high level. The conclusion that unemployment in this case is not caused by mismatch but by demand deficiency again rests on the assumption that labor within industries or occupations is sufficiently homogeneous.

In this study, we favor an indicator that accounts for intra-industry mismatch as well. Such an indicator can be constructed with the definition of maladjustment used by Dow and Dicks-Mireaux (1958; Hansen 1970; see section 2.4.2). They have defined maladjustment as the point at which unemployment equals vacancies ($u = v$). The higher this value, the more severe the mismatch. This definition can be used to develop an indicator that takes intra-industry mismatch into account and uses the lower value of either the unemployment or the vacancy rate:

$$mm_3 = \frac{1}{2} \sum_{j=1}^{n} e_j \, (u_j + v_j - |u_j - v_j|) \tag{3.28}$$

with: e_j = share of the industry in relation to total employment (E_j/E) or the labor force

This measure is highest if intra-industry maladjustment is great, but it assumes that mobility across industries is low.

Clearly, mismatch across industries and within industries depends not only on the pace of structural change and technological progress but also on the functioning of training and retraining systems. If training and retraining are provided by firms themselves (internal adjustment, Sengenberger 1984 and 1990), then mismatch would not occur in labor market statistics, although skill adjustments might be substantial. If training and retraining are provided externally, measured mismatch might be high. The type of training or retraining system is therefore an important variable for the adjustment ability of the economy (Soskice 1990) and for the extent that mismatch is measured by labor market statistics.

In chapters 5 and 6, different mismatch measures will be used and compared. It will not be possible, however, to compute every indicator for both countries because, as always, international comparative approaches inevitably suffer from data problems.

3.6 THEORETICAL EXPLANATIONS FOR CHANGING UNEMPLOYMENT RATES AND LABOR MARKET DYNAMICS

The various explanations for the changing level of unemployment rates in Germany and the United States that were developed in chapter 2 (summarized in section 2.6) can now be specified and linked to the indicators for labor market dynamics. The explanations for persistently high levels of unemployment emphasize either demand deficiency or the matching process. The latter is of primary interest here since developments in economics during the last few decades have inverted Richard Lipsey's (1965) suggestion that existing unemployment can be reduced through demand expansion until only structural unemployment is left. Today, it first has to be shown that structural factors are not preventing the economy from expanding and that quantitative measures, such as demand expansion or shorter working hours, are appropriate to reduce unemployment.

The theoretical hypotheses about persistent unemployment and mismatch in the labor market can be summarized under the following headings: (1) The wage structure has destroyed incentives for mobility; (2) the pace of structural change has increased; (3) insiders exclude outsiders from employment; (4) employers are reluctant to hire; (5) mismatch and bottlenecks have occurred; and (6) (long-term) unemployment is self-sustaining (hysteresis).

The wage structure has destroyed incentives for mobility. A great deal of research has been done on this hypothesis, and theoretical arguments as well as empirical evidence are presented in section 2.3.4 of this study. The available empirical data do not particularly support the view that the German wage structure has become more rigid. Recent research suggests that the explanation of the wage structure is more complex than the competitive labor market model suggests.

The pace of structural change has increased. The effect of a higher pace of structural change on labor market dynamics depends on whether the changes in the economy's structure occur when positive growth rates differ or whether they occur when there are positive and negative growth rates simultaneously. In the second case, one would expect higher flows into and out of employment and the labor market or between industries; adjustments will be greater. Different indicators for the pace of structural change are presented for both countries in section 4.3, and flows are analyzed in chapters 5 and 6.

Insiders exclude outsiders from employment. If these arguments are important, one expects decreasing flow ratios in and out of employment. The insider-outsider argument has also been used to explain low employment growth, which is said to be due to overly high wages paid to insiders. In this case, it is difficult to identify the "right" wage, as discussed in the wage section (2.3).

Employers are reluctant to hire. Reluctance to hire can be caused by greater uncertainty about future demand levels or future skill requirements. In any case, one would expect the accession rate (a) and the inflow ratios from unemployment and nonparticipation into employment to have decreased. Employers may have become more choosy, and this may have resulted in a prolonged duration of vacancies. The employment elasticity of economic growth should also have declined, according to this argument.

Mismatch and bottlenecks have occurred. If mismatch is a problem in the economy, one expects unemployment and vacancies to be high simultaneously. In the case of bottlenecks, certain occupations are expected to have very low unemployment rates, while labor demand (vacancies) is very high in these occupations. Depending on the distribution of declining and expanding occupations across industries, the industry-specific unemployment-vacancy relations will be affected differently. They could indicate mismatch, depending on the indicator used, if occupational bottlenecks are concentrated in certain industries, but they could indicate no mismatch if the occupational bottlenecks are distributed evenly across industries.

In a technologically progressive economy, one would expect strong intra-industry maladjustment if training or retraining is ineffective, in the sense that it does not allow adjustments of skills. The substitution rate should be high, indicating the exchange of employees (external adjustment). An effective training and retraining system and a high initial skill level might, however, lead to internal adjustments and "unidentified mismatch." In a technologically stagnant economy, on the other hand, we would expect no serious mismatch problems and no necessity for high substitution rates.

Although excess demand for labor in an industry might not affect the industry's unemployment, it might nevertheless have an effect on the labor market. Newly hired employees might come from unemployment in other industries (U_iE_j), from other industries' employment (E_iE_j), or from nonparticipation (NE_j). These possible patterns indicate very different labor market dynamics and different adjustment mechanisms in an economy. If newly hired employees are recruited from other industries or from nonparticipation, this would cause a discrepancy between trends in unemployment and vacancy rates and in their components. Vacancies might be filled in short periods, and unemployment might remain at high levels at the same time; a reverse trend would occur in the relationship of duration and changes in level in the vacancy and unemployment diagrams (Figure 3.3 and sections 5.4 and 6.4).

(Long-term) unemployment is self-sustaining (hysteresis). High rates of excess labor supply and long-term unemployment may have destroyed the working ability of the unemployed (one cause of hysteresis). This would result in long-term unemployment. Furthermore, the hiring rate (f) from unemployment would be low, but flow ratios from unemployment into nonparticipation would be high. Unless society provides alternative roles for dismissed persons, they may remain unemployed for long periods. The U.S. and German economies differ in their social security systems, which may have influenced the unemployment dynamics.

Has the (flow) equilibrium rate of unemployment increased over recent decades? If so, what has caused the increase? The theoretical arguments about labor market dynamics and developments in the U.S. and German economies will be investigated on an empirical basis in the following sections.

4

Job Boom and Job Decline: Global Economic Trends in the United States and Germany

4.1 DEVELOPMENT OF CENTRAL ECONOMIC INDICATORS SINCE THE 1960s

This section is an exploration of trends in the main economic indicators in the U.S. and the German economies. The data series start in the early 1960s in order to allow for the investigation of changes in the relations among the indicators. Because the United States experienced high unemployment during the 1960s when Germany's unemployment was low while the opposite—although at different levels—has been true for the mid-1980s, it is of particular interest whether other economic relationships have changed as well. Wages are not discussed in this section because empirical evidence on the wage issue was presented in section 2.3.

4.1.1 Population, Labor Force, and Unemployment

The unemployment rates displayed in Figure 4.1 show substantial differences in the 1960s, when Germany's unemployment rate was below the 1 percent level (except for the recession years of 1967 and 1968). During the same time, the United States experienced unemployment rates well above 3 percent and even above 5 percent. During these years, the puzzle in economics was to explain why the United States was doing so badly compared with Europe and Germany in terms of this central economic indicator (Killingsworth 1963). Times changed during the 1970s, however, when Germany's unemployment rate increased to 4 percent, and during the 1980s, when its rate rose above the 8

Figure 4.1
Unemployment Rates in the United States and Germany, 1963–1988

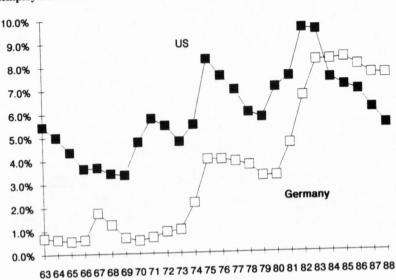

Source: Computations are based on OECD labor force statistics.
Note: Unemployment rates are the share of unemployment in the labor force; annual averages.

percent level. In the same period, the U.S. unemployment rate increased as well and was higher than the German rate in the 1970s, but the U.S. rate declined during the 1980s and fell below the German rate. Both economies are now experiencing levels of unemployment well above Germany's levels of the 1960s (see Figure 4.1).

The shift in the economic discussion, which now concentrates on explaining the persistently high levels of unemployment in Germany or, more generally, in Europe, was caused less by the success of the U.S. economy with respect to changes in its unemployment rate than by the success of the "Great American Job Machine." (For a discussion of the unemployment rate as an indicator for employment policy, see Peters and Schmid 1982; Schettkat 1989.)

The main development distinguishing the two economies from each other is the tremendous growth of jobs provided by the U.S. economy and the stagnating or slow job growth in the German economy (see Figure 4.3). This phenomenon, however, was already apparent in the 1960s. High rates of job growth and high rates of unemployment occurred simultaneously in the United States because the population and the labor force grew even faster than jobs did during most of the period analyzed. In Germany, by contrast, low levels of unemployment in the 1960s can be explained, to a substantial extent, by labor supply developments, which were characterized by a stagnating population of working age (15 to 65 years) and a slight decline in labor force participation (see Figure 4.2). The growing U.S. labor force has been the result not only of

Figure 4.2
Labor Force Participation Rates in the United States and Germany, 1963–1988

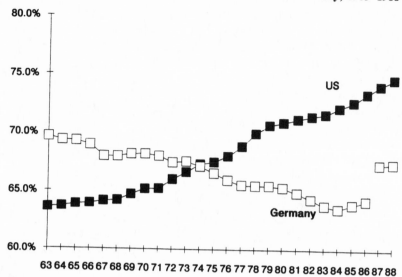

Source: Computations are based on OECD labor force statistics.
Note: Participation rates are computed as labor force (15/16 years +) divided by population (15/16 to 65 years). Figures for Germany from 1986 on are not comparable with those up to 1985, mainly because of marginal employment hidden in the values up to 1985.

population growth but also of a rising labor force participation rate, which grew from roughly 65 percent in the 1960s to about 75 percent in the late 1980s. In Germany, the labor force participation rate stagnated and even declined during this period. The overall trend was caused mainly by a shrinking rate for men, compensated by rate growth among women (for details, Schettkat 1987). The rise in the overall U.S. participation rate was caused by a growing female participation rate.

So far, the United States can be characterized as an economy with high secular rates of growth in employment, population, and labor force participation rates. The German economy can be summarized as stagnating with respect to these labor market indicators. It is important to note, however, that these trends are secular and not specific to certain periods. Furthermore, they have occurred with both high and low rates of unemployment, a fact that casts doubt on simple explanations of high unemployment through demographic variables.

4.1.2 Economic Growth and Productivity Growth

Output, as measured by GDP, roughly doubled in both economies from 1963 to 1986 (see Figures 4.3 and 4.4). Despite these similarities in economic growth, the number of jobs that were developed was very different. Total jobs (employment) in the United States rose by roughly 60 percent, whereas German employment declined slightly during this period. The number of employed persons, however, depends not only on economic growth but also on productivity increases and average working time.

Figures 4.3 and 4.4 display the overall hours worked in both economies as well. It is immediately clear from these series that the U.S. employment miracle cannot be explained in terms of working-time arrangements alone. U.S. job growth has been achieved mainly by an increasing number of working hours and not just by the effect of an expansion of marginal part-time employment. In Germany, on the other hand, the total number of hours worked dropped substantially, by roughly 20 percentage points, but the country's economic growth was still almost the same as that in the United States. Despite Germany's substantially shrinking number of working hours, the number of persons employed declined by only about 4 percentage points until the mid-1980s. Since then, the number of persons employed in Germany has increased, partly because of an underestimation of marginal employment that was discovered by the census and, in the last few years, because of the enormous demand expansion in Eastern Europe, including the former German Democratic Republic. The less than proportional decline in employment is the result of a decrease in average working time in Germany, a reduction achieved by an increased number of holidays, the introduction of a shorter work week, and an expansion in the overall share of part-time work (for the importance of the different components for historical trends, see Reyher and Kohler 1988).

Obviously, the same rate of output growth produced much more additional employment in the United States than in Germany. In other words, the employment elasticity of economic growth was much higher in the United States (.63 for the period 1963 to 1986) than in Germany (−.05). Still, the negative sign for the employment elasticity of economic growth in Germany cannot be interpreted as a causal relationship. It simply illustrates that additional variables influence the employment outcome associated with economic growth. Most prominent in this context are wages, productivity, and average working time.

The per-hour productivity trends shown in Figures 4.3 and 4.4 illustrate the huge productivity increases in Germany compared with the United States, where productivity growth was even negative in some years. Germany has never experienced a decline in productivity, but productivity growth rates have nevertheless followed a secular declining trend. Except for a few years, productivity in Germany grew at a higher rate than output, whereas the opposite has been true for the United States. Based on the data presented in Figures 4.3 and 4.4 simple univariate regressions for the period 1964 to 1987 produced higher coefficients of regression for GDP changes on productivity growth, the Kaldor-Verdoorn relationship, for Germany ($b = 0.5$ [standard error $= 0.1$], $R^2 = 0.5$) than for the United States ($b = 0.3$ [standard error $= 0.03$], $R^2 = 0.4$). In other words, the productivity increases in Germany are more sensitive to output variations than in the United States although the relationship in Germany seems to

Figure 4.3

U.S. Productivity (per Hour), Employment, and Hours Worked; and U.S. Annual Changes of GDP and Productivity, Overall Economy

GDP, employment, hours of work, and productivity in the US

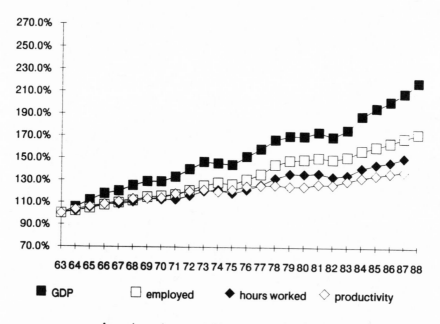

Annual growh rates of GDP, and productivity in the US

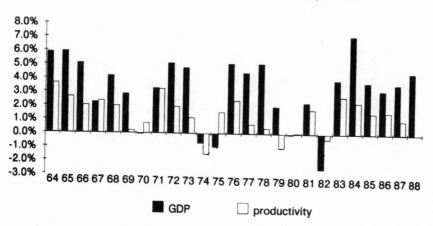

Source: Computations are based OECD statistics, BLS data for hours worked.

Figure 4.4
German Productivity (per Hour), Employment, and Hours Worked; and German Annual Changes of GDP and Productivity, Overall Economy

GDP, employment, hours of work, and productivity in Germany

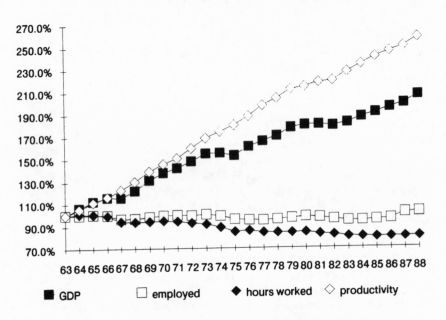

Annual growth rates of GDP and productivity in Germany

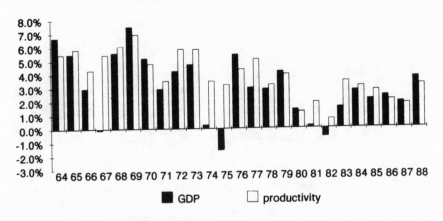

Source: Computations are based OECD statistics, IAB data for hours worked.
Note: The increase in employment in Germany in 1987 is due to new figures based on the census. Figures before 1987 are not corrected.

have weakened since the mid-1970s (Kalmbach 1983). The result is compatible with the findings of Julio Rotemberg and Laurence Summers (1988), who argued that, procyclically, productivity growth is mainly caused by labor hoarding, since one would expect labor hoarding to be more important in Germany, with its more restrictive labor laws. In light of this explanation it is surprising that productivity growth in the United States was even negative in some years but always positive in Germany.

It has been shown in several studies (Sengenberger 1987; Abraham and Houseman 1988) that hours worked in Germany are adjusted to demand variations as quickly as they are in the United States. In the United States, labor input is varied more by persons being hired or dismissed, while in Germany, the average hours per employee vary and the number of employed persons remains very stable in the short run. In the long run, however, both economies vary the number of persons employed. If the reaction of hours worked is similar in the two economies, we would expect similar coefficients of regression. The fact that they differ and that the United States has experienced negative productivity growth may then be caused by either a different structure of the economies or different "production regimes" (Boyer 1987).

One explanation of Germany's high productivity increases is that they are caused by the slow growth of services, which are regarded as low-productivity (stagnant) industries. In essence, a bigger share of services reduces productivity. Based on productivity data from the Bureau of Labor Statistics (BLS) (Jablonsky, Kunze, and Otto 1990) and the ifo-institute in Munich, detailed productivity trends for specific industries in the private sector have been analyzed. Productivity figures are difficult to compare, and the validity of the figures depends heavily on the reliability of volume estimates of the GDP. It is well known that tremendous difficulties exist with national accounting data, especially at constant prices, and that results therefore should not be interpreted too rigorously. Nevertheless, national accounting data are the main data source for economic analysis. Although small changes may be caused entirely by measurement errors, it is hard to believe that substantial differentials are the result of measurement errors alone. The analysis is restricted to labor productivity and uses only trends, since it can be assumed that trends are less affected by measurement errors (see Figure 4.5).

Based on the available data mentioned above, a very similar picture emerges in every industry in the private sector. Germany's productivity trend is well above the U.S. productivity increases over the whole period. It may well be that the share of low-productivity industries has grown faster in the United States than in Germany, which would have reduced productivity increases in the United States relative to Germany. The overall productivity trend has therefore been decomposed into a component that describes productivity trends under the assumption of constant industry-specific productivity but with a changing industry structure (structural component). Another component has been computed under the assumption of a constant industry structure, with produc-

Figure 4.5
Components of Productivity Trends in the United States and Germany, Private Sector, 1963–1987

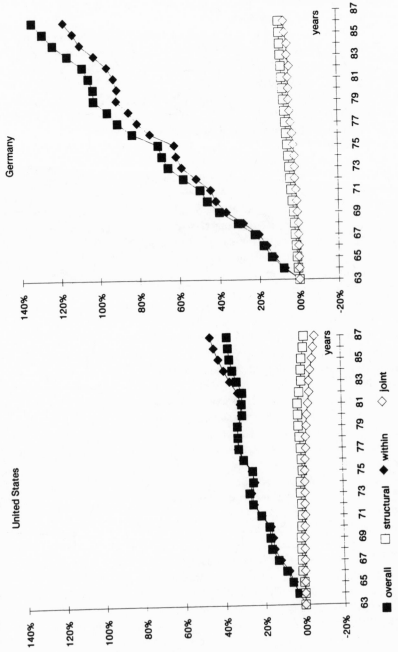

Source: Computations are based on BLS data for the US and ifo data for Germany.
Note: Base year for the computation is 1963. The values for the various components give the relative difference to the 1963 productivity.

tivity growth within industries (within components) being allowed for. A third component the joint effect, appears because of simultaneous changes in the other two components.

The trends of the productivity components based on 9 industries of the private sector are displayed in Figure 4.5. The structural component has reduced the overall U.S. productivity trend, especially since 1980. Without sectoral shifts, overall productivity growth would have been higher in the United States. The reverse has been true for Germany. The structural component has increased the overall productivity trend. Although the shift to service industries has been less pronounced in Germany than in the United States, the service sector nevertheless has grown as a share of overall employment in Germany as well (see section 4.2). Service industries like banking, however, are not low-productivity industries in Germany. This is not the place to address problems related to productivity measurement, but it is hard to believe that measurement is the only explanation for the divergent productivity trends. William Baumol, Sue Blackman and Ed Wolf (1989) have argued that the slowdown in American productivity growth is mainly caused by the expansion of service industries that are stagnant with respect to productivity trends. It was less a demand shift to services than the inevitable growth of its employment shares in the case of "cost disease" (Baumol 1967) that led the service sector to expand and overall productivity to decline (see Williamson 1991). These arguments are basically in line with the results presented here and higher overall productivity growth in Germany might be due to "catching up," but the question remains why German service industries seem to be less affected by cost diseases than U.S. services.

4.1.3 Cost and Final Demand Components of GDP

Since the end of the 1960s, compensation of employees has been, with some variations, about 60 percent of the GDP in the United States; this share was substantially lower in Germany. Furthermore, it has declined in Germany since 1981, when it reached its highest level, 57 percent of the GDP. In 1986, the ratio was almost at the level of 1970. A symmetrical trend has emerged in the ratio of operating surplus. It is higher in Germany than in the United States and has been rising since 1982. The U.S. profit ratio declined, with variations, until 1982, when it reached its lowest level—16.6 percent. Since then, the ratio has increased slightly. The consumption of fixed capital has risen in both economies since the 1970s, reaching levels of roughly 12 percent in the 1980s (Table 4.1).

Germany's high labor productivity gains may have been caused by a more capital-intensive organization of the production process. Consumption of fixed capital divided by GDP in the two economies has roughly been developing in similar directions (Table 4.1). Gross fixed capital formation (measured in constant 1980 prices) divided by labor (either employed persons or hours worked)

Table 4.1
Cost Components of GDP (In Percentage of GDP, Current Prices)

years	US				Germany			
-------	compen- sation of employees	opera- tional surplus	consumption of fixed capital	indirect taxes	compen- sation of employees	opera- tional surplus	consumption of fixed capital	indirect taxes
1963	57.2	24.1	10.1	09.0	50.2	27.8	09.2	13.8
1966	57.7	24.4	09.6	08.5	51.4	26.6	09.8	13.4
1971	60.3	19.9	10.6	09.4	54.3	23.9	10.3	13.1
1976	60.2	19.4	12.0	08.6	56.2	22.1	11.1	12.7
1981	60.4	18.1	13.4	08.4	57.2	19.6	12.2	12.9
1986	60.1	19.7	12.5	08.3	53.5	24.0	12.4	12.2
1989	60.3	20.2	12.3	08.1	52.4	24.8	12.4	12.4

Source: Calculations based on OECD National Accounts Statistics, current prices.

is lower in the United States than in Germany and in Europe in general, but it has occurred not only during periods of high German unemployment but also during the 1960s and early 1970s, when unemployment was much lower in Germany than in the United States (see also Gordon 1988, 276). However, gross fixed capital formation per hour worked almost doubled in Germany from 1963 to 1986 whereas this ratio increased only by roughly 40 percent in the United States.

In the United States, total domestic expenditures have always been higher than the GDP (see Table 4.2), and the ratio of these two variables increased in the 1980s. As a result, the import ratios (imports divided by the GDP) are higher than the export ratios, revealing the widely discussed increasing gap between the two indicators in the 1980s. The situation in Germany has been completely different. In most years, Germany consumed less than it produced. In contrast to developments in the United States, Germany's exports increased considerably in the 1980s, and the gap between the import and export ratios widened. Moreover, the values of the ratios were much higher for Germany than for the United States, but in both countries, the series show a positive trend. It is immediately clear that the German economy depends much more on the world market than does the U.S. economy.

Perhaps surprisingly, the governments' final consumption expenditures have been very similar in both countries as a ratio to GDP and have been very stable over the whole period (see Table 4.2). A substantial difference has been apparent in private consumption expenditures. Again, this difference was already occurring in the 1960s and has persisted with some variations over the whole period. Investment ratios (gross fixed capital formation) have remained around 20 percent during the whole period in the United States, dipping to their lowest value of 17.2 percent in 1982. Investment ratios in Germany declined from

Table 4.2

Components of Final Demand (In Percentage of GDP, 1980 Prices)

years	total domestic demand	private final consumption expenditure	government final consumption expenditure	gross fixed capital formation	exports	imports
			US			
1963	101.3	59.7	20.6	20.4	5.7	7.1
1966	101.9	59.4	20.3	20.9	5.9	7.8
1971	103.3	62.2	20.1	20.2	6.4	9.7
1976	102.4	64.8	18.3	18.4	8.5	10.9
1981	100.8	62.7	18.6	18.4	9.8	10.6
1986	105.8	65.9	19.6	19.8	8.7	14.5
1989	101.2	65.1	17.8	17.9	10.5	11.9
			Germany			
1963	99.0	51.9	20.6	26.0	15.7	14.8
1966	99.1	51.9	19.6	26.5	17.3	16.3
1971	101.0	54.7	19.1	26.6	21.0	22.1
1976	99.1	56.0	20.2	21.2	25.2	24.3
1981	97.8	56.5	20.5	21.6	28.5	26.3
1986	96.5	56.0	20.0	20.1	31.0	27.5
1989	98.0	56.8	18.9	21.0	33.7	31.8

Source: Calculations based on OECD National Accounts Statistics, 1980 prices,
1985 prices for 1989.

values of about 26 percent in the 1960s to values of roughly 20 percent in the 1980s. This change, however, has been closely related to trends in investments in buildings and is not surprising since the German population has been stagnating (see also Appelbaum and Schettkat 1990a). If one adds consumption and investment as two private demand categories, one arrives at a slightly decreasing ratio (77.9 percent in 1963 to 76.1 percent in 1986) for Germany, as opposed to an increasing ratio (80.1 percent in 1963 to 85.7 percent in 1986) for the United States. The main difference between the two economies seems to be that domestic demand in the United States has become more important, whereas foreign demand has gained importance in Germany.

4.1.4 Income per Capita: Different Measures

Leaving aside the well-known and serious criticism of the concepts of the GDP and the national accounting framework (Zapf 1979; Leipert 1975), a rate of economic growth equal to the rate of population or labor force growth is necessary to hold the income per capita constant. In order for the economic situation of the population to improve, a rate of economic growth higher than the rate of population growth is required. A steady-state rate of economic growth would result in a constant ratio of economic output (measured as the GDP at constant prices) to population. The most comprehensive denominator is the nation's total population (indicator 1), but since younger and older persons usually do not participate in the labor market, the population of working age (15 to 65 years) is another suitable denominator (indicator 2). The difference between these two indicators is influenced mainly by demographic factors. For example, a high birth rate (and thus a high proportion of very young persons) would cause indicator 1 to grow at a lower rate than indicator 2.

Since income per capita is an indicator of the efficiency of the economy, it is useful to compare it to other measures of the efficiency of the economy. These are the GDP per labor force (indicator 3), the GDP per employed person (indicator 4), and the GDP per hour worked (indicator 5). All five indicators will change at the same rate if the proportion of the working age population in the total population remains constant, if the participation rate remains unchanged, if the unemployment rate is steady, and if average working hours are fixed. Therefore, these indicators can be used to describe different types of increasing efficiency in the economy and different forms of the division of labor.

The GDP per employed person, for instance, could grow very quickly, but this might be accompanied by increasing unemployment and, hence, by less growth of indicator 3 (GDP per labor force). Another example would occur if the proportion of part-time work increased or working hours were generally reduced this would reduce the growth rates of indicator 4 (GDP per employed person). This situation reflects more the distribution of work than changes in the efficiency of production, which is much better described by indicator 5 (GDP per hour worked). The latter might even be influenced positively by shorter working hours or part-time work (Schettkat 1984).

Table 4.3 gives a more systematic overview of the relations between the different indicators and the intervening variables. The two economies experienced almost an inverse order of growth rates for the various indicators. In the United States, the GDP per capita (indicator 1) increased at a much higher rate than the GDP per hour worked (indicator 5), and the growth rate of the latter is higher than the GDP per employed person (indicator 4) as shown in Figure 4.5. In Germany the GDP per hour worked (indicator 5) increased at the highest rate, followed by GDP per employed person (indicator 4), while the lowest growth appeared for the GDP per capita in the working-age population (indicator 2) (see Figure 4.6). These inverse developments of the different efficiency indicators in the United States and Germany are also shown by the high and negative rank order correlation coefficient ($-.7$) for the growth rates of these different indicators between the two countries.

As mentioned in section 4.1.2, the productivity (GDP per hour worked) of the German economy developed very well. Economic growth in Germany was thus brought about not by population growth but by the increasing efficiency of the production process. Part of the increased efficiency per hour has been used to reduce average working hours in Germany, as shown in Figure 4.6 by

Table 4.3

Overview of Different Indicators for the Efficiency of an Economy

indicators				
GDP per capita (total population)	GDP per capita (population 15-65 years)	GDP per labor force (civilian)	GDP per employed person	GDP per hour worked (productivity)
1	2	3	4	5

Relations between growth rates

1 = 2	Constant share of working-age population in relation to total population
1 > 2	Increasing share of working-age population in relation to total population
1 < 2	Decreasing share of working-age population in relation to total population
2 = 3	Constant labor force participation
2 > 3	Increasing labor force participation
2 < 3	Decreasing labor force participation
3 = 4	Constant unemployment rate
3 > 4	Decreasing unemployment rate
3 < 4	Increasing unemployment rate
4 = 5	Constant average working hours
4 > 5	Increasing working hours
4 < 5	Decreasing working hours

line 4, which runs below line 5. The curve for the GDP per labor force (line 3) is below line 4, however, indicating an inefficient use of the labor force or high and increasing unemployment. Since GDP per total population (line 1) is highly influenced by demographic factors (the age structure), it is not a particularly good indicator of economic efficiency. The GDP per capita of the working-age population (line 2) is influenced mainly by changes in labor force participation, so it is a good indicator for the division of labor in the economy. This curve shows a slight overall decrease in the participation rate in Germany.

In the United States, the growth of the GDP per capita for the total population (line 1) and for the population in the working-age category (line 2) was higher than that of the other indicators. This fact reflects the increasing participation rates in the United States. Lines 3 and 4 are below line 5 in the United States, which reflects decreasing average working hours (caused mainly by an increasing proportion of part-time work). Most importantly, the growth of the GDP in the United States is related largely to an increasing labor force, whose expansion has been caused by both a growing population and increasing participation rates. By contrast, Germany's economy might be characterized as a productivity miracle. Income per capita has increased at a higher rate than in the United States as a result of faster productivity growth, which in economics is often equated with technological progress. Still, the U. S. economy has been

Figure 4.6
GDP per Capita, per Labor Force, per Employed Person, and per Hour Worked, 1963–1988

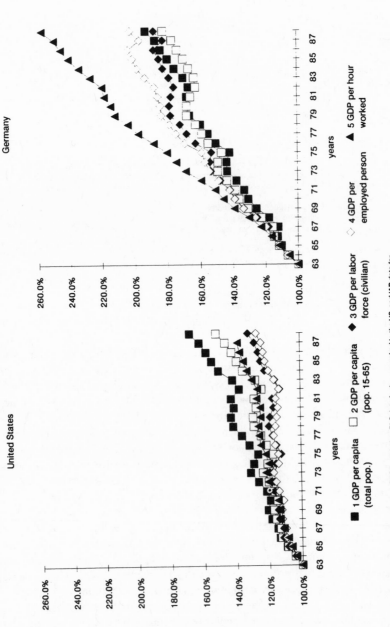

Source: Computations are based on OECD statistics, BLS data for hours worked in the US, and IAB data for hours worked in Germany.

Note: The increase in employment in Germany in 1987 is due to new figures based on the census. Figures before 1987 are not corrected.

more successful at integrating a high share of the population into the production process. Work is obviously more evenly distributed in the United States than in Germany. Of course, the distribution of work cannot be equated with the distribution of income (see Burtless 1990; Levy 1987; Danziger, Gottschalk, and Smolensky 1988; Haveman 1988).

4.2 THE STRUCTURE OF THE ECONOMIES

Both the U. S. and German economies have experienced a decline in agriculture and manufacturing and, consequently, an expansion of the service sector. To that extent, the developments are in line with the Three-Sector-Hypothesis. The share of manufacturing declined in the United States from 1963 to 1973 by 2 percentage points. In the following decade, however, and mainly after 1979, it fell by 5 percentage points, a development that provided the basis for discussions about deindustrialization (Bluestone and Harrison 1982; Cohen and Zysman 1987). In Germany, the share of manufacturing was stable in the 1960s, but from 1973 to 1983, this sector's share of overall employment dropped by 7 percentage points. Germany's overall net employment losses in the 1960s were caused solely by the shrinking primary (agricultural) sector, while the German manufacturing sector has been shrinking since 1973. In relative terms, however, many more persons are still employed in manufacturing in Germany than in the United States (see Figure 4.7). In the United States, only 28 percent of civilian employment was found in the secondary sector, compared to 41 percent in Germany at the end of the analyzed period.

Accordingly, the service sector's share is much smaller in Germany than in the United States (54 percent compared to 69 percent; for a detailed discussion of differences between statistical concepts, see Appelbaum and Schettkat 1991). This share increased in Germany at a higher rate in the 1970s and 1980s (8 percentage points from 1973 to 1983, compared to 5 percentage points in the United States). The United States seems to be much more advanced in the development of the service society (for a discussion of this concept, see Scharpf 1990; Stille 1990; Cohen and Zysman 1987). Common views on the high adaptability of the U. S. economy, and especially of the U. S. labor market, seem to be supported by these figures.

Besides the changing structure of the economy, one must investigate the economy's overall performance. There are different reasons for the growth or decline of an economy. The first is changes in the population. A growing population, for example, requires a higher output but not necessarily a different structure of the output. It is less of an adjustment burden, for example, if every sector grows at the same rate, leaving the structure constant. The structure of an economy might also change because of demand shifts combined with stagnating overall economic growth; in this case, resources have to be shifted from one sector to another. Again, growth of the overall economy allows for easier adjustments. In extreme cases, when "old" sectors stay at their absolute size,

Figure 4.7
The Sectoral Composition of the Economies in the United States and Germany, 1963–1986

US

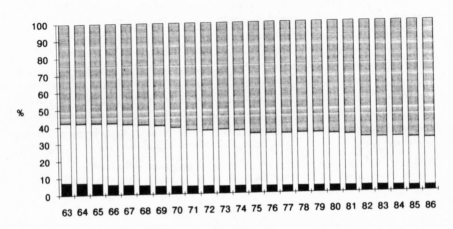

Germany

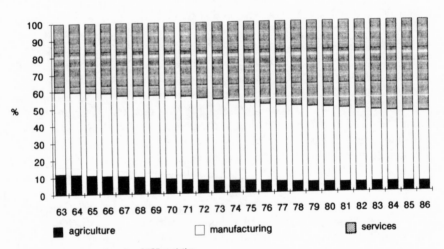

■ agriculture   ☐ manufacturing   ▨ services

Source: Computations are based on OECD statistics.

additional resources need to be directed only to the expanding sectors. Adjustment processes are much more difficult to deal with when an economy is shrinking and changing its structure at the same time (see Pasinetti 1981 and chapters 1, 2, and 3).

Within this rough framework, the U.S. economy can be characterized overall as a growing economy experiencing structural change. Throughout the period from 1963 to 1986, only the primary sector was shrinking. Both manufacturing and services employed more persons in 1986 than in 1963. The changing structure was achieved by different positive growth rates. In Germany by contrast, the decline of both primary and secondary sectors' employment was partly compensated for by the expanding service sector. Negative and positive rates of growth underlay the changing structure of the economy, at least after 1973. For this reason, one might expect that the stagnating or even shrinking German economy (with respect to employment) has had more difficulty managing structural change than the growing U.S. economy. The shares of the sectors are, of course, influenced by the degree of the division of labor, the degree of vertical integration, and classification problems. Nevertheless, the observed differences cannot be explained by measurement errors only.

4.3 THE PACE OF STRUCTURAL CHANGE

Adjustment processes in the labor market are more difficult when developments in individual industries differ, and easier in a situation of uniform trends. If some sectors are growing and others are shrinking, some employees have to move from one sector to another or across labor market boundaries. In other words, the higher the pace of structural change in the economy, the higher the required flexibility in the labor market. This is especially true if total employment in the economy is stagnating or, even worse, if it is shrinking. Although structural change is not the only source of labor mobility (chapters 2, 3, 5, and 6), this section will focus on the changing structure of the U.S. and German economies. In the following paragraphs, some indicators for the pace of structural change are discussed, and empirical results for both countries are presented.

Table 4.4 shows the shares of nine industries in total employment, as well as an index for employment growth. Again, it can be seen that employment in the United States was growing in almost every sector, whereas Germany's employment was expanding in only a few sectors (electricity, finance, and community services). The sectoral distribution is influenced by the classification of industries across countries and even within countries over time (for details on the United States and Germany, see Appelbaum and Schettkat 1990a). Classification problems have only a limited influence on the sectoral distribution, however.

In this more detailed classification, the main differences between the two countries in 1986 in the distribution of employment across industries occurred

Table 4.4
The Structure of the U.S. and German Economies by One-Digit Industries

year	Total	Agriculture	Mining	Manufacturing	Electricity	Construction	Trade, Restaurants	Transport	Finance	Community
					US shares (in % of total)					
1963	100.0	7.1	0.8	26.6	1.3	6.3	—	—	57.8	—
1966	100.0	5.6	0.8	27.8	1.2	6.3	—	—	58.3	—
1976	100.0	3.9	0.9	22.8	1.2	5.9	21.8	5.6	7.5	30.3
1986	100.0	3.1	0.8	19.1	1.1	6.6	22.2	5.4	10.7	31.0
					1973 = 100					
1963	79.7	134.8	86.3	85.6	93.4	77.2	—	—	73.5	—
1966	85.7	114.8	85.7	96.1	92.2	82.6	—	—	79.8	—
1976	104.3	96.7	123.7	96.2	108.0	94.5	108.0	101.2	101.2	101.2
1986	128.8	93.8	137.1	99.6	125.0	131.0	135.7	120.5	120.5	120.5
					Germany shares (in % of total)					
1963	100.0	11.9	1.8	37.7	1.0	8.2	14.6	5.8	3.3	15.7
1966	100.0	10.6	1.6	38.2	0.9	8.3	14.9	5.9	3.7	16.0
1976	100.0	6.7	1.4	35.1	0.9	7.5	15.0	6.1	5.4	21.8
1986	100.0	5.3	1.3	32.2	0.9	6.6	15.1	6.0	6.7	25.9
					1973 = 100					
1963	99.7	163.4	121.6	102.2	133.5	95.7	98.5	94.5	66.6	80.5
1966	105.0	165.9	116.8	114.1	109.3	115.8	103.9	100.8	71.9	77.2
1976	94.9	87.4	89.9	90.8	104.9	83.3	96.6	95.8	103.8	106.6
1986	95.7	69.9	79.9	83.8	115.0	73.9	97.9	95.0	129.7	127.7

Source: Calculations based on OECD statistics.

Note: Detailed data on service industries in the US are not available for the 1960s.

in manufacturing (19 percent in the United States, 32 percent in Germany), trade and restaurants (22 percent and 15 percent, respectively), and community services (31 percent and 26 percent respectively). It might be surprising from the European point of view that the United States has a higher proportion of employment in community services than Germany does. Part-time work cannot explain the difference; it is instead partly the effect of differences in the organization of education (schools in the United States versus apprenticeship in Germany; see Appelbaum and Schettkat 1990a).

The high share of U.S. employment in trade and restaurants is consistent with common views of the "U.S. job machine." Taking changes in industry-specific employment into account, however, one sees that manufacturing employment in the United States has actually expanded. By contrast, employment in Germany's manufacturing sector has declined. "Deindustrialization" would therefore better characterize the trends in the German economy than those in the United States, although the share of employment in manufacturing is still high in Germany (for some explanations, see Appelbaum and Schettkat 1990a).

Important to labor market dynamics is the pace of structural change in the economy. Different indicators of the pace of structural change are given in the literature. In principle, one can use the shares of industries, the growth rates of industries, and the contribution of industries to overall change in the economy. Indicators from each of these principal groups will be used and discussed in this section.

To compare various economies, Johnson and Layard (1986) have used an indicator based on the absolute differences between the share of employment accounted for by nine International Standard Industry Classification (ISIC) industries:

$$\sum_{j=1}^{n} |e_{j,t} - e_{j,t-1}| \qquad (4.1)$$

with: $e_j = E_j/E$
        E = employment
        j = index for industries, and
        t = time index.

The lower limit for this indicator is zero; the higher the value of the index, the higher the pace of structural change. Johnson and Layard have used a centered, five-year moving average for the computation of the shares, and their last reported value is for 1979 (see Table 4.5). The indices used by Johnson and Layard (1986) show a much higher pace of structural change for Germany until the mid-1970s. By the end of the 1970s, the indices for both countries are close together. In the column next to the series by Johnson and Layard (1986), a similarly constructed index is shown. The only difference between this index and the former one is that this index is computed from actual values, not from a moving average. Thus, this series is more sensitive to short-term variations in the structure of the economy. With respect to movements in the labor market, short-run variations are relevant as well, of course. In particular, demand variations are commonly not distributed evenly over the sectors and can cause mobility between sectors, as well as an increase in unemployment or nonparticipation in the short run. For the 1980s, this last index shows a higher rate of structural change for the United States than for Germany. This result would be consistent with hypotheses emphasizing rigid German (or European) labor markets as an impediment to structural change.

Thomas Jessen and Diana Winkler (1979) have mentioned that the indicator computed by formula 4.1 has the disadvantage that the same absolute changes of the shares are equally weighted regardless of whether they occur in large or small sectors. They have suggested dividing the differences in the shares in consecutive years by the initial size of the sector. This procedure gives equal absolute changes a higher weight if they occur in small sectors. It is not clear in terms of labor market adjustments why equal absolute changes should be weighted according to the sector size. The amount of labor reallocation is relevant no matter what the nominal size of the labor sectors is. All of the indicators discussed by Jessen and Winkler (1979) vary together closely, however.

An alternative index for structural change can be constructed using the growth rates of the individual sectors. Lilien (1982) and Abraham and Katz (1986) have used such an indicator:

$$\left(\sum_{i=1}^{n} e_{j,t}(\Delta \ln E_{j,t} - \Delta \ln E_t)^2 \right)^{\frac{1}{2}} \tag{4.2}$$

This formula weights the growth rate differences by the relative size of the sectors. Weighting in this formula compensates for high growth rates that in some sectors might be caused by small absolute employment changes. The values based on this formula also show a high pace of structural change in Germany during the 1960s, a convergence of the U.S. and German economies in the 1970s, and higher values for the United States in the 1980s. Nevertheless, the indicators based on formulas 4.1 and 4.2, as displayed in Table 4.5 (columns 2, 3, 6, and 7), correlate highly ($r = .92$ for the United States, $r = .98$ for Germany), showing that it does not make a big difference in practical terms whether changes in industries' shares of overall employment or growth rates are used to describe structural change.

Since it does make a difference for labor market adjustments whether growth rates differ and whether the economy as a whole is expanding, a third index of structural change, based on the contributions of individual sectors to total employment changes, can be used (Appelbaum and Schettkat 1990a):

$$\sum_{j=1}^{n} \left| \frac{E_{j,t} - E_{j,t-1}}{E_t - E_{t-1}} \right| \qquad\qquad (4.3)$$

This indicator is lowest if all sectors are growing at a uniform rate and is highest if some sectors are growing and others are shrinking at the same time. If total employment is stagnating and individual industries are developing in different directions, this indicator produces very high values. Since it is more difficult for labor markets to adjust to structural changes in a stagnating economy than in an expanding one, this indicator seems particularly well suited to our purposes. Important additional information can be obtained if the direction of overall employment developments is taken into account.

As shown in Table 4.5, this indicator produces higher values for Germany than for the United States, except for a few years. This is also true for the mid-1980s. The differences in the underlying patterns of the changing structure of the two economies can be demonstrated by the correlation coefficients. In the United States, the correlation coefficients between the series based on formulas 4.1 and 4.2 (columns 2 and 3) on the one hand, and the series based on formula 4.3 (column 4) on the other hand, are comparatively high (.83 and .77, respectively). In Germany, the correlation coefficients are very low (.18 [columns 6, 8] and .24 [columns 7, 8], respectively) because structural change in Germany has consisted of increasing employment in some sectors and decreasing employment in others, a situation where mismatch is most likely to cause problems. Of course, intrasectoral changes that can cause adjustment problems as well are not identified by the indicators presented above.

4.4 SUMMARY: DIFFERENT DYNAMICS

The U.S. economy has created enormous job growth and integrated a high share of its population into the labor force and employment; in Germany employment and the integration of the working-age population into the labor force have worsened. At the same time productivity growth has been relatively low in the United States but grew at a much higher rate in Germany, a difference that also emerges in comparisons between the United States and Western Europe as a whole (Gordon 1987b, 715).

This summary of the two economies does not describe new trends. They were already apparent in the 1960s. U.S. employment growth has always been higher than job creation in Germany, although unemployment rates were lower in Germany during the 1960s. The difference in job creation cannot be explained by differing rates of economic growth but rather by different degrees of productivity growth and, hence, by the efficiency of the manner in which the production process is organized.

The employment elasticity of economic growth was .63 for the whole period (1963 to 1986) in the United States, but −.05 in Germany. Of course, these

Table 4.5
Indicators of Structural Change

year	United States				Germany			
	sum of absolute changes of shares (Johnson/ Layard)	sum of absolute changes of shares	standard deviation of growth rates (logs. weighted. multip. by 100)	sum of absolute contributions to overall growth	sum of absolute changes of shares (Johnson/ Layard)	sum of absolute changes of shares	standard deviation of growth rates (logs. weighted. multip. by 100)	sum of absolute contributions to overall growth
	1	2	3	4	5	6	7	8
1964	1.0	1.1	1.8	125.8	2.2	1.3	2.1	1405.2
1965	1.2	1.0	1.8	118.5	2.2	1.5	2.1	358.5
1966	1.2	1.7	3.1	142.3	1.8	1.4	2.0	343.5
1967	1.2	1.2	2.8	133.7	2.0	3.0	3.4	118.4
1968	1.6	1.3	1.5	103.7	2.1	1.8	2.3	1471.8
1969	1.9	1.2	2.0	121.5	2.9	2.4	3.0	192.4
1970	1.7	2.5	2.7	223.4	2.8	1.8	2.4	189.6
1971	1.6	3.7	4.2	375.5	2.7	5.6	6.5	946.9
1972	1.7	1.1	1.3	109.4	2.6	2.1	2.4	501.1
1973	2.1	1.6	1.8	108.7	2.8	1.3	2.0	195.0
1974	1.8	1.5	1.6	104.8	2.1	2.3	2.9	181.6
1975	1.9	4.2	4.8	352.1	2.0	2.9	3.6	125.5
1976	2.0	0.9	1.5	116.9	2.0	1.9	2.3	215.0
1977	1.9	0.9	1.4	117.3	1.8	1.5	2.2	806.1
1978	1.4	1.4	1.9	115.6	1.4	1.3	1.6	181.5
1979	1.5	0.9	1.3	110.0	1.4	1.6	2.1	130.8
1980		1.9	2.4	416.6		0.9	1.2	114.5
1981		1.3	2.0	137.6		1.6	1.9	235.5
1982		3.4	3.9	342.6		1.9	2.3	123.5
1983		2.3	3.3	206.3		1.7	1.9	120.9
1984		1.6	2.0	126.9		1.1	1.1	506.3
1985		1.7	2.2	129.3		1.1	1.7	208.7
1986		1.2	1.9	113.2		1.0	1.2	139.1
coefficient of variation	20.5	54.0	41.8	58.6	21.7	53.8	47.3	88.3

Source: Calculations based on OECD data (OECD labor force statistics).
Note: The index of Johnson andLayard (1986) used the same data source as the computations, but it is a centered. five-year moving average. For definitions of the indicators, see text.
The U.S. indicators are based on 6 sectors only for 1964 to 1967; otherwise, 9 sectors.

indicators cannot show causality, but they do illustrate the difference in job creation in the two economies. Although the difference already existed in the 1960s, it sharpened in the 1970s and 1980s. Employment elasticity in the United States was .54 from 1963 to 1973 and .8 from 1973 to 1986; in Germany, it was 0 and −.16 in the same periods. The growth of industries in which the "American productivity problem" was most pronounced (i.e., services) may have pushed up the employment elasticity of economic growth.

There have been substantial differences in the structure of the two economies. The United States has had a high share of its workers employed in services (about 65 percent), whereas this share has been relatively low in Germany (about 55 percent). Both economies have been integrated to very different degrees into the world economy. Germany exported much of its production to the rest of the world and had a positive external trade balance. The United States, by contrast, was less integrated into (and less dependent on) the world economy. At the same time, the United States was a net importer. U.S. consumption was higher than its GDP, whereas the opposite was true of Germany.

U.S. employment growth and the structure of its economy were substantially influenced by U.S. population growth. A growing population creates domestic demand. This relation explains some of the higher share of services in the United States compared to Germany (see Appelbaum and Schettkat 1990a). In the 1980s, both the United States and Germany experienced high interest rates. Tight money policies were accompanied by expansionary budget policies in the United States, but the German government followed a policy of budget consolidation and thus forced domestic consumption to grow more slowly than the GDP.

If one were to take productivity growth as an indicator of technological progress, the German economy would be characterized as progressive, while that of the United States would appear stagnant. Global productivity developments cannot, however, be connected to technology alone; they are influenced by the structure of the economies as well. Economies with a high share of employment in personal services are likely to have lower productivity growth. At the same time, structural factors cannot explain all of the divergent productivity developments. It is mainly the productivity trend within industries that determines overall productivity growth.

It has often been argued that Germany's economic structures are overly rigid. One never knows what is "enough," but in comparison with the United States, the German economy seems to have adjusted very well. With respect to productivity, it is more progressive than the United States; with respect to structural change, it also seems to be more flexible than the U.S. economy. More or less the same rate of structural change occurred in both countries when employment rates were stagnating in Germany, whereas employment was growing substantially in the United States. Restructuring in Germany was thus more difficult than in the United States.

A comparison of different indicators of efficiency in the economy shows that the comparatively high German productivity growth was produced by only a small part of the population, even though average hours worked have been reduced substantially. The United States, by contrast, has distributed work (but not wages) more evenly over its population. This has not been the result of work redistribution, however, but rather of low growth in productivity.

The picture that emerges from this empirical analysis contradicts the common wisdom. The German economy has adjusted to structural change at least as fast as the United States, but it has failed in job creation. How are these developments in the two economies related to labor market dynamics? Can Germany be characterized as a big "primary" labor market that favors insiders and does not hire outsiders? Is the United States a labor market where insiders let outsiders in? How are changes in the structure of the economies linked to flows of workers across sectors? Is there evidence that the matching processes in Germany are less effective than those in the United States? Has the equilibrium rate of unemployment moved upwards, or has it been simply demand deficiency that let unemployment rates rise? To answer some of these questions, the dynamics of the U.S. and German labor markets are analyzed in the following chapters.

5

Labor Market Dynamics in the United States

5.1 THE U.S. FLOW DATA

Labor market data in the United States is gathered by household surveys and establishment data. The latter type of information is regarded as more reliable with respect to the structural composition of the economy (Employment and Earnings 1989, 233). These data sources, however, have incongruencies. Two or more jobs held by the same person will be counted twice (or more) in establishment data, but are counted once in household data. Paid and unpaid absenteeism is classified as employment in household data, but only paid absenteeism counts as employment in establishment data. The establishment data refer only to wage and salary nonagricultural employment, while household data include all sectors (for a comprehensive discussion, see Green 1969). Until 1981, flows based on the establishment data were computed. These flows included all accessions and separations, but, unfortunately, this series was ended in 1982 (Employment and Earnings 1982).

The main data source for labor market information on workers, rather than on jobs, is the Current Population Survey (CPS). The CPS is a monthly survey of about 57,000 households. It covers the civilian noninstitutional population aged sixteen years and over. The overall CPS sample is divided into eight panels. Households from each panel are interviewed in four consecutive months; they are then removed from the sample for the next eight months and are interviewed again during the following four months (see National Commission on Employment and Unemployment Statistics 1979). One panel of households enters the sample and one panel leaves it every month. Likewise, one panel enters the noninterview eight-month period and one panel leaves it every month. Six panels, or 75 percent of the households, are therefore interviewed in consecutive months. For these panels, the month-to-month changes in labor force status can be compared, and gross flows can be computed. Since the period between the first and the final interview covers sixteen months, it is also possible to compute year-by-year changes in labor market status. The inquiry refers to the labor market status in terms of the calendar week (Sunday through Saturday), which includes the twelfth day of the month. The interview is conducted in the following week.

The flow data from the CPS are time discrete, but since the interval between interviews is only one month, these data offer a good approximation to flows measured continuously (see section 3.3.3). Since survey data, especially panel data, may contain errors, however, the quality of the data will be investigated in the following pages. Indeed, the Bureau of Labor Statistics (BLS) stopped the publication of the flow data in 1952 because of inconsistency between data based on the whole CPS and the flows, which are based on a fraction of the overall survey.

If there is no bias in the data, each panel should produce the same estimates of labor market status, except for random variations. Investigations of the reliability of the data show substantial variations between the panels, however. Furthermore, there are differences in the net changes in the level of employment, unemployment, and labor force participation based on gross flow data (which is only a fraction of the overall sample) and in those estimates based on the overall sample (conventional cross-section data). Flaim and Hogue (1985, 8) have offered two main reasons for discrepancies between net changes calculated from the published data and those calculated from flow data: (1) Error cumulation in the flow data or (2) the fact that flows are calculated from a subset of the overall CPS. Another major reason for differences in the net changes computed from the two data sets is that the flow data are based on the assumption that the population remains constant, a circumstance that builds in a systematic bias. Indeed, there are substantial differences between net changes computed from cross-sectional data and those computed with flow data (see the upper part of Table 5.1).

The different sources of biases in the flow data that are obtained from the CPS panels are discussed in the following section. A correction procedure for the biases is then presented.

5.1.1 Error Cumulation

Since the sample for the computation of the gross changes is a subsample of the overall CPS, any error in the subsample (for example, response variability or coding errors) would affect the overall sample as well. In the conventional cross-sectional estimates, errors are assumed to cancel each other out, whereas, in the gross flow data, they can cumulate. The report of the National Commission on Employment and Unemployment Statistics (1979, 215) gives the following extreme illustration: There are two respondents, one employed for two consecutive months and the other unemployed for both months. If, in the second month, the first respondent is incorrectly recorded as unemployed and the second respondent is incorrectly recorded as employed, these errors will cancel each other out in the cross-sectional statistics. In the gross change data, however, the errors will cumulate rather than cancel, because both workers will be counted as having changed their status.

This extreme example applies, of course, to the resulting overstatement of mobility, but it cannot explain differences in net changes computed with the whole CPS and the subsamples. After all, randomly distributed misclassifications will cancel each other out in both the conventional cross-sectional statistic and in the calculations of net change based on longitudinal (gross flow) data. If it is assumed that response errors cancel each other out, then this should occur for net changes computed with flow data as well. Misclassifications can inflate flows, but this distortion cannot explain differences in net changes.

5.1.2 Subsample Biases

Errors caused by the fact that the flow data are based on a subsample of the CPS might be labeled as (1) rotation group bias, (2) nonresponse and mover effects, and (3) differences between the labor force behavior of panel members and that of those who drop out of the panels.

The rotation group bias is the result of the reinterview process that conditions the respondent and the interviewer in panels (Bailar 1975). Analyzing the responses of the different panels in the CPS, Barbara Bailar found that panels' reports differed significantly according to the length of time that respondents had been in the panel. Unemployment was generally higher for the first interviews and declined in the following months. It was found that the unemployment rate of the first-month respondents was about 10 percent higher than the unemployment rate in the overall sample (Flaim and Hogue 1985, 13). Therefore, it is most likely that the flow from unemployment to another labor market status may be overestimated by the panel data. It is assumed that unemployment is classified in the later months as nonparticipation, so that the flow from unemployment into nonparticipation increases (Smith and Vanski 1979, 142).

The unit of observation in the CPS is the household living at the interview address. Persons who move out of the household (away from the address) during the interview cycle are deleted from the sample. About 2 percent of American people move each month, and movers are generally younger and more mobile with respect to labor force status than older people are. The result is that total labor force flows are slightly underestimated (Flaim and Hogue 1985, 11). An additional source of misclassification is variability in responses because different household members may answer the questions in different interviews. Moreover, "telescoping," i.e., interviewing by telephone, is used in the fol-

Table 5.1
Net Changes (In Percentage of the Preceding Year) in Major Labor Market Categories, Based on U.S. Stock and Flow Data (Corrected and Uncorrected)

year	popu-lation	labor force	employ-ment	unem-ployment	popu-lation	labor force	employ-ment	unem-ployment
	flow data (uncorrected)				stock data			
1968	0.00	-0.79	-0.40	-10.69	0.15	0.15	0.17	-0.44
1969	0.00	-0.65	-0.34	-8.98	0.17	0.21	0.22	0.04
1970	0.00	-0.26	-0.26	-0.39	0.19	0.21	0.08	3.71
1971	0.00	-0.27	-0.03	-4.86	0.23	0.16	0.07	1.88
1972	0.00	-0.23	0.01	-4.01	0.17	0.26	0.29	-0.22
1973	0.00	-0.28	-0.05	-4.10	0.17	0.23	0.30	-0.88
1974	0.00	-0.18	-0.24	0.92	0.17	0.23	0.17	1.52
1975	0.00	-0.34	-0.26	-1.65	0.16	0.17	-0.09	4.47
1976	0.00	-0.16	0.04	-2.23	0.15	0.21	0.28	-0.55
1977	0.00	-0.25	0.07	-4.00	0.15	0.25	0.31	-0.47
1978	0.00	-0.22	-0.02	-2.86	0.15	0.27	0.37	-0.94
1979	0.00	-0.26	-0.12	-2.43	0.15	0.22	0.24	-0.09
1980	0.00	-0.27	-0.18	-1.76	0.12	0.16	0.04	2.04
1981	0.00	-0.27	-0.26	-0.39	0.10	0.13	0.09	0.69
1982	0.00	-0.25	-0.37	1.10	0.09	0.12	-0.07	2.42
1983	0.00	-0.31	-0.04	-2.84	0.10	0.10	0.11	0.03
1984	0.00	-0.28	-0.14	-1.60	0.09	0.15	0.34	-1.69
1985	0.00	-0.29	-0.24	-0.98	0.11	0.14	0.17	-0.22
1986	0.00	-0.25	-0.16	-1.50	0.10	0.17	0.19	-0.08
1987	0.00	-0.21	-0.06	-2.19	0.08	0.14	0.22	-0.82
1988	0.00	-0.20	-0.06	-2.38	0.05	0.13	0.19	-0.81
	flow data corrected (Poterba/Summers)				flow data corrected (Abowd/Zellner)			
1968	0.00	0.00	0.00	0.08	0.00	-0.20	-0.01	-4.85
1969	0.00	0.06	-0.02	2.30	0.00	-0.07	0.01	-2.31
1970	0.00	0.23	-0.08	6.61	0.00	0.23	0.06	3.79
1971	0.00	0.32	0.08	4.09	0.00	0.31	0.27	0.91
1972	0.00	0.24	0.08	3.11	0.00	0.25	0.27	-0.09
1973	0.00	0.20	0.04	3.58	0.00	0.20	0.21	0.09
1974	0.00	0.27	-0.08	6.56	0.00	0.29	0.08	4.12
1975	0.00	0.27	-0.05	3.83	0.00	0.22	0.12	1.38
1976	0.00	0.31	0.10	2.89	0.00	0.33	0.32	0.40
1977	0.00	0.26	0.13	1.86	0.00	0.25	0.35	-1.18
1978	0.00	0.24	0.07	2.95	0.00	0.24	0.26	-0.08
1979	0.00	0.21	0.02	3.42	0.00	0.19	0.18	0.42
1980	0.00	0.19	-0.03	3.23	0.00	0.17	0.14	0.48
1981	0.00	0.20	-0.08	3.76	0.00	0.16	0.07	1.32
1982	0.00	0.23	-0.16	4.05	0.00	0.19	0.01	2.06
1983	0.00	0.20	0.06	1.55	0.00	0.15	0.27	-1.00
1984	0.00	0.18	0.00	2.37	0.00	0.14	0.17	-0.21
1985	0.00	0.19	-0.05	3.50	0.00	0.15	0.10	0.90
1986	0.00	0.17	-0.04	3.01	0.00	0.14	0.13	0.27
1987	0.00	0.14	0.01	2.23	0.00	0.14	0.19	-0.72
1988	0.00	0.07	-0.02	1.74	0.00	0.07	0.16	-1.39

Sources and definitions:
Bureau of Labor Statistics. Stock data: published data based on the CPS; flow data: unpublished data based on the CPS. Net changes computed with monthly average flow data are a ratio to the stock in t-1. All figures refer to the civilian labor force 16 years and older. Corrections are based on the results of Poterba/ Summers (1986) and Abowd/ Zellner (1984) as displayed in Table 5.2.

THE UNITED STATES AND GERMANY IN TRANSITION

low-up interviews (Flaim and Hogue 1985, 13), thereby changing the interview situation.

The data that can be used in the flow statistics (75 percent of the overall CPS sample at maximum) are further reduced by mover and nonmatching effects. "In practice about 7.5 percent of all (weighted) respondents in the current month who are eligible for matching cannot be matched. An additional 7.5 percent of all respondents in the previous month who are eligible for matching cannot be matched" (Abowd and Zellner 1984, 46). All these circumstances produce misclassification that is assumed to cancel itself out in cross-sectional computations but not in the flow data (see above).

It may be not only that the magnitude of the flows is overestimated but also that misclassification is more likely to occur in one direction than in another. This would lead to a bias in net changes. James Poterba and Lawrence Summers (1984 and 1986) investigated possible misclassifications in the U.S. flow data by making use of the CPS Reinterview Surveys, which are carried out one week after the original interviews. They found that flows were substantially overestimated and that conventional studies therefore overestimated labor mobility in the United States. A comparison of the labor market status in the interview with that of the reinterview (one week later) showed that a spurious transition, specially with movements from unemployment, was occurring (Poterba and Summers 1986, 1,325). They therefore suggested corrections to reduce the off-diagonals of the transition matrix and increase the diagonals (Poterba and Summers 1986, 1,327). Table 5.2 displays the ratios of the corrected transition probabilities to the uncorrected probabilities. Critics have emphasized that Poterba's and Summers's adjustment method relies on the CPS-reinterview data, which may contain their own reinterview-interview bias (Horvath 1984, 97, and 1982; McIntire 1984, 64) and that their method possibly leads to overadjustment (Shapiro 1984, 98).

Assuming that misclassification due to response errors is invariant over time, one can use these ratios to correct the original flow data. This leads not only to different magnitudes of the flows but also to different net changes as displayed in the lower part of Table 5.1. With the adjusted series corrected by the values arrived at by Poterba and Summers (1986), employment trends are positive and similar to cross-sectional changes, at least in direction. Nevertheless, the values are still well below the cross-sectional ones.

5.1.3 Constant Population

The panels constructed with the subsamples of the CPS are biased because they do not allow for population growth, only for decline. This can be demonstrated with the matrix in Figure 3.2. All movements out of the labor market (from employment [EN] or unemployment [UN]) into nonparticipation are measured correctly by the CPS if one abstracts from the response errors discussed above. Movements from the main matrix (E, U, and N) to outside the covered population (EO, UO, NO) are not counted in the flow statistics because these persons do not have matches; they thus disappear from the sample (Abowd and Zellner 1984). Movements from outside the population into the sample population (flows OE, OU, ON) likewise cannot be counted in the flows since, by definition, the movements can only be identified with those persons who were in the sample at least once before. The age restriction in the CPS (persons sixteen years and over) and the restriction to the noninstitutional population lead to inflows and outflows because of aging and switching between the institutional and noninstitutional populations. Ignoring all movements from outside the population (O) into the panels leads to a systematic downward bias of flows into the labor market.

Taking the net changes that are produced by the flow data and comparing them with those produced by the overall CPS, one finds that the selection bias caused by the design of the CPS seems to be an important source of discrepancies. It has been discovered that the flow into nonparticipation has most likely been overestimated. With the exception of a few years, the net changes based on the unadjusted flow data indicate a decline in employment, unemployment, and, consequently, in the labor force as a whole (Table 5.1). But the stock data display increases in employment and in the labor force in almost every year. These systematic downward biases are likely to be caused in part by the assumed constant population in the flow data.

The CPS covers persons sixteen years and older. It is therefore limited at the lower end of the age scale (no person younger than sixteen years is included), but it has no upper age limit. This does not cause a bias in the overall CPS, which is a cross-sectional set of data, but it does cause a bias in the flow data because all persons who enter the relevant population are included in the overall CPS of $t+1$. The six panels used to construct the flow data do not include those persons who were below the age limit (younger than sixteen years) in the first interview but who would have been included in the later interviews when they were above the age limit. The same arguments can apply for immigrants. There is, of course, no way to enter already existing cohorts. The population in the flow data is assumed to be constant (see Table 5.1), and no inflows are allowed for. Therefore, the flows reported in the statistics are based solely on variations in labor force status but not on flows caused by the natural inflow of younger persons and of immigrants into the labor market. The CPS excludes very young persons in consecutive observations, and this is exactly the group that is most likely to move from nonparticipation into the labor force. The composition of the inflows according to the estimates of Abowd and Zellner (1984) is shown in the last column of Table 5.2.

Since the CPS has no upper age limits and since leaving the labor force is more likely to happen at a higher age, this situation overestimates the outflow from the labor force compared to the inflow and thus produces underestimations of overall labor force growth. These conditions do not affect the cross-sectional results of the CPS, however, since they also include persons who did not ex-

Table 5.2
Ratios of Adjusted to Unadjusted Transition Probabilities

labor market status in t

	employment (E)	unemployment (U)	nonparticipation (N)
employment (E)	1.0326 (1.0227)	0.7059 (0.8143)	0.2121 (0.6249)
unemployment (U)	0.7294 (0.9341)	1.3545 (1.3317)	0.4211 (0.7135)
nonparticipation (N)	0.1489 (0.6025)	0.5926 (0.8746)	1.0562 (0.9998)
population inflow (overall = 100)	25%	54%	20%

labor market status in t-1

Definitions and sources:
Ratios without parentheses are computed on the basis of Poterba and Summers (1986).
Ratios in parentheses and the composition of the population inflow are computed on the
basis of Abowd and Zellner (1984).

ceed the age limits in the month before. It can therefore be assumed that the overall CPS produces more reliable estimates for overall labor force developments.

Besides those who turn 16 during the survey month, there are also immigrants and persons who return to the noninstitutional population either from military or from institutions. At the same time, people are leaving the noninstitutional population by emigrating or entering the military or institutions. As displayed by the cross-sectional results in Table 5.1, the U.S. population grew every year during the period analyzed by John Abowd and Arnold Zellner (1984, 47). They have concentrated their adjustments of the flow data to make the margins of the flow tables fit with those of the whole CPS and have argued that population growth is unimportant as a source of misclassification compared to "missings" (nonmatchers). In the sample that they investigated, they found 8,404 missings compared to a population increase of only 141 persons.

The method of adjustment developed by Abowd and Zellner (1984 and 1985) takes misclassification (spurious transition) into account just as Poterba and Summers (1984 and 1986) did. But Abowd and Zellner also adjusted the flows for nonmatchers and for population inflows and outflows. As shown in the matrix of Table 5.2, the results of their method diverge from those of Poterba and Summers. The lower part of Table 5.1 shows net changes computed with corrected flow data. The corrections are based on the coefficients of Table 5.2. That is, flows between the labor market categories are reduced. In addition, variation of the noninstitutional population, sixteen years of age and older (see Table 5.1), is allowed for—the assumption being that the composition of the population increase is as shown in the last row of Table 5.2.

With the corrections by Poterba and Summers (1986) and Abowd and Zellner (1984), the net changes based on the corrected flow data differ from the net changes computed from stock data, but the differences are lower and the variation between the series is smaller. The coefficient of correlation roughly doubles from .3 for uncorrected net changes computed with flow data with stock data changes up to .6 for the corrected series in stock changes. The corrections bring the net changes based on flow data closer to the net variations in stock data. The most important finding, however, is that the Abowd and Zellner (1984) and Poterba and Summers (1986) corrections suggest substantially lower flows in the U.S. labor market.

In the following section, flow data that are adjusted with the Abowd and Zellner method and combined with a correction for population increase are used because net changes computed with these data come closest to the net changes based on stock data. It is assumed, however, that corrections are invariant over time, an assumption that seems reasonable since Abowd and Zellner (1985, 269) have found strong seasonal influences but no time trend in the ratios of corrected to uncorrected data. With respect to the inflow into the noninstitutional population, the assumption of a constant composition of the inflow into unemployment, employment, and nonparticipation is probably wrong, because demographic waves and so forth will influence the inflow composition. This is, however, the best available approximation even though the inflow will appear to be more stable than it actually is.

5.2 AGGREGATE FLOW ANALYSIS

5.2.1 Flows into and out of Employment

The employment inflow and outflow ratios in Figure 5.1 are computed with the BLS unpublished gross flow data and are adjusted with the Abowd and Zellner (1984) coefficients as shown in Table 5.2. In general, the substitution rate, which expresses the part of labor turnover not caused by variation in the employment level, shows a slightly downward trend. Exchange between employment and unemployment or nonparticipation that is not caused by variations in the level of employment—the substitution rate—has declined in the United States over time, although the time trend is not very strong (1.5 percentage points over a ten-year period). The two flow ratios representing exchange between employment and nonparticipation (EN and NE) correlate highly ($r = .96$), and the same is true for the exchange with unemployment (EU and UE, $r = .94$). The two groups of ratios show inverse trends, however. The first (EN, NE) has been declining, whereas the flow ratios between employment and

Figure 5.1
Employment Inflow and Outflow Ratios in the United States, 1968–1988 (Gross Flows Divided by Initial Employment)

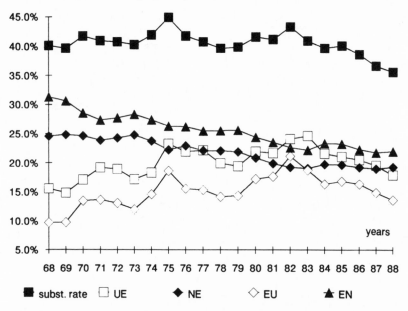

Source: Computations are based on unpublished BLS gross flow data. Note: For abbreviations see text.

unemployment (EU) and vice versa (UE) were increasing slightly until the early 1980s.

Nonparticipation has thus lost importance as a source of recruitment as well as a destination for nonemployed workers according to the corrected BLS flow ratios. This trend may be caused by demographic variables, such as smaller teenager cohorts, or by the changed labor force participation of women, who are more strongly integrated into the economy today than they were in the 1960s. Workers who lose their jobs seem to become unemployed to an increasing degree, and this can explain part of the increased unemployment inflow in the United States (see section 5.2.2).

The flows discussed so far are flows between employment and nonemployment and do not include direct movements from one job to another. Such movements are included in the accession rates, which are based on establishment data but which are available up through 1981 only (see section 5.1). The substitution rate of the overall accession and overall separation rates has declined over time but shows clear variations over the business cycle (see Figure 5.2). One must remember that the U.S. economy is a growing economy but that the rates express the flow relative to initial employment. The substitution rate is, therefore, determined mainly by the separation rate, but the two rates vary together closely.

Figure 5.2
Accession and Separation Rates in the United States, 1963–1981

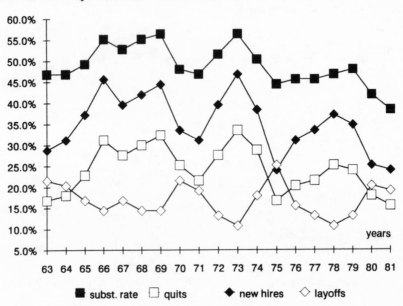

Source: Computations are based on BLS establishment data. Note: Manufacturing sector only.

In the establishment data, hiring can be broken down into new hires and recalls of laid-off workers; a similar differentiation between quits and layoffs can be made for separations. The curves in Figure 5.2 show high correlations between the different rates: The substitution rate, which gives the value of accessions and separations not caused by variation in the number of employees, correlates positively with quits ($r = .92$) and new hires ($r = .94$), but negatively with layoffs ($r = -.52$). Taken together with the extremely high correlation between quits and new hires ($r = .96$), these figures indicate that a substantial part of overall accessions is caused by direct movements between different jobs. Quits result in vacancies and new hires, especially in a growing economy, and thus cause a chain of mobility. The positive correlation between new hires and quits confirms the view that good labor market conditions are favorable for the voluntary mobility of workers (Akerlof, Rose, and Yellen 1989). The variation of both rates is parallel to the business cycle.

5.2.2 Unemployment Dynamics

Although the U.S. unemployment rate was substantially lower in the 1960s than in the 1980s (see Table 4.1), it was well above the German rate in the 1960s. The U.S. rate peaked in 1975 and 1982–1983, when the U.S. economy experienced a serious recession. Since then, unemployment has declined continuously. The composition of overall unemployment with respect to the inflow component and duration has not changed much over time. Both components increased when unemployment rose, and both peaked during the recessions, with duration following the inflows by a short time lag (Figure 5.3). This pattern seems to be an unemployment process that has not changed its function over time.

The same picture occurs if the composition of unemployment is analyzed by duration (see Table 5.3). There is some variation but no trend in the share of the duration categories over time. In general, the duration of unemployment is more or less constant, a result that sharply contrasts with the German experience (see section 6.2.2). There are several reasons for this difference. One explanation would be that the unemployed in the United States are more easily reemployed. This situation might occur because unemployment in an economy with high labor turnover does not brand a jobless person as a "lemon" in the eyes of potential employers, as might be the case in the more stable German economy. Another explanation would be based on the institutional set-up of the U.S. unemployment insurance system. Unemployment benefits are paid for no longer than six months, during which time the replacement rate is only about 35 percent (Schmid 1990). Therefore, the unemployed may search more intensively or even be forced to accept lower paying jobs because an alternative does not exist. Still another explanation is that unemployment duration, as measured with the CPS, is unreliable because the unemployed may be discouraged about seeking work and may not report themselves as unemployed persons who are actively seeking work. Light can be shed on these explanations with the analysis of the composition of flows between unemployment, employment, and nonparticipation.

If the unemployed are easily reemployed, then one would expect the flow from unemployment into employment (UE) to account for a large share of the total outflow out of unemployment. If discouragement is an important variable, then one would expect the share of the flow into nonparticipation (UN) to be high. Making use of the BLS gross flow data, one finds that the shares of these two flows are surprisingly stable. The flow into employment fluctuates by plus or minus 2 percentage points around the 55 percent level, and the flow into nonparticipation hovers around the 45 percent level. Thus a substantial part of the unemployed leaves into nonparticipation.

In Figure 5.4, the risk of becoming unemployed is computed based on the BLS gross flow data (flow EU) and adjusted with the correction ratio of Abowd and Zellner (1984), as shown in Table 5.2. For the years before 1968, the inflow into unemployment from employment was estimated as a constant share of the overall unemployment inflow given in the unemployment statistics. As expected, changes in the risk of becoming unemployed correlate negatively with changes in the GDP ($r = -.45$ for the period 1964 to 1987). A time lag of one year worsens rather than improves the relation, a finding that is not surprising, for the U.S. economy is expected to adjust employment to output

Figure 5.3
Indices of Unemployment Duration and Unemployment Inflow in the United States, 1963–1987

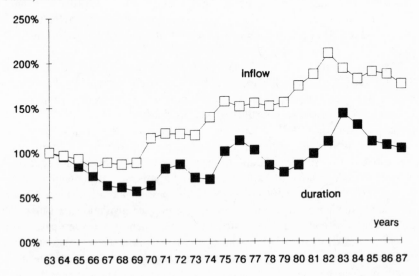

Source: Computations based on BLS data.
Note: The inflow into unemployment is estimated by unemployment of less than 5 weeks. The duration is computed with the steady-state assumption.

Table 5.3
Unemployment by Duration in the United States

years	total (persons in 1000s)	unemployment duration (weeks) (distribution in %)				average duration	median duration
		< 5	5 - 14	15 - 26	> 27		
1973	4,093	58.8	26.0	9.0	6.1	10.0	5.2
1974	5,093	57.9	25.9	9.4	6.9	9.8	5.2
1975	7,413	41.8	25.4	13.0	19.3	14.2	8.4
1976	6,892	45.2	27.6	11.6	15.6	15.8	8.2
1977	6,304	48.1	27.9	10.8	13.3	14.3	7.0
1978	5,679	53.6	27.8	9.1	9.5	11.9	5.9
1979	5,658	50.2	31.6	8.6	8.1	10.8	5.4
1980	7,288	43.1	30.7	14.8	11.4	11.9	6.5
1981	7,477	46.2	28.9	12.2	12.7	13.7	6.9
1982	10,289	38.7	29.8	14.4	17.2	15.6	8.7
1983	9,469	39.9	26.1	11.4	22.7	20.0	10.1
1984	7,833	43.4	28.7	11.1	16.7	18.2	7.9
1985	7,711	46.0	28.8	10.6	14.6	15.6	6.8
1986	7,706	44.9	29.2	11.2	14.7	15.0	6.9
1987	6,678	49.8	25.7	10.9	13.6	14.5	6.5
1988	6,148	52.4	25.9	10.0	11.7	13.5	5.9

Source: BLS, employment and earnings.

Figure 5.4
The Risk of Becoming Unemployed and Economic Growth in the United States, 1964–1987

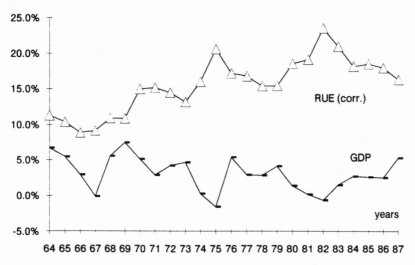

Note: The risk of becoming unemployed for the years 1968 to 1987 is computed with unpublished BLS gross flow data adjusted with the coefficients of Abowd/Zellner 1984. Before 1968 it is assumed that 47% of the overall inflow into unemployment originates in employment.

variations quickly (Sengenberger 1987, Abraham and Housemann 1988), but this effect cannot be fully detected in annual data.

5.3 LABOR AND JOB TURNOVER

5.3.1 Labor Turnover

Different sources for the computation of labor turnover will be used in this section to analyze industry-specific turnover. One source is the establishment data that allowed for the computation of turnover rates until 1981. These data give every accession and every separation, but they are limited to manufacturing and wage and salary earners. The other data source is gross flows based on the household information provided by the CPS (see section 5.1). The last data source covers employment outside manufacturing as well, but the industrial classification is broad and not always consistent with conventional statistics. Self-employed and unpaid family workers, for example, are grouped into an extra "industry" and are excluded in the following analysis.

Table 5.4 displays labor turnover data based on the uncorrected CPS gross flows for the overall period from 1968 to 1982 and for two subperiods. For the years after 1982, the gross flow data cannot be distinguished by industries. Perhaps most surprising is the stability of the industry-specific rates in the two

Table 5.4
Labor Turnover by Industry in the United States

industry	accession rate	separation rate	substitution rate	stability rate	share of switchers on inflow	share of switchers on outflow
			1968 to 1982			
Agriculture	27.7	28.9	27.7	71.1	54.3	54.2
Mining	16.3	16.0	15.8	84.0	86.0	84.5
Manufactusing	8.9	8.9	8.7	91.0	65.7	63.8
Construction	20.1	20.5	20.0	79.5	64.4	63.4
Transport	9.9	9.7	9.7	90.3	75.1	73.4
Trade	15.2	15.3	15.1	84.7	61.1	62.1
Other Services	14.5	14.9	14.5	85.1	56.9	56.7
Government workers	8.0	8.0	7.9	92.0	56.4	56.4
Self empl. & unpaid	17.3	17.4	17.1	82.6	61.0	58.4
Average (unweighted)	15.3	15.5	15.2	84.5	64.6	63.6
			1968 to 1975			
Agriculture	28.1	29.3	28.1	70.7	53.5	53.7
Mining	16.2	15.9	15.8	84.1	87.6	86.3
Manufacturing	8.8	8.8	8.6	91.1	66.2	64.3
Construction	19.0	19.4	18.9	80.6	64.9	63.6
Transport	9.3	9.1	9.1	90.9	74.3	72.5
Trade	15.4	15.5	15.3	84.5	60.8	61.5
Other services	14.7	15.2	14.7	84.8	54.5	53.9
Government workers	7.9	7.8	7.8	92.2	55.8	55.4
Self empl. & unpaid	15.9	16.4	15.9	83.6	58.5	56.2
Average (unweighted)	15.0	15.3	14.9	84.7	64.0	63.0
			1976 to 1982			
Agriculture	27.2	28.5	27.2	71.5	55.3	54.8
Mining	16.4	16.2	15.9	83.8	84.3	82.4
Manufacturing	9.0	9.1	8.8	90.9	65.2	63.2
Construction	21.2	21.8	21.2	78.2	63.8	63.0
Transport	10.6	10.5	10.3	89.5	76.0	74.4
Trade	14.9	15.1	14.9	84.9	61.5	62.7
Other services	14.3	14.5	14.3	85.5	59.6	59.9
Government workers	8.1	8.2	8.1	91.8	57.2	57.5
Self empl. & unpaid	18.8	18.6	18.5	81.4	63.9	60.9
Average (unweighted)	15.6	15.8	15.5	84.2	65.2	64.3

Source: Computations based on unpublished BLS flow data.
Unadjusted monthly averages.
Note: The substitution rate is the lower value of either the accession or the separation rate.
The stability rate gives the share of stayers in the particular sector in proportion to initial employment.

subperiods. All rates vary only very slightly and should not be interpreted too strictly, considering the measurement problems mentioned in section 5.1. Industries in which seasonal variations of employment are high have high labor turnover rates. By far the highest substitution rates—labor turnover not caused by variations of employment levels—are computed for agriculture and construction. Manufacturing, transport, and government are clearly below the average for turnover. Other services, trade, and mining are close to the average. The relatively low value for trade is surprising, since trade, together with some other service industries, is often regarded as the sector with the most unstable employment.

The stability rate presented in Table 5.4 is based on the number of employees who did not switch industry, divided by the number of employees initially employed in that industry. The relation between stability and turnover is summarized in Figure 5.5, in which the industries are classified as high or low with respect to average employment stability and turnover. Agriculture, construction, and mining have high substitution rates but low stability rates; in other words, unstable employment is a common characteristic in these industries. The reverse is true for manufacturing, transport, and government, where turnover is low and employment stability is high. In these sectors, stable employment is common. Trade and other services are low with respect to both indicators.

Within the broad sectors displayed in Table 5.4, labor turnover is not determined by the growth or decline of the industries but rather by other factors. The accession and separation rates are close together within every industry, and the two rates (excluding self-employment) correlate positively with a coefficient of almost 1. Since the stability rate is computed here as that fraction of the work force that remains in employment in this particular sector, it must correlate negatively with the substitution rate with a coefficient of close to 1. The relation between stability and the share of switchers (defined here as those accessions [separations] that come from [move to] other industries or nonemployment) in terms of inflow or outflow is comparatively weak, however; the correlation coefficient is only about .25. The high share of switchers in the inflows indicates that access to an industry's jobs is spread widely and does not seem to depend greatly on former work experience in the particular sector.

Based on the establishment data, accession and separation rates are available for manufacturing up to 1981. The values of the turnover figures displayed in Table 5.5 are based on the September figures for each year. To arrive at an estimate for annual flows, one can multiply the September figures by 12 (months), an operation that produces values of more than 100 percent. The figures are higher in durable manufacturing than in nondurable manufacturing but are generally quite high if one takes into account that overall manufacturing is the industry with the lowest substitution rates—except for government workers—according to the CPS gross flow data (Table 5.4).

Figure 5.5
Industries Classified by Substitution and Stability Rates, United States

		stability rate	
		low	high
substitution rate	low	1 trade other services	2 manufacturing transport government
	high	3 agriculture mining construction	4

note: low = below average, high = above average

Although the turnover rates shown in Table 5.5 seem to be lower in the second period (1976–1981) than in the first (1968–1975), the industry pattern was almost stable between the two periods. The correlation between the accession (columns 1 and 7), separation (columns 3 and 9), substitution (columns 6 and 12), and layoff rates (columns 5 and 11) between the two periods was well above .90. This finding indicates strong industry-specific patterns. In other words, industrial relations, innovative activity, market environment, and, quite probably, the average establishment size seem to be extremely important variables when it comes to explaining labor turnover.

5.3.2 Job Turnover

Data on job turnover is not provided by the official statistical institutions in the United States, but some job-flow data obtained by the exploitation of existing data sources has become available. Data on job turnover has been produced for Wisconsin (Leonard 1987b), Pennsylvania, and the U.S. manufacturing sectors (Davis and Haltiwanger 1989; Dunne, Roberts, and Samuelson 1989). The following paragraph draws on the Pennsylvania data regarding job turnover and on manufacturing data from Steve Davis and John Haltiwanger (1989).

Although the overall net effect of job turnover is comparatively small (see columns 1, 2, and 3 in Table 5.6), substantial job turnover is taking place in U.S. industries if the Pennsylvania data can be taken to represent approximately the U.S. economy. The individual industries, however, show much bigger net effects. In general, the well-known pattern of a growing service sector and a shrinking manufacturing sector is occurring. Most of the expansion and most of the contraction stem from existing establishments rather than from the founding and closing of establishments. Establishment turnover seems to be of

Table 5.5
Labor Turnover in U.S. Manufacturing (Unweighted Averages of September Values)

Industry	No.	labor turnover rates (average 1968-1975)						labor turnover rates (average 1976-1981)					
		acces-sions	new hires	sepa-rations	quits	lay-offs	substi-tutions	acces-sions	new hires	sepa-rations	quits	lay-offs	substi-tutions
		1	2	3	4	5	6	7	8	9	10	11	12
Lumber	24	6.4	5.7	7.8	5.7	1.1	6.4	5.4	4.5	6.5	4.1	1.4	5.4
Furniture	25	7.7	6.8	7.3	5.3	0.7	7.3	6.1	5.1	5.7	3.7	0.9	5.7
Stone, clay	32	4.7	3.9	5.7	3.6	1.0	4.7	3.7	2.8	4.3	2.3	1.1	3.7
Primary metals	33	3.6	2.3	4.7	2.3	1.4	3.6	2.8	1.4	3.7	1.1	1.6	2.8
Fabricated metals	34	5.5	4.5	5.8	3.4	1.2	5.5	4.4	3.3	4.4	2.2	1.2	4.4
Machinery. nonelectrical	35	3.5	2.7	3.8	2.1	0.9	3.5	3.0	2.2	2.9	1.5	0.7	2.9
Machinery. electrical	36	4.3	3.2	4.5	2.7	0.8	4.3	3.5	2.5	3.5	1.8	0.7	3.5
Transport equipment	37	4.8	2.8	4.6	2.2	1.4	4.6	4.5	2.2	3.5	1.4	1.3	3.5
Instruments	38	3.6	2.9	3.9	2.4	0.6	3.6	2.8	2.3	3.2	2.1	0.5	2.8
Miscell. manufacturing	39	7.5	6.3	7.0	4.6	1.1	7.0	6.5	5.2	6.2	3.6	1.3	6.2
Durable maoufacturing		5.2	4.1	5.5	3.4	1.0	5.2	4.3	3.1	4.4	2.4	1.1	4.3
Food	20	9.1	6.8	9.9	5.8	3.1	9.1	7.7	5.5	8.8	5.2	3.1	7.7
Tobacco	21	6.9	5.1	5.3	3.0	1.3	5.3	5.3	2.9	3.6	1.6	1.1	3.6
Textile	22	6.5	5.3	6.8	5.0	0.7	6.5	4.5	3.6	4.9	3.2	0.7	4.5
Apparel	23	6.4	4.8	6.6	4.2	1.5	6.4	6.1	4.3	6.1	3.8	1.4	6.1
Paper	26	3.9	3.4	5.0	3.4	0.7	3.9	2.9	2.3	3.7	2.0	0.9	2.9
Printing	27	4.1	3.5	4.2	2.8	0.7	4.1	3.9	3.4	3.8	2.5	0.6	3.8
Chemicals	28	2.6	2.1	3.3	2.0	0.5	2.6	1.7	1.3	2.2	1.1	0.5	1.7
Petroleum	29	2.3	2.1	3.2	1.9	0.5	2.3	2.5	2.0	2.8	1.2	0.6	2.5
Rubber	30	6.1	5.1	6.5	4.2	0.9	6.1	5.2	4.1	5.6	3.2	1.3	5.2
Leather	31	7.0	5.4	8.5	5.5	1.9	7.0	6.8	5.1	8.1	5.2	2.0	6.8
Nondurable manufacturing		5.5	4.4	5.9	3.8	1.2	5.5	4.7	3.5	5.0	2.9	1.2	4.7
Total manufacturing		5.3	4.2	5.7	3.6	1.1	5.3	4.5	3.3	4.7	2.6	1.1	4.5

Source: BLS establishment data. employment and earnings. different volumes.

more importance in the service sector, where the average size of an establishment tends to be smaller as well. In services, the net effect caused by establishment turnover is as much as 35 percent of the overall net effect.

The sector of financial services is comparatively stable with respect to both job turnover and labor turnover. This industry has the lowest job turnover rate. Nevertheless, 8 percent of all jobs in financial services were exchanged annually on average during the ten-year period. This job turnover was not caused by variation in the level of employment but just by new jobs being substituted for existing ones (see substitution rate in column 10 of Table 5.6). Manufacturing appears to be a stable industry with respect to labor turnover and job turnover as well. Perhaps surprisingly, about 10 percent of the jobs were newly created every year in this shrinking industry. At the other end of the scale were construction, trade, and hotels/restaurants (the last including personal services in Table 5.6). In these industries, the average establishment size used to be small, a characteristic that can influence measured job turnover, of course. But these are also industries in which labor turnover is high, indicating the less stable employment relationships in these industries in general.

Labor turnover as well as job turnover and wage differentials for manufacturing are shown in Table 5.7. The wage differentials (columns 11 and 12) are taken from Krueger and Summers (1987). As mentioned earlier, controlling for labor quality, which includes variables like education, age, occupation, sex, race, and a central city dummy (see Krueger and Summers 1987, 21), does not substantially change the relative position of industries. Both series (columns 11 and 12) correlate highly, and Krueger and Summer found strong empirical evidence for industry-specific wage differentials independent of quality differentials. Furthermore, these differentials seem to be very stable over time (see also section 2.3). If industry-specific institutional variables rather than skill or individual productivity differentials account for wage differentials, one would expect quits, that is voluntary labor mobility, to be low in high-wage industries. In fact, there is a strong negative correlation ($r = -.80$) between wage differentials (column 12) controlled for labor quality and quits (column 4). Additional empirical evidence (based on other data) supporting these results was found by Krueger and Summers (1987). Workers in high-wage industries seem to try to remain there.

These results refer to labor turnover, which might be different from job turnover. With the theory of compensating wage differentials, one would expect industries with unstable jobs to have positive wage differentials because employees in these industries should be compensated for the employment risk they are carrying. More stable jobs and employment, conversely, should result in "wage reductions." This relation should occur especially if the "quality of labor" is controlled for. Assuming the validity of the dual labor market theory, on the other hand, one would expect a reverse relation where industries with unstable employment and jobs pay lower-than-average wages and vice versa. Negative components of jobs should cumulate rather than compensate. In other

Table 5.6
Job Turnover by Industry in the United States

industry	net effects			average of annual changes in Pennsylvania, 1976-1985						substitution rates			turn-over rate[∘]
				job gains			job losses						
	over-all	exp. & contract.	new & closed	over-all	expan-sion	new	over-all	con-traction	closed	over-all	exp. & contract.	new & closed	
	1	2	3	4	5	6	7	8	9	10	11	12	13
Energy, mining	-2.8	-3.2	0.4	12.9	7.0	5.9	15.7	10.2	5.5	12.9	7.0	5.5	28.7
Intermediate goods	-2.2	-2.6	0.3	9.9	5.0	4.9	12.2	7.6	4.6	9.9	5.0	4.6	22.1
Consumer goods	-1.4	-0.9	-0.5	9.9	5.1	4.8	11.3	6.0	5.3	9.9	5.1	4.8	21.2
Manufacturing[∞]	-1.8	-1.8	-0.1	9.9	5.1	4.9	11.8	6.8	5.0	9.9	5.1	4.7	21.7
Construction	0.2	-0.2	0.5	19.9	12.0	7.9	19.6	12.2	7.4	19.6	12.0	7.4	39.7
Transport, communic.	0.5	0.1	0.4	11.2	6.3	4.9	10.7	6.2	4.5	10.7	6.2	4.5	21.8
Trade	2.3	1.0	1.2	15.0	7.7	7.3	12.8	6.7	6.1	12.8	6.7	6.1	27.7
Finance, insurance	2.9	2.4	0.5	11.1	6.4	4.7	8.2	4.0	4.2	8.2	4.0	4.2	19.3
Business services	3.2	2.0	1.2	13.1	8.3	4.8	9.9	6.3	3.6	9.9	6.3	3.6	23.1
Hotels, rest. incl. personal services	3.9	2.5	1.4	18.3	9.9	8.4	14.4	7.4	7.0	14.4	7.4	7.0	32.6
Services	2.8	1.6	1.2	14.9	8.0	6.9	12.1	6.4	5.7	12.1	6.4	5.7	27.0
All industries	0.7	0.1	0.7	13.3	7.1	6.2	12.5	7.0	5.5	12.5	7.0	5.5	25.8

Source: OECD 1987.
Notes: [∘] sum of columns 4 and 7. [∞] unweighted average of intermediate and consumer goods.
exp. & contract. = expansion and contraction

Table 5.7
Job and Labor Turnover in U.S. Manufacturing

Industry	No.	turnover rates labor (averages Sept. 1980, 81) [o]						job (annual 1980-83) [oo]			job / labor turnover	estimated wage differentials	
		accession	new hires	separations	quits	layoffs	substitution	job gains	job losses	substitution		uncontrolled	controlled [ooo]
		1	2	3	4	5	6	7	8	9	10	11	12
Lumber	24	4.6	3.0	6.2	2.7	2.6	4.5	10.0	17.0	10.0	2.5	-0.027	-0.048
Furniture	25	4.7	3.5	4.3	2.4	1.0	4.3	7.0	12.0	7.0	2.1	-0.098	-0.033
Stone, clay	32	3.3	2.0	4.0	1.5	1.6	3.3	7.0	14.0	14.0	2.9	0.357	0.082
Primary metals	33	3.3	1.0	3.9	0.8	2.3	3.3	4.0	15.0	4.0	2.7	0.357	0.179
Fabricated metals	34	3.9	2.3	4.0	1.6	1.6	3.9	7.0	14.0	7.0	2.7	0.143	0.061
Machinery, nonelectrical	35	2.7	1.6	2.8	1.2	1.0	2.6	8.0	15.0	8.0	4.2	0.335	0.187
Machinery, electrical	36	3.1	1.9	3.0	1.4	0.9	3.0	9.0	11.0	9.0	3.3	0.185	0.105
Transport equipment	37	4.2	1.4	3.4	1.0	1.7	3.4	7.0	13.0	7.0	2.6	0.370	0.189
Instruments	38	2.5	2.0	3.0	1.9	0.5	2.5	9.0	10.0	9.0	3.5	0.232	0.131
Miscell. manufacturing	39	5.5	4.1	5.1	2.6	1.4	5.1	9.0	16.0	9.0	2.4	0.004	0.001
Durable manufacturing		3.8	2.3	4.0	1.7	1.4	3.8	14.0	13.7	13.7	3.6		
Food	20	7.1	4.6	7.9	3.5	3.4	7.1	8.0	11.0	8.0	1.3	0.085	0.072
Tobacco	21	4.9	2.9	3.5	1.4	0.9	3.5	6.0	8.0	6.0	1.7	0.356	0.294
Textile	22	3.5	2.7	3.9	2.2	0.8	3.5	6.0	11.0	6.0	2.3	-0.114	-0.022
Apparel	23	5.8	4.0	5.6	3.2	1.6	5.6	11.0	16.0	11.0	2.4	-0.327	-0.156
Paper	26	2/5	1.7	3.4	1.5	1.2	2.5	6.0	8.0	6.0	2.4	0.241	0.126
Printing	27	3.6	3.0	3.6	2.3	0.7	3.6	8.0	9.0	8.0	2.4	0.119	0.083
Chemicals	28	1.6	1.2	2.1	1.0	0.5	1.6	6.0	9.0	6.0	4.1	0.362	0.238
Petroleum	29	2.0	1.6	2.6	0.9	0.8	2.0	8.0	12.0	8.0	4.4	0.594	0.382
Rubber	30	4.6	3.1	4.6	2.2	1.4	4.5	8.0	13.0	8.0	2.3	0.038	0.035
Leather	31	6.0	4.6	6.7	3.8	1.9	6.0	8.0	14.0	8.0	1.7	-0.245	-0.126
Nondurable manufacturing		4.2	2.9	4.4	2.2	1.3	4.2	7.5	11.1	7.5	2.2		
Total manufacturing		4.0	2.6	4.2	1.9	1.4	4.0	10.8	12.4	10.8	2.9		

Source: BLS establishment data, employment and earnings, Davis and Haltiwanger 1989;
Krueger and Summers 1987.
[o] September values, unweighted average; [oo] annual values, unweighted average;
[ooo] controlled for labor-quality variables.

words, if wages compensate for employment instability, it should result in a positive correlation between turnover variables and wage differentials. If, on the other hand, negative components cumulate, it should result in negative correlation coefficients.

For labor mobility, we have already found that the relationship is negative, and this was especially true for voluntary mobility (quits). Correlations between the job-gain rate and the job-loss rate (columns 7 and 8 in Table 5.7), on the one hand, and quality-controlled wage differentials (column 12), on the other, both produced negative coefficients of about $-.46$. In other words, manufacturing industries with high job-gain and job-loss rates are industries that tend to pay lower wages. This result is consistent with the dual labor market theory, according to which negative job assets will cumulate rather than compensate.

The ratio of job to labor turnover should eliminate the impact of job turnover on labor turnover. Without any measurement errors or inconsistencies, one would get values equal to or less than 1 for the ratio of job turnover to labor turnover (column 10). Measurement problems, however, cause the ratio between job turnover and labor turnover to be higher than 1 in Table 5.7. Labor turnover is measured by the average of the September values for 1980 and 1981; the figure thus represents labor turnover per month. Job turnover, on the other hand, is measured on a year-to-year basis. Although the absolute values cannot be interpreted in this case, the relative values can be. If labor turnover is caused to a substantial degree by job turnover, one expects the coefficient of variation for the ratio to be lower than the coefficient of variation for labor turnover. Indeed, the ratio of job to labor turnover (column 10) produces a coefficient of variation that is 85 percent of the coefficient for labor turnover itself. Thus, the variation is reduced, but most of the labor turnover in U.S. manufacturing industries is obviously not caused by job turnover.

Another indication that negative job characteristics cumulate rather than compensate is the correlation between the controlled wage differentials and the ratio of job to labor turnover. If labor turnover is caused mainly by job turnover—that is, if labor mobility is unvoluntary—we expect the ratio of job turnover to labor turnover to be high in high-wage industries, and vice versa. This is consistent with the positive correlation ($r = .55$) between controlled wage differentials (column 12) and the ratio displayed in column 10 of Table 5.7. In other words, workers tend to stay in industries with high wages, and mobility in these industries is "enforced" by job turnover.

5.4 MISMATCH

5.4.1 Measurement Issues

Vacancy data for the United States is constructed with the "help-wanted index," which is based on the number of help-wanted advertisements in the classified section of newspapers in fifty-one large cities of the United States.

These metropolitan areas account for about 49 percent of nonagricultural employment in the United States, and the data collection method has remained unchanged since its inception (Abraham 1987, 208). It is the number of advertisements that is counted in the index, not the number of job openings, even though an advertisement might list several openings. The base year for the index is 1967. To control for the expansion of the economy, the help-wanted index is normalized by the division through the number of nonagricultural employees (see Medoff 1983). A comparison of the normalized help-wanted index with vacancy data collected in surveys in some states has shown that the normalized help-wanted index seems to be a reasonable proxy for vacancies (Abraham 1987, 213).

As with German vacancy data, it is not clear whether and when advertised jobs are available, and the advertising practices of employers may change over time. The shift from blue-collar to more heavily advertised white-collar work may have caused an upward drift in the "help-wanted index," and concentration in the newspaper business may have resulted in a higher index, since only one major metropolitan newspaper is used to compute the index in each area. Abraham (1987) has adjusted the U.S. "help-wanted index" to correct for these possible shifts. Both series, the adjusted as well as the unadjusted, are displayed in Figure 5.6.

5.4.2 The U.S. Beveridge Curve

The adjustments of the help-wanted index shift its values downward, but do not change the general picture, which suggests an outward shift of the U.S. Beveridge curve from the 1960s to the 1980s (see Figure 5.6). The Beveridge curve shows a rightward shift with every recession from 1963 to 1982, but since then, the curve seems to have shifted leftwards. These outward shifts are less pronounced in the adjusted than in the unadjusted data, but they are visible in both curves.

Information on the duration of "vacancies" is not available in the United States (for estimates, see Abraham 1987), so the relation between duration and changes in vacancies (Figure 3.3) cannot be analyzed. This relation can, however, be investigated for unemployment (Figure 5.7). Three main cycles can be distinguished. The first covers the 1960s and early 1970s, the second goes from 1973 to the late 1970s, and the third covers the 1980s. The duration of unemployment clearly shifted outwards in the United States over these three business cycles, but by the late 1980s it had returned to the values of the early 1960s. This picture is perfectly consistent with the shifts in the Beveridge curve. Shifts in the Beveridge curve as well as shifts in the duration curves may be explained by differences in the pace of structural change during the periods. When the duration of unemployment peaked in 1971-1972, 1975-1976, and 1982-1983, the indicators for structural change displayed in Table 4.5 reached high values as well.

Figure 5.6
The U.S. Beveridge Curve, Unadjusted and Adjusted

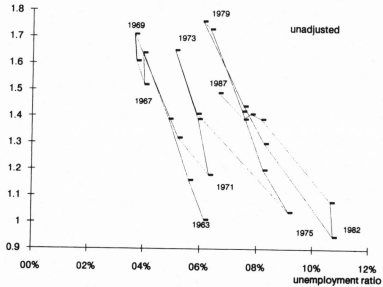

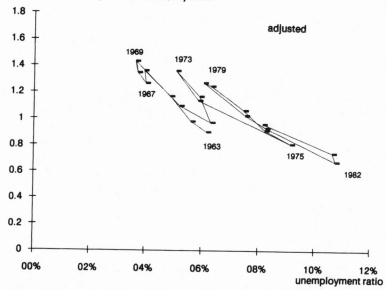

Source: Computations are based on BLS data for the unadjusted help-wanted index; Abraham 1987 for the adjusted help-wanted index.
Note: The unemployment ratio and the normalized help-wanted index are computed with employment as denominator.

Figure 5.7
Change-Duration Curve for Unemployment in the United States

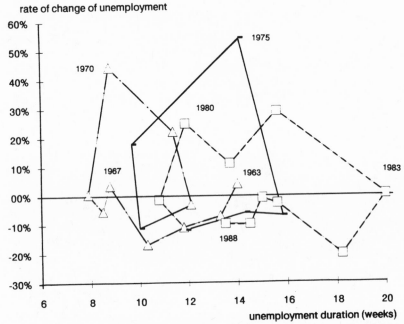

Source: computations based on BLS data. Note: average duration is computed with the steady-state assumption.

Although the outward shifts coincided with high paces of structural change, the indicators computed with formulas 4.1 and 4.2 are not different enough at the peak levels in the three business cycles that these could explain the outward shift. If anything, this shift should point in the opposite direction. The indicators for structural change are slightly lower in the 1980s than in the 1970s. It may well be, however, that individual industries are causing this trend or that some occupations—perhaps evenly distributed across industries—are the main cause of the outward shift in unemployment duration.

An outward shift of the average duration of unemployment at every rate of change in unemployment can be found in every U.S. industry (Figure 5.8). Nevertheless, the overall picture shows that unemployment duration in the United States at the end of the 1980s returned to levels known in the 1960s, a pattern obviously different from the German trends (see section 6.4).

5.4.3 Mismatch Indicators

Since vacancy data for individual industries or occupations are not available in the United States, the analysis of mismatch indicators is limited to those indicators that rely on unemployment rates only. The variances in the annual unemployment rates (mm2, formula 3.27) are presented in Table 5.8. Industry mismatch as measured with mm2 has reached a level in the late 1980s that is comparable to those of the early 1970s. As with the indicators discussed above, mismatch is high when unemployment in general is high. The highest value for industry mismatch occurred in 1982-1983, when the United States experienced a serious recession (see section 4.1). Recessions are also the periods when economic restructuring has been strong (see section 4.3), however.

In the United States, the shift in the occupational structure has been far less publicized than industrial restructuring, but it is equally dramatic (Kutscher 1990). Ronald Kutscher (1990) has noted that changes in the occupational structure are concentrated in a few major occupational groups. The growth in the share of employment of "executive, administrative, and managerial" personnel, "professional workers," and "technicians and related support workers" was about 25 percent of overall U.S. employment in 1986 and is projected to increase to 27 percent by the year 2000. "These three occupational groups have two things in common: First, they nearly all require some post-secondary training or education and two, these occupations are increasing not only in the rapidly growing service-producing industries but also in many of the declining manufacturing industries" (Kutscher 1990). Two other major occupational groups—"sales workers" and "service workers"—have shown increasing shares in overall employment as well, but these two groups differ in at least two aspects from the groups mentioned before. They are growing primarily in the service sector, and they usually do not require post-secondary education or training. This pattern of the changing occupational structure in the United States is therefore the result of a shift to service industries but also of changes in the organization of the production process within most industries. It is a trend similar to those in Germany (Warnken and Ronning 1989).

The occupational classification used in the United States was changed in 1982, and comparisons between the two periods are possible with caution only (see Rumberger 1981; Kutscher 1990). These changes have also affected the computation of the indicator for occupational mismatch even if broad occupational groups are used. In the earlier periods, the classifications were broader, so there are inconsistencies between the periods before the 1970s and after 1982. Differences of the indicators' values for occupational mismatch should thus be interpreted with caution. For example, by omitting 1980 and 1981 from the data in Table 5.8, the indicators for industry mismatch and for occupational mismatch vary closely ($r = .71$) in the period from 1970 to 1988.

5.5 RISING EQUILIBRIUM RATES OF UNEMPLOYMENT IN THE UNITED STATES?

The analysis so far suggests that no substantial changes in U.S. labor market dynamics have occurred in recent decades. The flow ratios seemed to be fairly constant over the periods analyzed. Making use of formula 3.22, one can compute estimates for equilibrium rates of unemployment based on flows between

Figure 5.8
Industry-Specific Change-Duration Curves for Unemployment in the United States

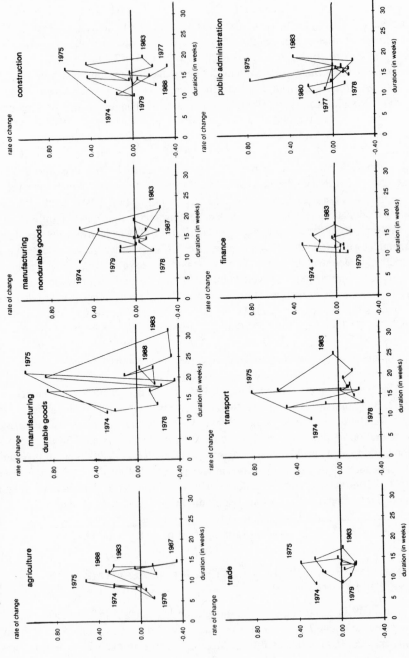

Source: computations based on BLS data. Note: average duration is computed with the steady-state assumption.

Table 5.8
Mismatch Indicators for the United States

year	industries		occupations	
	mm2	1977 = 100	mm2	1977 = 100
1963	5.6	84.8	9.4	124.7
1968	3.4	51.5	3.2	42.4
1973	4.5	68.2	4.0	53.2
1974	5.3	80.3	6.3	82.8
1975	8.2	124.2	17.5	232.0
1976	7.3	110.6	10.1	133.3
1977	6.6	100.0	7.6	100.0
1978	5.6	84.8	6.3	82.8
1979	5.5	83.3	6.5	85.6
1980	6.9	104.5	–	–
1981	7.3	110.6	–	–
1982	9.3	140.9	9.7	128.3
1983	9.2	139.4	9.6	127.0
1984	7.1	107.6	7.5	99.2
1985	6.8	103.0	7.2	95.2
1986	6.6	100.0	7.0	92.6
1987	5.8	87.9	6.2	82.0
1988	5.2	78.8	5.5	72.8

Source: Computations based on BLS unemployment rates for 9 industries.
Occupational mismatch is computed with 10 groups for 1963 and 1968.
with 11 groups in the 1970s, and with 16 groups in the 1980s.
Classifications of occupations differ over these 3 periods.

employment and unemployment rather than on inflation-unemployment relations. The discussion of the "natural rate of unemployment" (or the "steady-
state rate of unemployment") in section 3.4.2 showed clearly that this rate
depends on the duration of unemployment, the separation rate, the share of
flows between unemployment and employment, the overall inflow into employment, and the share of the flow between employment and unemployment in the
overall outflows out of employment.

Since the values of the variables in formula 3.22 change with the actual labor
market situation, that is, for example, that the unemployment duration is longer
in periods of slack labor markets than otherwise, some "base" values that are
close to a steady-state situation must be found. Since the focus is on the impact
that structural change and employment dynamics have on unemployment, the
substitution rate of the employment system seems to be a good indicator to use
in formula 3.22. Although the substitution rate for employment might not be
independent of unemployment itself, it can nevertheless be taken as an approximation of the inherent employment dynamics.

If one takes the stand that hirings and separations in a slack labor market are
determined mainly by the dynamics of the employment system, then the substitution rate on the whole seems to be an adequate indicator. Use of the lower
value of either the hiring or the separation rate also seems to be suggested by

Table 5.9
Labor Market Flow Ratios and Estimations for Flow-Equilibrium Rates of Unemployment in the United States

years	separation rate of employment (EX/E)	hiring rate of employment (XE/E)	ratios (in %) substitution rate (1 or 2)	y (UE/XE)	z (EU/EX)	y/z²	duration of unempl. (weeks) (U/XU)	estimates for flow-equilibrium rates of unemployment (in %) all	varying variables y/z²	varying variables substitution rate	varying variables duration of unempl.	none	unemployment rate. OECD data (in %)
	1	2	3	4	5	6	7	8	9	10	11	12	13
average 1968-1969	40.7	39.9	39.9	38.1	24.0	6.7	9.4						
1968	41.0	40.1	40.1	38.9	23.6	7.0	9.6	1.1	1.0	1.1	1.1	1.1	3.4
1969	40.4	39.6	39.6	37.4	24.3	6.3	9.2	1.1	1.1	1.1	1.0	1.1	3.4
1970	42.0	41.7	41.7	41.0	32.0	4.0	9.2	1.8	1.8	1.1	1.1	1.1	4.8
1971	41.0	43.0	41.0	44.6	33.3	4.0	10.7	2.1	1.8	1.1	1.2	1.1	5.8
1972	40.8	43.2	40.8	43.8	32.0	4.3	10.4	1.9	1.7	1.1	1.2	1.1	5.5
1973	40.3	41.9	40.3	41.0	29.7	4.6	9.7	1.6	1.5	1.1	1.1	1.1	4.8
1974	42.0	42.0	42.0	43.5	34.8	3.6	9.4	2.1	2.0	1.1	1.1	1.1	5.5
1975	44.9	45.5	44.9	51.1	41.5	3.0	12.1	3.4	2.4	1.2	1.4	1.1	8.3
1976	41.8	44.8	41.8	48.9	37.3	3.5	11.9	2.7	2.0	1.1	1.4	1.1	7.5
1977	40.8	44.2	40.8	50.0	37.5	3.6	11.7	2.5	2.0	1.1	1.3	1.1	6.9
1978	39.7	42.0	39.7	47.4	35.7	3.7	10.6	2.1	1.9	1.1	1.2	1.1	6.0
1979	39.9	41.3	39.9	47.0	35.9	3.7	10.4	2.1	1.9	1.1	1.2	1.1	5.8
1980	41.6	42.7	41.6	51.3	41.4	3.0	11.2	2.9	2.4	1.1	1.3	1.1	7.0
1981	41.2	41.5	41.2	52.1	42.9	2.8	11.5	3.1	2.5	1.1	1.3	1.1	7.5
1982	43.7	43.3	43.3	55.6	48.3	2.4	12.8	4.3	2.9	1.2	1.4	1.1	9.5
1983	40.9	43.7	40.9	56.3	45.9	2.7	14.2	4.0	2.6	1.1	1.6	1.1	9.5
1984	39.7	41.3	39.7	52.2	41.2	3.1	12.0	2.9	2.3	1.1	1.4	1.1	7.4
1985	40.1	40.7	40.1	51.7	42.0	2.9	11.3	2.9	2.4	1.1	1.3	1.1	7.1
1986	38.6	39.8	38.6	51.6	42.3	2.9	11.5	2.9	2.4	1.0	1.3	1.1	6.9
1987	36.7	38.6	36.7	50.7	40.6	3.1	11.2	2.5	2.3	1.0	1.3	1.1	6.1
1988	35.6	37.2	35.6	48.1	38.3	3.3	10.9	2.2	2.1	1.0	1.2	1.1	5.4

Source: Computations based on unpublished CPS flow data, adjusted with coefficients of Abowd and Zellner 1984.

Note: The flow-equilibrium rates of unemployment are computed with formula (3.22)
$u^* = 1/(1+y/z^2 \ 1/(subr \ avdur))$. The average duration of unemployment is computed with the steady-state assumption. For abbreviations, see text.

the results of recent research that shows that voluntary labor mobility is a function of opportunity and that voluntary mobility is most likely to be direct mobility from one job to another. Therefore, it can be assumed that most separations into unemployment are involuntary movements.

Questions about the impact that changes in the average characteristics of the employment process have on the "flow-equilibrium rate of unemployment" can be answered by using formula 3.22. What would the rate of unemployment be if only the separation rate of employment had changed while the other variables determining the steady-state rate of unemployment—that is, the share of unemployment in the outflow and inflow, together with the duration of unemployment—had remained constant? As discussed in the first section of this chapter, there is some inconsistency in the U.S. flow data computed with the CPS. The corrections suggested by Poterba and Summers (1984) or Abowd and Zellner (1984) can, however, reduce the difference between net changes based on gross-flow data and those based on cross-sectional data. Although some inconsistencies remain, Poterba and Summers (1984) and Abowd and Zellner (1984) are the only adjustment methods available. For the computations in Table 5.9, the adjustment ratios of Abowd and Zellner (1984; see also Table 5.2) were used.

Table 5.9 shows the actual unemployment rate in the United States as published by the OECD (column 13). This rate is much higher than either the steady-state rate of unemployment (column 8), as computed with the values for each year, or the flow equilibrium rates of unemployment (columns 9 to 11). The difference is caused by the fact that the rate in columns 9 to 11 takes only the flows between employment and unemployment into account, whereas the actual unemployment rate (column 13) is, of course, influenced by flows between unemployment and nonparticipation. In addition, the actual rate is influenced more by variations of employment growth than are the flow-equilibrium unemployment rates that eliminate at least part of the influence of employment trends.

Although the duration of unemployment (column 7) varied slightly, this did not change the unemployment rate very much, as has already been suggested by the analysis in section 5.2.2 with other data. The substitution rate of employment (column 3) was almost constant during the period of analysis. The share of unemployment in relation to employment in- and outflows (columns 4 and 5) has contributed most to the rise in the flow-equilibrium rate of unemployment. These trends, however, are not independent of the overall labor market situation. The ratio is higher in periods of slack labor market conditions than otherwise. But there is also a trend in the variable; unemployment, instead of nonparticipation, has become more common as a destination for employees leaving employment. It can be concluded that changes in employment dynamics have contributed little to the increase in the unemployment rate in the United States but that the rise was caused to a substantial degree by the entrance of nonparticipants into the labor market, a phenomenon that took place via unemployment.

6

Labor Market Dynamics in Germany

6.1 THE GERMAN FLOW DATA

Information on labor market dynamics in Germany can be gathered from two principal sources: (1) surveys (the microcensus and an inflow-outflow survey of the unemployed) and (2) data on employment, unemployment, and job openings (Beschäftigtenstatistik) as gathered by German employment agencies mainly for administrative purposes. The microcensus (Mikrozensus) is a survey of 1 percent of the German population; it classifies as employed all persons who worked at least one hour during the survey week (usually the last week in April or the first week in May). For some consecutive years, the Mikrozensus data (for details, see Mayer and Wolny 1980) have allowed a comparison of labor market status from one year to the next.

The Beschäftigtenstatistik is based on information from the social security insurance system and covers all those employees who are eligible for the insurance. The Beschäftigtenstatistik is thus not a survey; it covers instead all employees who contribute to social security insurance. In principle, this means all employees, except for those who are only marginally employed (those who earned less than DM 470 a month in 1990), the self-employed, unpaid family workers, and "Beamte" (civil servants who have a special status in the German employment system and who are not insured by the social security system; for details, see Wermter 1981). In actuality, these employment statistics cover about 80 percent of all employed persons. In recent years, data on flows in and out of employment have been provided by the Beschäftigtenstatistik (Wermter and Cramer 1988), and, since the late 1970s, the Federal Institute for Labor

Market and Vocational Research (IAB) has provided information on labor market flows based on a longitudinal sample drawn from the Beschäftigtenstatistik (Cramer 1986b; Rudolph 1986). Recently, the Beschäftigtenstatistik has also been used to provide information on job turnover (König and Weißhuhn 1989; Cramer and Koller 1988). In addition, the IAB has established the so-called Arbeitskräftegesamtrechnung (gross labor market accounting framework; Reyher and Bach 1988), a statistic that provides information on gross changes in the aggregate labor market.

Employment agencies collect information on inflows into and outflows from unemployment for the period of May and June each year. The data are gathered mainly for administrative purposes and provide information on vacancies, flows in and out of unemployment, and job placements by the employment agencies.

The various data sets have to be differentiated according to the statistical concepts used for the flows. The Mikrozensus data compare the labor market statuses of identical persons between two years but neglect movements within this period. Data based on the Beschäftigtenstatistik usually refer to continuous flows—that is, every movement in and out of employment or other labor market categories is counted, including movements between establishments within one sector. These differences result in higher measured mobility in the data based on the statistics of the employment agencies compared with the Mikrozensus data. Furthermore, the IAB survey identifies any employee whose establishment registration number changes as a "switcher," even though this registration number can change simply for administrative reasons. In the IAB survey, switchers are therefore not necessarily those employees who have changed establishments; they can be misclassified. In this respect, the real labor market movement of switchers is likely to be overestimated in the IAB data. Switchers between establishments are defined as those who are reemployed within seven days after leaving their former jobs. This is exactly the category in which misclassifications are most likely to occur. This argument, however, does not apply to nonswitchers who have had a spell of unemployment or nonparticipation between two employment contracts. Since the IAB data are based on the Beschäftigtenstatistik, they do not include marginally employed workers (those workers not covered by social security insurance) who may be the most likely to change their labor market status more often. All the data sources mentioned will be used to analyze German labor market dynamics in the following sections, and comparisons will be made where possible.

6.2 AGGREGATE FLOW ANALYSIS

6.2.1 Flows into and out of Employment

Flows into and out of employment partly reflect variations in the number of persons employed. With growing employment, the inflow ratio is expected to increase while the outflow ratio is expected to decrease, and vice versa. But

Figure 6.1
Employment Inflow and Outflow Ratios in Germany, 1970–1989 (Gross Flows Divided by Initial Employment)

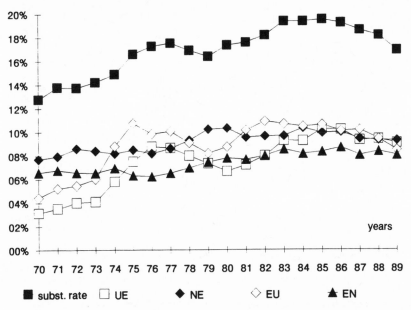

Source: Computations based on the Arbeitskraeftegesamtrechnung (Reyher and Bach 1988).
Note: For definitions, see text.

there are inflows in and outflows out of employment that are not caused by variation in the number of persons employed. The magnitude of these effects can be identified by the substitution rate (formula 3.6), which is defined as the lower value of either the inflow or outflow ratio. It gives that part of the movement that is not caused by changes in the overall level of employment.

In general, there was an upward trend in both the inflow and the outflow ratios (and thus in the substitution rate) until the middle of the 1980s (see Figure 6.1). That is, the exchange between employment and unemployment or nonparticipation increased during the 1970s and early 1980s, quite the opposite of what one would expect from hypotheses that purport to explain high unemployment by insider-outsider relations or by an excessively low hiring rate. Over a period of five years, the substitution rate increased by about 2 percentage points. According to the Arbeitskräftegesamtrechnung (Reyher and Bach 1980), turnover between employment and nonemployment (nonparticipation and unemployment) clearly increased in recent decades when unemployment rose substantially. Most surprisingly, substitution rates have risen in recessions (see also Burda and Wyplosz 1990).

New hires are recruited not only from unemployment or nonparticipation but also from employment itself. Intra-employment hiring is included in the series

Figure 6.2
Accession Rate and Employment Inflow Rate in Germany, 1963–1987

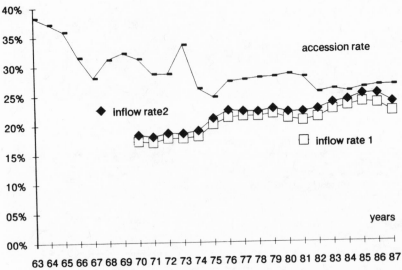

Source: Computations based on the Arbeitskraeftegesamtrechnung (Reyher and Bach 1988), Rudolph 1984 and other data of the Bundesanstalt fuer Arbeit.
Note: Hiring of apprentices is not included in the accession rate. The denominator includes all employees.

of total accessions, which showed a decreasing trend from the 1960s on. The rate of total hirings (the ratio of all accessions to employees) decreased from about 40 percent in the early 1960s to roughly 28 percent in the early 1970s, when unemployment was still less than 1 percent. Since then, the accession rate has remained more or less at that level (see Figure 6.2). The distance between the two series—that is, between total hiring and hiring from nonemployment—narrows and thus shows the decreasing importance of intra-employment hiring directly from other firms. This, however, is a typical pattern in labor markets that move from excess demand to excess supply of labor. In tight labor markets, a greater share of hires has to come directly from other employment—producing vacancies and a mobility chain (Akerlof, Rose, and Yellen 1988).

In Germany, the flow from employment into unemployment has to be broken down into a flow of "normal" employees and a flow consisting of persons who have participated in an apprenticeship program. As unemployment has risen, apprenticeship has gained importance as a source of the inflow into unemployment. Although youth unemployment is relatively low in Germany (see Evans, Franz, and Martin 1984), the apprenticeship program has been unable to prevent unemployment from rising in this category, partly because apprenticeships in occupations that already have an excess labor supply are still numerous (Becker

1983). Nevertheless, the apprenticeship program is certainly an important channel for recruitment, although not all apprentices have been employed after finishing the training period (Semlinger 1990, 39).

The ratio for the flow originating in nonparticipation increased only slightly, from roughly 8 percent in the early 1970s to about 9 percent in the middle of the 1980s, with some peaks in the late 1970s and early 1980s. In contrast, the inflow ratio for formerly unemployed persons increased substantially, from about 3 percent in the early 1970s to roughly 10 percent in the 1980s. This change, however, reflects the larger reservoir of unemployed that has existed in Germany since 1974 and especially since 1983, when unemployment jumped well above the two million level. Although the average duration of unemployment increased during the last decade, (see section 6.2.2), there has been a substantial flow from unemployment into employment.

Parallel to the inflow ratios originating in unemployment, the outflow ratios destined for unemployment also increased. Increases occurred in 1974 and 1975, but since then the ratio has remained high, never again reaching the low levels that had prevailed before the oil price shock. In the late 1980s, when the labor market improved, the curves showed a slightly downward trend. The flow ratio culminating in nonparticipation did not show as large an increase. Nevertheless, this ratio did increase as well, hitting a peak in 1975, because of the combined effects of the recession and the introduction of the so-called flexible retirement age that was introduced in 1973. Since the mid-1970s, firms have increasingly made use of a Sozialplan (a negotiated compensation and severance payments), in combination with one year of unemployment and early retirement (usually at 60 years of age), to dislocate workers (see also section 6.3.1).

Flows in and out of the employment system (flows 3, 4, 5, and 6) in Figure 3.1 are not the only sources of labor mobility; movements of labor between jobs can occur within the employment system (flows 1 and 2 in Figure 3.1). Figure 6.2 presents the overall accession rate, which includes hirings from unemployment and nonparticipation but also from other employment. Although total accessions should not be interpreted too strictly (Rudolph 1984, 171), the accession rate shows a downward trend in the 1960s and early 1970s, with procyclical variations. In other words, the accession rate was low in the recession years of 1967 and 1974-1975, and it ran above the trend in recovery years. This finding is perfectly consistent with the view that labor mobility is a function of opportunities as outlined by Akerlof, Rose, and Yellen (1988) and others. Over the whole period, however, the overall accession rate declined whereas the hiring rate from unemployment and employment, which is available for the period from 1970 only, increased. Both rates were closest when unemployment was highest (in the mid-1980s). Thus, one can conclude that if insufficient mobility was a problem for the German labor market, it was not because hiring from nonemployment was too low but rather because of decreasing mobility within the employment system itself. This relation, however, can be explained by changing opportunities. In tight labor markets, every move from one job to another causes a vacancy and will result in hiring activities of the firm that lost a worker. Hiring in tight labor markets creates mobility chains.

Thus, the aggregate flow data do not support the view that the German labor market has been static. The opposite seems to be true. Labor mobility increased with respect to movements into and out of employment during the period of rising unemployment. The nonhiring hypothesis is not supported by this aggregate analysis, nor is there strong evidence that insiders keep outsiders out of employment. The empirical evidence for Germany supports a relation of flows between employment and unemployment in both directions, a relation characterized by high flows when unemployment is high and low flows when unemployment is low.

6.2.2 Unemployment Dynamics

The unemployment rate (registered unemployment) in Germany in the mid-1970s jumped from less than 1 percent to 4 percent and remained at this level until the beginning of the 1980s. In 1983, registered unemployment rose to more than 2 million persons, a rate of more than 8 percent. As mentioned, average annual unemployment is composed of inflows into unemployment and duration of unemployment. Until 1973, the average duration of unemployment was well under 10 weeks. In the late 1970s, it already averaged 16 weeks, and duration doubled to more than 30 weeks in the 1980s. Figure 6.3 shows clearly that the increase in Germany's unemployment rate has been caused mainly by a longer duration of unemployment rather than by an increase of the inflows, a result that contrasts with what was found generally by Jackman, Layard, and Savouri (1990). The average duration rose especially in those years when unemployment increased substantially. Nevertheless, the flow ratios also doubled from the 1960s to the 1980s.

The average duration of unemployment—computed under the steady-state assumption—hides information on the distribution of duration that is displayed in Table 6.1. Clearly, the share of persons unemployed for more than 52 weeks increased enormously, as did the share of those unemployed for more than 2 years (104 weeks). This distribution of unemployment, based on the duration of continuing unemployment spells, thus confirms the picture derived from the average duration of unemployment displayed in Figure 6.3. Both measures are biased. The average duration is computed under the steady-state assumption, which is almost never true, and the distribution of duration is computed by the unemployment duration of those who are unemployed at the end of September each year, which is an upward, biased measure (see chapter 3). But both series indicate the same phenomenon very well: A rise in unemployment in Germany has been overwhelmingly caused by longer duration rather than by increasing inflows. This development contrasts with U.S. trends (see section 5.1).

One frequently mentioned explanation for high German unemployment is the

Figure 6.3
Indices of Unemployment Duration and Unemployment Inflow in Germany,
1963–1987

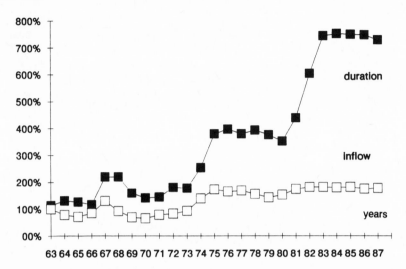

Source: Computations are based on data of the Bundesanstalt fuer Arbeit.
Note: Duration is computed with the steady-state assumption.

generosity of unemployment benefits. In fact, however, the share of unemployed persons who obtained unemployment benefits, which could be either unemployment insurance benefits or unemployment assistance (see Schmid, Reissert, and Bruche 1987), decreased from around 75 percent in the 1960s to roughly 65 percent in the 1980s. Furthermore, the share of the unemployed who obtain unemployment benefits is higher when the unemployment rate is low. The correlation coefficient between the unemployment rate and the share of unemployment beneficiaries for the period from 1963 to 1987 is $-.67$. The composition of unemployment benefits has changed in favor of unemployment assistance (Arbeitslosenhilfe), which is means-tested and lower than unemployment benefits. In the beginning of the 1970s, less than 10 percent of the unemployed received unemployment assistance, but in the mid-1980s, this share rose to more than 25 percent. At the same time, the share of the unemployed who received unemployment insurance benefits decreased from 65 percent to less than 40 percent (Cramer 1986a; Ermann 1988). Not only did the share of beneficiaries decrease but the monetary incentive (the replacement rate) decreased as well. This result is evidence against attempts to explain high German unemployment rates by pointing to unemployment benefits. A similar result was obtained for the United States (Burtless 1983).

The decreasing share of beneficiaries among the unemployed might be explained by a different composition of unemployment sources. A higher inflow from nonparticipation would bring about a decline in the share of those who

Table 6.1
Unemployment by Duration in Germany

years	unemployed (total)	duration in weeks in % of total						average duration (weeks)	share of benificiaries (in %)
		< 4	4 - 12	12 - 26	> 26	> 52	> 104		
1975	1006554	16.4	25.5	21.2	36.8	8.3	1.3	16.2	76.1
1976	898314	16.6	24.8	17.8	40.8	13.6	4.3	16.9	73.5
1977	911257	16.0	25.6	18.1	40.3	11.7	6.9	16.2	69.9
1978	864243	15.7	25.1	17.8	41.4	11.3	9.0	16.8	67.8
1979	736690	16.6	25.2	18.3	39.9	11.6	8.3	16.0	66.4
1980	822701	17.7	27.5	18.6	36.2	9.6	7.4	15.0	64.8
1981	1256396	15.9	26.4	19.5	38.1	10.4	5.8	18.7	68.2
1982	1818638	12.0	23.4	18.3	46.4	15.2	6.1	25.7	66.4
1983	2133900	9.2	19.9	16.7	54.1	19.2	9.3	31.7	66.4
1984	2143008	9.3	19.7	15.8	55.1	18.6	14.2	32.1	64.3
1985	2150897	12.3	20.2	15.8	51.7	16.9	14.1	31.9	63.1
1986	2045837	12.2	20.0	15.6	52.2	16.3	15.6	31.9	62.9
1987	2106950	12.1	20.3	16.0	51.6	15.8	16.1	31.1	63.3
1988	2099638	11.7	20.1	16.0	52.2	16.1	16.5	31.8	65.8

Source: Computations are based on data from the Bundesanstalt fuer Arbeit.
Note: The original data is grouped by the month. Weeks are therefore only approximations.
The average duration of unemployment is computed with the steady state assumption.

are eligible for unemployment benefits. In other words, the composition of the inflow into unemployment by origin might be important. The inflow from nonparticipation into unemployment as a share of the overall inflow rose substantially from the mid-1970s, while flows from employment into unemployment dropped accordingly.

Nonparticipation as a source of the unemployment inflow has gained importance, but only those coming from employment are usually eligible for unemployment benefits. Thus, the composition of the inflow partly explains the decreasing share of recipients of unemployment benefits. At the same time, the long duration of unemployment can itself explain the decrease in the share. The period during which unemployed persons can receive unemployment insurance benefits is limited to 12 months (for some exceptions, which extended the periods in the mid-1980s, see Maier and Schettkat 1990). After that period, the unemployed might receive unemployment assistance, which is less than the insurance benefits, and eligibility for unemployment assistance depends on household income (income-tested).

The outflows out of unemployment showed the opposite trend. Outflows into employment gained importance in the 1980s, and outflows into nonparticipation lost importance. At first glance, this result seems to contradict hysteresis theories, but it does not if there is a segmentation of unemployment into one group that experiences long duration and another group with only short unemployment spells. It may also be that unemployment as the first stage in the process of entering (or reentering) the labor market has gained importance, as the in-

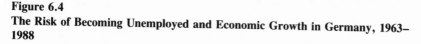

Figure 6.4

The Risk of Becoming Unemployed and Economic Growth in Germany, 1963–1988

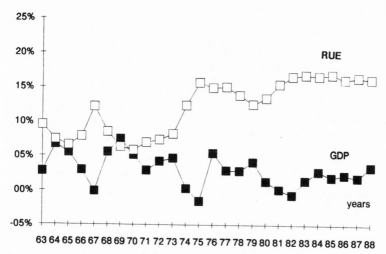

Source: Computations are based on OECD data (GDP in 1980 prices) and data of the Bundesanstalt fuer Arbeit.

Note: GDP = annual changes; rue = risk of becoming unemployed, computed by the flow form employment to unemployment devided by employment covered by social security insurance.

creased flow from nonparticipation suggests. Another explanation would be the greater share of former apprentices who have entered unemployment but who are likely to be hired after only a short spell of unemployment.

The risk of becoming unemployed, which is computed by the ratio of the flow from employment into unemployment divided by initial employment, depends, as do other labor market flows, on several factors, such as seasonal variation in production and the composition of the economy's employment by skills, innovative activity, structure, and other criteria (see Schettkat 1989). These factors are important if the level of the risk of becoming unemployed is to be explained but they are fairly constant over time. In the longitudinal perspective, one expects the risk of becoming unemployed to be negatively correlated with economic growth. Figure 6.4 illustrates the risk of becoming unemployed and the variation in the economy's output (real GDP). Changes in real GDP and changes in the risk of becoming unemployed do correlate negatively ($-.80$).

Variation over time, however, is only a small part of the overall risk of becoming unemployed and of employment flows in general. It is, therefore, of particular relevance whether this risk and labor market flows vary across industries and how they are related to job turnover and other measures of employment stability. These relations will be investigated in the following section.

6.3 LABOR AND JOB TURNOVER

6.3.1 Labor Turnover

The sectoral distribution of the inflow and outflow ratios displayed in Table 6.2 clearly shows that employment stability varies greatly from one sector of the economy to the next. Different data sources based on different concepts are used to gain an impression of effects related to different measurement methods and to investigate different aspects of mobility and flexibility. Still, in general, very similar pictures appear regardless of the different indicators. Based on the IAB sample (columns 1 to 7) and the employment statistics that count every movement between jobs (columns 8 to 10), exceptionally high values for the accession and separation rates appear in agriculture (I) and the construction industry (IV), both sectors with strong seasonal variations in production. In trade (V), transport and communication (VI), and other services (VIII), where marginal employment is more likely to be used, the substitution rates are well above the average as well (see also Table 6.5).

Finance and insurance (VII), on the other hand, where a high degree of loyalty is expected in exchange for high employment stability, displays rates well below the average. Even lower rates occur in mining, electricity, and water supply (II), which can be explained in part by the strong influence of unions as well as by the fact that energy, gas, and water suppliers are quasi-public services in Germany. In public service, including government and social security (X), the rates are somewhat higher, but nevertheless remain well below average. The values of the IAB sample, however, represent annual averages of labor turnover for a time period of six years (from 1976 to 1981), whereas the data from the employment statistics (columns 8, 9, and 10) cover 1985 only. The rates computed from these two data sources correlate highly, with coefficients of more than .97, which also indicates very stable industry patterns over time. Nevertheless, the levels are different and in most industries lower in 1985 than in the IAB sample.

In each sector, the accession and separation rates are quite close together (Table 6.2, columns 1, 2, 8, and 9). Hence, no sector shows very much net change in employment; there is neither much employment growth nor much decline. It follows that most of the labor market mobility cannot be explained by sectoral differences in employment growth or decline. Instead, it has to be explained by other factors, such as variation of employment in individual establishments within the sector (job turnover), seasonal variations in production and employment, outflows into retirement or other nonparticipation, and unemployment that may stem from skill adjustments. If employment and jobs are totally fixed and movements into and out of the labor force are the only source for "natural" mobility, and if a working life of 40 years is assumed, one arrives at a "natural" substitution rate of 2.5 percent which would equate the accession and separation rates. A shortening of the working life by a reduction of the retirement age, for example, or by the extension of education would increase the "natural" labor turnover. That is exactly what has happened in Germany. The retirement age was reduced, and, from 1984 to 1988, a special program was implemented that subsidized the substitution of younger workers for older ones (Landenberger 1990; Maier and Schettkat 1990). In the 1970s, several other measures also reduced the labor force participation of older workers. The labor force participation rate of 60-to-65-year-olds dropped from about 70 percent in 1970 to 44 percent in 1982. In addition, the educational periods were extended (Bangel 1990; Schettkat 1987). The reduction of the working life can thus explain part of the increase in employment inflow and outflow ratios (see Figures 6.1 and 6.2).

If one compares the substitution rates computed with the IAB sample (continuous flows) with those of the Mikrozensus (time-discrete flows, columns 14 to 23 in Table 6.2), one sees that the latter are much lower. This was to be expected on the basis of the considerations made in section 3.3.3. The differences are extremely high, however, in agriculture (I), construction (IV), trade (V), and transport/communication (VI). Part of the difference may be due to the different time periods underlying the data collection, but measurement differences and the type of mobility that is covered by the data sources seem to be more important. The IAB sample counts every movement into and out of employment, including multiple movements and direct movements from one job to another. In the Mikrozensus data, on the other hand, all short-run movements during the year and intraindustry mobility are hidden. Thus, the high rate of marginal, unstable employment in these industries seems to explain the high differences. This view is supported by the job turnover figures, which are high in these industries as well (see also Table 6.4).

Intuitively, one would expect sectors with low substitution rates to have high employment stability. Sectors with lower turnover rates are not necessarily sectors with high stability of employment from the employee's perspective, however, since it could well be that with the same substitution rate, the number of affected persons varies (see section 3.4.1). That is, in one sector labor turnover may be high because of the multiple movements of a few persons in and out of employment, whereas in other sectors the burden may be more evenly distributed over a greater population. While the substitution rate measures turnover not caused by variations of the level of employment, the stability rate gives the share of employees who remain with their sectors or establishments during a certain period. Substitution and stability rates thus have different denominators and different ranges of values: Stability rates can range from zero to 100 percent, whereas the substitution rate can assume values that range from zero to infinitely large. The two rates thus cannot be compared directly, but the difference between them gives some impression of how strongly stability is concentrated in each sector.

The stability rate in Table 6.2 (column 7) shows the stability of employment from the employee's perspective. The stability rate is defined by Ulrich Cramer

Table 6.2
Labor Turnover by Industry in Germany (Percentages)

Industry	IAB Sample (1976-1981), unweighted annual averages						stability rate 1980	Employment statistics (1985)			Unemployment statistics risk of becoming unemployed		
	rates			share of switchers° on				rates					
	acces-sion	sepa-ration	sub-stitution	accessions total	intraind.	sepa-ration		acces-sion	sepa-ration	sub-stitution	1977	1980	1985
	1	2	3	4	5	6	7	8	9	10	11	12	13
I Agriculture	64.8	66.3	64.8	20.0	8.0	19.0	34.5	66.7	69.2	66.7	30.0	25.9	38.2
II Mining, energy	16.0	12.7	12.7	47.0	18.0	37.0	68.2	12.0	12.7	12.0	4.2	3.7	3.3
III Manufacturing	25.2	25.1	25.1	32.0	20.0	31.0	58.2	22.4	20.5	20.5	10.6	8.4	9.7
IV Construction	47.3	46.9	46.9	28.0	17.0	28.0	46.3	47.1	53.4	47.1	28.0	17.4	38.4
V Trade	38.5	37.4	37.4	33.0	19.0	36.0	47.2	28.6	28.9	28.6	15.6	12.3	13.2
VI Transport, comm.	40.3	36.0	36.0	35.0	18.0	36.0	50.8	30.7	29.4	29.4	11.3	9.8	10.4
VII Finance	19.9	16.7	16.7	48.0	31.0	50.0	68.8	12.9	11.3	11.3	5.1	3.7	3.5
VIII Other services	47.3	44.4	44.4	28.0	16.0	29.0	42.2	39.7	36.5	36.5	15.5	12.7	14.1
IX Nonprofit org.	34.4	28.1	28.1	35.0	10.0	36.0	47.1	30.4	25.4	25.4	12.5	10.3	11.7
X Government	24.3	21.4	21.4	37.0	15.0	32.0	60.3	20.1	17.9	17.9	8.0	8.2	10.7
Total	33.4	31.8	31.8	31.0	18.0	32.0	52.3	28.6	27.5	27.5	13.2	10.4	13.1

Industry	Mikrozensus 1976/77					Mikrozensus 1980/81				
	rates			share other sectors		rates			share other sectors	
	acces-sion	sepa-ration	sub-stitution	acces-sion	sepa-ration	acces-sion	sepa-ration	sub-stitution	acces-sion	sepa-ration
	14	15	16	17	18	19	20	21	22	23
I Agriculture	13.8	18.3	13.8	30.6	27.5	15.1	17.5	15.1	38.7	35.7
II Mining, energy	17.7	21.8	17.7	86.5	51.8	23.4	18.0	18.0	86.3	91.1
III Manufacturing	14.9	13.8	13.8	64.9	63.0	17.0	17.4	17.0	71.0	68.8
IV Construction	17.5	22.8	17.5	74.1	65.2	21.9	23.0	21.9	80.3	81.9
V Trade	16.5	18.7	16.5	65.4	69.3	19.1	21.7	19.1	71.0	75.4
VI Transport, comm.	11.6	13.9	11.6	75.4	72.0	14.8	14.4	14.4	72.9	77.8
VII Finance	7.9	8.2	7.9	64.8	57.8	8.4	6.3	6.3	70.0	71.4
VIII Other services	41.2	37.2	37.2	58.9	62.1	51.0	42.4	42.4	65.7	67.4
IX Nonprofit org.	20.7	21.2	20.7	68.9	66.2	26.0	28.9	26.0	74.4	80.9
X Government	14.2	14.1	14.1	76.1	73.4	16.0	14.7	14.7	79.2	79.7
Total	17.2	17.7	17.2	65.2	63.2	20.4	20.2	20.2	70.9	71.8

Source: calculations are based on Mikrozensus data, IAB-data (Cramer 1986; Rudolph 1986), Amtliche Nachrichten Bundesanstalt für Arbeit, and Schettkat 1989a.
Note: accession and separation rates are computed as: flow/employment covered by social security (midyears).
° switchers are those employees who are reemployed within 7 days.

(1986b) as the share of employees who have remained with the same establishment during the whole six-year period of the investigation (from 1976 to 1981). Because of the method of data collection (see above), these values are certain to underestimate the stability of employment, since some people are counted as job switchers even though they did not really switch but were misclassified. When high turnover is evenly distributed across the employees in a particular sector, it results in a low stability rate in that sector; multiple movements would be low. If high turnover is concentrated on a few employees, it would result in a comparatively high stability rate; multiple movements would be concentrated.

Especially sharp differences between the substitution rate and the stability rate occur in agriculture (I), in which the stability rate is much lower than the substitution rate, indicating that unstable employment is a common characteristic faced by many employees in this sector. On the other hand, high and evenly distributed stable employment occurs in mining and electricity (II), finance (VII), and government (X), in which stability rates are high and substitution rates are low. In general, a high negative correlation (r = −.94) between the stability and the substitution rate exists across industries, indicating that both rates describe similar phenomena. According to the substitution rates from the Mikrozensus, agriculture and transport/communication would move from cell 3 to cell 1 in Figure 6.5. As in other services and nonprofit organizations, these industries would then be characterized as industries with below-average separation rates in the year-to-year perspective.

With the IAB sample, a distinction between switchers and nonswitchers can be made (columns 4, 5, and 6 in Table 6.2). Switchers are defined as those employees who are reemployed within 7 days; nonswitchers have a period of nonemployment, unemployment, or nonparticipation lasting more than 7 days between employment contracts. In all sectors, most outflows out of employment culminate in, and most inflows into employment originate in, nonparticipation or unemployment, as indicated by the high proportion of nonswitchers. This result is expected from the aggregated flow ratios in Figure 6.1. Nonswitchers cannot be distinguished by detailed destination or origin, respectively, but other flow data show that about 60 percent of all inflows and outflows go into or come from registered unemployment (Reyher and Bach 1988). This is especially true for employees covered by the social security system since they are most likely to be entitled to unemployment insurance benefits. There is little reason to expect them not to register at the employment agencies. This argument is supported by the very high correlation between the flow from employment into unemployment divided by the number of employees—the risk of becoming unemployed (columns 11, 12, and 13 in Table 6.2)—and the share of nonswitchers in separations (r = 0.99). Similar values occur for the risk of becoming unemployed and the separation rate (column 2; r = 0.95). Although the series varies closely together, there are substantial differences between the values of the separation rate (column 2) and the risk of becoming unemployed

Figure 6.5
Combinations of Separation and Stability Rates in Germany

| | | stability rate | |
		low	high
substitution rate	low	1 other services nonprofit organization (agriculture) (transport)	2 mining manufacturing finance government
	high	3 agriculture construction trade transport	4

note: low = below average, high = above average

(columns 11 to 13). These differences can be explained fairly well by divergences in the definition and scope of the two ratios.

First, the presented separation rate includes not only movements into unemployment but also into nonparticipation, which counts for 11 percentage points of the separation rate. Second, the separation rate includes direct movements between sectors and companies (switchers), which account for about 30 percent of the overall outflow or roughly 10 percentage points of the outflow ratio. Taking these two factors into account, the overall risk of becoming unemployed and the "corrected" separation rate for 1980 are 10 percent and 11 percent respectively.

With respect to the sectoral distribution, it is worth noting that the two sectors with the lowest separation rates—mining (II) and finance (VII)—are those in which the accession rates have the highest share of switchers (column 4 in Table 6.2). In finance, they are furthermore overwhelmingly switchers within the sector (column 5). In other words, they were previously employed at other finance or insurance establishments. This can be explained by high sector-specific human capital and by the high employment security in this sector (the highest stability) that allows employees to change if the opportunities are favorable. In addition, perhaps the stigma of unemployment has led them not to be accepted in the financial sector in the first place.

Table 6.3 presents accession and separation rates for occupational groups. Different signs and values for net changes indicate skill restructuring within the economy. Without giving too much weight to these one-year changes, other investigations have shown that the occupational flexibility in Germany has been quite high and that labor supply has responded very sensitively to demand changes. Not one of 39 occupational groups had decreasing unemployment from

1980 to 1985, but labor supply grew in the expanding occupations and shrank in the decreasing ones (Schettkat 1989, 68). Substitution rates and net changes for occupational groups correlated negatively (r = −.47), however, indicating that substitution rates tended to be higher in the shrinking occupations. In other words, the German economy seems to have shifted to more stable skill groups. This may have caused an increasing equilibrium rate of unemployment since hiring for more stable jobs may be more time-consuming.

Access to jobs equipped with new technologies, which are the jobs with better prospects, is influenced by employment stability as well. An analysis of the personal characteristics of workers in jobs with new technologies, as compared with those in jobs with old technologies, showed that companies tend to introduce new technologies with those workers who already have work experience in the sector. Skilled workers are more likely to gain access to jobs with new technologies, and those working in jobs with such technologies feel significantly less in danger of losing their jobs than those working in jobs with old technologies (Schettkat 1989, 112–13). This conclusion corresponds to the view that employment stability depends not only on sectoral characteristics but that personal characteristics are also relevant. In general, employment stability increases with age and the level of education. But it is not education itself that guarantees stable employment; it is the specific skills that are required mainly in the more stable sectors (Cramer 1986b).

6.3.2 Job Turnover

Job turnover focuses on gross changes of positions rather than on employment contracts. The number of gross job changes is influenced by economic growth, business cycles, structural change, and competition within industries. If job turnover is measured under the continuous flow concept, industries with seasonal fluctuations will show high job turnover. This variation is more important, however, for labor turnover, since seasonal variations do not change the economy substantially. The concept of job turnover is used to investigate the more permanent changes in the economy, and most measures of job turnover, therefore, measure gross changes from year to year or over even greater periods. In this section, data on annual flows, as well as gross changes over a six-year period, will be used.

Job turnover can occur because existing establishments grow and shrink or because new establishments are founded and old ones disappear. In Figure 6.6, different sources for aggregate job turnover based on yearly data are presented. The net effect follows a business cycle, with job losses in 1981–1982 and job gains before and after this recession. Highly correlated with the net effects are the reduction rates (r = .97) and expansion rates (r = .95) of jobs in existing establishments. The correlation is much weaker for newly founded establishments (r = .36) and closed establishments (r = .22).

Most of the variation caused by the expansion and contraction of jobs in

Table 6.3
Accession and Separation Rates for Occupational Groups in Germany, 1985 (In Percentage of Employment Covered by the Social Security Insurance)

occupational group	no	accession rate	separation rate	substitution rate	net change
agriculture, animal breeding, fishing	01-06	70.3	70.5	70.3	-0.1
miners (coal and mineral)	07-09	18.5	20.7	18.5	-2.3
stone workers, masons, suppl. of build. mat.	10-11	67.7	74.9	67.7	-7.2
potters and glass manufacturers	12-13	21.4	18.5	18.5	2.9
chemical/plastic processing workers	14-15	23.8	20.8	20.8	3.0
makers of paper and paper products	16	27.1	25.5	25.5	1.5
printers	17	20.8	19.2	19.2	1.6
wood preparation, woodworking	18	35/5	39.6	35.5	-4.1
producers of metal and metal goods	19-24	20.5	16.8	16.8	3.7
fitters, mechanics and allied occ.	25-30	24.9	23.3	23.3	1.6
electricians	31	24.2	21.5	21.5	2.8
mechanical and metal fitting occupations	32	31.9	25.2	25.2	6.7
textiles and clothing	33-36	25.1	25.7	25.1	-0.6
leather and fur processing	37	26.5	29.5	26.5	-3.0
food, drinks and tobaccos related occ.	39-43	46.7	46.1	46.1	0.6
construction workers	44-47	58.8	65.8	58.8	-7.0
building trades, fitting & furnishing, upholstery	48-49	43.4	50.1	43.4	-6.7
joiners, pattern making occ.	50	30.2	32.4	30.2	-2.2
painters, varnishers and allied occ.	51	52.9	54.9	52.9	-2.0
checkers and packers	52	29.1	27.4	27.4	1.7
unskilled laborers without specified tasks	53	56.2	51.2	51.2	4.9
machinists and allied occupations	54	22.0	24.5	22.0	-2.5
engineers, chemists, physicists, math.	60-61	15.9	12.7	12.7	3.2
technicians	62	12.7	11.1	11.1	1.7
technical specialists	63	18.7	15.8	15.8	2.8
trades occupations	68	26.5	26.4	26.4	0.1
goods and services, sales	69-70	15.4	12.9	12.9	2.5
transport occupations	71-74	33.8	33.2	33.2	0.6
organizers, administrative and clerical staff	75-78	18.0	16.6	16.6	1.4
law and order, security	79-81	29.6	27.8	27.8	1.8
journalists, interpreters. librarians	82	22.4	18.7	18.7	3.7
artists and allied occ.	83	64.4	63.7	63.7	0.7
health service, diagnosing/treatment occ.	84-85	28.2	24.7	24.7	3.5
social work, educationalists, researchers	86-89	33.2	27.8	27.8	5.4
personal hygiene	90	40.6	38.9	38.9	1.7
hotel staff	91	75.7	74.5	74.5	1.2
domestic services	92	44.6	44.8	44.6	-0.2
cleaning staff	93	31.4	31.9	31.4	-0.5
other	97-99		68.5	64.9	-3.6
overall		64.9 28.5	27.3	27.3	1.2

Source: Computations based on data from the Bundesanstalt fuer Arbeit, Beschaeftigtenstatistik.
Note: Employment includes those employees covered by the social security insurance.

Figure 6.6
Aggregate Job Turnover Components in Germany

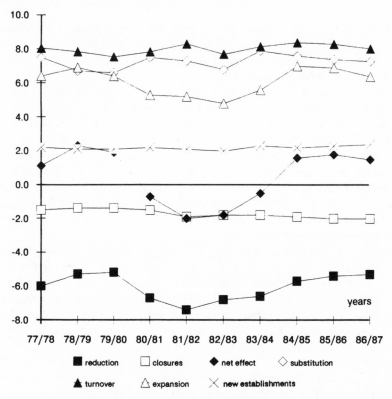

Source: Computations based on data in Cramer and Koller 1988.
Note: For definitions, see text. All rates are based on employment covered by the social security insurance.

existing establishments and the net effect of these two components vary pro-cyclically with the overall net effect. The difference between newly founded and closed establishments, on the other hand, was positive over the whole period.

In Table 6.4, the job turnover components of industries are shown in terms of their average annual changes from 1980 (June) to 1986 (June) as well as for that period as a whole. Both series are constructed from the same principal data source but use different measurement concepts. The first series is a measurement of job turnover on a yearly basis. The second series is a measurement for the whole period from June 1980 to June 1986 and computes gross job growth for newly founded and closed establishments. For existing establishments, it provides the net effects only. The recession of 1982 falls in the middle of the period analyzed. It can, therefore, be expected that turnover will be underestimated in the second data source because all movements caused by short-lived establishments or jobs and by the effects of the business cycle are hidden.

Surprisingly, the substitution rate, computed by the foundation and closure of establishments, is very similar in the two data sets. The yearly data (column 12 in Table 6.4) produces a value of 10.8 percent (6 times 1.8) for the entire six-year period, while the second data source produces a value of 11.4 percent (column 29). The substitution rates in column 12, however, are determined by the closure rates (column 9), whereas the substitution rates in column 29 are determined by the foundation rate (column 21), except for the expanding industries of services and finance. If use is made by the closure and the foundation rates directly, the difference between the two data sets becomes greater. The foundation rate is 13.2 percent (column 6), compared with 11.4 percent (column 21), and the closing rate is 10.8 percent (column 9), compared with 12.2 percent (column 25). These values are lower than either the founding or the closure rate. Furthermore, the series of the two data sets correlate highly, with coefficients around .90.

Keeping the classification problems in mind, one must note that the rates are not that different. This lack of divergence, however, is the effect of the relatively stable foundation and closure rates over that period and of the fact that most of the job turnover was caused by the expansion and reduction in employment in existing establishments. It also indicates that job turnover caused by very short-lived establishments was not that important in the overall German economy, at least not during the first half of the 1980s.

Job turnover as measured in these and other data is a function of the average establishment size. The smaller the establishments, the more likely that turnover will occur. The substitution rates in columns 30 to 32 of Table 6.4 show that most of the turnover caused by the foundation and closure of establishments was concentrated in small establishments (fewer than 20 employees, column 30). A comparison with the average establishment size (columns 33 and 34) shows that industries with bigger establishments had a tendency toward lower turnover figures. The correlation coefficient for overall job turnover divided by labor turnover (column 13) and for the job substitution rate (column 10) with the average establishment size (excluding transport, for which data on establishment size were not available) is about $-.80$. The subcomponents of job turnover—job contraction and job expansion (columns 11 and 12)—also correlate negatively with the average establishment size ($r = -.62$ and $r = -.77$, respectively).

The average establishment size is a quasi constant for industries since it does not change very much over time (compare columns 33 and 34 in Table 6.4). It cannot be distinguished from other industry-specific factors in this analysis. Moreover, job turnover is highly industry-specific, a characteristic that might be caused solely by the average establishment size. Dummies for industries explain 92 percent of the variation in the job substitution rates in a pooled data set covering the years from 1978 to 1985 and the industries listed in Table 6.5 (excluding transport, the regression is not displayed in Table 6.5). Again, financial services and basic industries (including energy production and chemicals) are the most stable industries, followed by the manufacturing of investment goods. It is not only that employment stability is high in these industries but also that jobs are very stable. Finance, however, is also a growing industry (column 5 of Table 6.4), mainly through the expansion of existing establishments (column 6). It is very seldom, however, that new financial institutions are founded in Germany; more often, of course, new establishments are set up by already existing firms.

If labor turnover is caused mainly by job turnover, then one would expect the ratio of job turnover to labor turnover to eliminate variations across industries. Column 13 in Table 6.4 presents the ratio of job turnover to labor turnover. The ratio is well below 100 percent, partly because job turnover and labor turnover figures are measured with different concepts. Labor turnover counts every movement on a continuous basis, whereas job turnover counts job differences from year to year. Short-run variations are therefore hidden in job turnover data. The coefficient of variation (standard deviation divided by the mean), however, is much lower for the ratio of labor turnover (0.15) than for labor turnover (0.37) or for job turnover (0.28), which indicates that part of the variation in labor turnover is caused by job turnover but that labor turnover is not caused entirely by job instability.

The relationship between the ratio of job to labor turnover and employment stability seems to be negative. Industries with above-average levels of employment stability (mining, the manufacturing of investment goods, and finance; see the coefficients for the industry dummies in Table 6.5, column 3) have comparatively high ratios of job to labor turnover (see the coefficients listed in column 2 of Table 6.5). Industries with particularly high labor turnover (low employment stability), like trade, transport, and services, have comparatively low ratios of job turnover to labor turnover. Especially in finance, where the ratio of job to labor turnover is above the average, significantly more labor turnover, which is low, is caused by job turnover. In other words, a substantial part of the low labor turnover in this industry is caused by low job turnover, most likely within multi-establishment firms. This finding is another sign of the extremely high employment stability in this industry.

One must keep in mind that job turnover counts the gross change of positions on the level of the establishment and that job shifts between different production sites in multi-establishment firms thus count as job flow. In addition, there are statistical problems. First, the establishment is identified in the data by an administrative number, which may change for purely administrative reasons (see section 6.1). Second, sectoral definitions are broad. Measured job turnover is, therefore, overestimated by data based on German employment statistics. The size of this effect is not known, and it is believed that it is generally small but may be more substantial in some sectors, like finance, where firm turnover

Table 6.4
Job Turnover by Industry in Germany

Industry	net effect			job gains			job losses			substitution rates			turnover
	over-all	exp.& contract.	new & closed	over-all	expan-sion	new	over-all	con-tract.	closed	over-all	exp.& ontract.	new & closed	job / labor
	1	2	3	4	5	6	7	8	9	10	11	12	13
Energy, Basic industries	-1.1	-1.4	0.3	4.6	3.7	0.9	5.7	5.1	0.6	4.6	3.7	0.6	28.3
Investment goods	-0.2	-0.5	0.3	6.3	5.3	1.1	6.5	5.7	0.8	6.3	5.3	0.8	37.3
Consumption goods	-2.3	-2.1	-0.2	6.6	5.1	1.6	8.9	7.2	1.7	6.6	5.1	1.6	32.5
Construction	-2.7	-2.5	-0.2	9.8	7.0	2.8	12.5	9.5	3.0	9.8	7.0	2.8	27.1
Trade	-0.8	-1.3	0.5	9.7	6.4	3.3	10.5	7.7	2.8	9.7	6.4	2.8	35.7
Transport	0.6	0.2	0.5	9.3	6.6	2.7	8.6	6.4	2.3	8.6	6.4	2.3	26.1
Finance	1.2	1.0	0.3	6.4	4.8	1.6	5.1	3.8	1.3	5.1	3.8	1.3	37.8
Services	2.3	1.2	1.1	11.6	7.9	3.7	9.3	6.7	2.6	9.3	6.7	2.6	29.3
Non-profit org.	2.2	1.3	0.9	10.2	6.8	3.4	8.0	5.5	2.5	8.0	5.5	2.5	27.2
Intermed. serv.	2.3	1.1	1.2	13.0	9.1	3.9	10.7	8.0	2.7	10.7	8.0	2.7	31.4
overall	-0.3	-0.6	0.4	8.0	5.8	2.2	8.3	6.4	1.8	8.0	5.8	1.8	28.7

average of annual changes 1980 (June) to 1986 (June) (unweighted, in %)

Table: employment trends for surviving, newly founded, and closed establishments (net effects)

Industry	employ-ment 1980 (in 1000)	overall total	overall sur-vivor	overall new & closed	survivor 1-19	survivor 20-499	survivor >500	new establishments total	new 1-19	new 20-499	new >500
	14	15	16	17	18	19	20	21	22	23	24
Energy.											
Basic industries	2137	-6.9	-5.9	-1.0	0.4	-0.5	-5.8	4.2	1.1	2.1	1.0
Invest. goods	4545	-1.5	-0.8	-0.7	1.1	0.1	-2.0	7.0	2.8	3.1	1.1
Consumer goods	2451	-12.0	-5.2	-6.7	1.8	-4.5	-2.5	7.4	3.5	3.7	0.2
Construction	1699	-15.1	-7.8	-7.3	0.4	-7.2	-1.0	12.0	7.5	4.4	0.1
Trade	2893	-5.2	-5.1	0.0	1.1	-4.4	-1.8	16.0	10.8	5.0	0.2
Transport											
Finance	762	8.0	7.8	0.2	2.4	4.8	0.6	3.8	2.6	1.0	0.2
Services	2177	13.9	3.9	10.0	3.4	0.6	-0.1	28.3	21.1	6.8	0.4
Overall	16663	21.0	-2.6	-0.8	1.4	-1.9	-2.1	11.4	6.9	3.9	0.6

Industry	closed establishments total	closed 1-19	closed 20-499	closed >500	substitution rates total	subst. 1-19	subst. 20-499	subst. >500	average establishment size 1980	1986
	25	26	27	28	29	30	31	32	33	34
Energy.										
Basic industries	5.2	1.2	2.8	1.1	4.2	1.1	2.1	1.0	73.3	69.7
Invest. goods	7.7	2.2	4.4	1.2	7.0	2.2	3.1	1.1	40.5	37.3
Consumer goods	14.2	4.6	8.9	0.6	7.4	3.5	3.7	0.2	17.8	16.6
Construction	19.3	9.0	10.1	0.2	12.0	7.5	4.4	0.1	12.7	11.2
Trade	16.1	10.6	5.4	0.1	16.0	10.6	5.0	0.1	9.1	8.6
Transport										
Finance	3.6	2.2	1.4	0.0	3.6	2.2	1.0	0.0	24.1	24.0
Services	18.3	14.4	3.9	0.1	18.3	14.4	3.9	0.1	5.8	5.8
Overall	12.2	6.2	5.4	0.6	11.4	6.2	3.9	0.6	14.7	13.6

Source: Computations based on data in Kramer and Koller 1988, König and Weißhuhn 1989, and Weißhuhn et al. 1988.

Note: exp. & contract. = expansion and contraction

157

Table 6.5
Explorative Regressions of Different Turnover Indicators

independent variables	dependent variables			
	job substitution rate	turnover jobs/labor	labor turnover	risk of becoming unemployed
	1	2	3	4
Constant	5.05	0.23	24.41	9.47
	(+20.08)	(+15.78)	(+21.88)	(+6.61)
Investment goods	0.34	0.06	-1.25	0.55
	(+1.39)	(+4.23])	(-1.09)	(+0.39)
Consumer goods	2.39	0.03	7.26	2.15
	(+9.80)	(+1.88)	(+6.30)	(+1.50)
Construction	5.35	-0.007	27.04	17.4
	(+21.95)	(-0.49)	(+23.47)	(+12.14)
Trade	5.01	0.06	13.05	3.48
	(+20.55)	(+3.75)	(+11.33)	(+2.43)
Transport	3.64	-0.02	20.76	1.03
	(+14.93)	(-1.23)	(+18.02)	(+0.72)
Finance	0.73	0.1	-3.53	-6.02
	(+2.99)	(+6.68)	(-3.06)	(-4.20)
Services	3.38	-0.003	19.11	
	(+13.86)	(-0.22)	(+16.59)	
1978-79	-0.88	-0.01	-1.38	-1.61
	(-3.21)	(-0.72)	(-1.19)	(-1.05)
1979-80	-0.90	-0.03	0.53	-2.06
	(-3.30)	(-2.36)	(+0.46)	(-1.34)
1980-81	-0.39	-0.02	-0.24	0.24
	(-1.42)	(-1.47)	(-0.21)	(+0.15)
1981-82	-0.70	0.01	-2.48	2.3
	(-2.57)	(+0.52)	(-2.15)	(+1.50)
1982-83	-1.06	0.01	-4.53	2.08
	(-3.90)	(+0.61)	(-3.93)	(+1.36)
1983-84	-0.46	0.03	-5.94	1.36
	(-1.70)	(+2.29)	(-5.15)	(+0.89)
1984-85	-0.73	0.03	-5.63	1.78
	(-2.66)	(+2.30)	(-4.88)	(+1.16)
1985-86	-0.36			
	(-1.33)			
1986-87	-0.48			
	(-1.74)			
R**2	0.94	0.75	0.97	0.88
SEE	0.55	0.03	2.3	2.87
F	4.95	3.04	29.59	7.52
n	80	64	64	56

Note: The omitted variables are: Energy, basic industries and 1977-78;
t-values in parentheses.
Sources: See Table 6.4.

tends to be small. Nevertheless, the employment statistics are the most reliable labor market data in Germany.

Regression analysis (not displayed in Table 6.5) shows that labor turnover variations are influenced more by closures than by reductions in jobs in surviving establishments. If, however, industries are controlled for by dummies in a pooled regression covering the period from 1978 to 1985 and the industries listed in Table 6.4 (with a detailed service sector), then "closure" loses its significance. In other words, closure is industry-specific. On the basis of the pooled data set, only the dummies for the year of 1979–1980 are above the

value of the omitted year of 1977–1978. These two years, however, were periods of slight recovery, and all other years show negative values; that is, labor
turnover was lower in those years. The risk of becoming unemployed (column
4 in Table 6.5), on the other hand, was higher in the 1980s than in 1977–1978.
Again, this result is consistent with a positive relation between voluntary labor
mobility and the business cycle.

Formula 3.13 provides an answer to the question of how much job turnover
is caused by structural change. Values of 1 will appear if all job turnover is
caused by intra-industry turnover, while values of zero indicate job turnover
caused by structural change only. High values occur in the years 1977–1978,
1980–1981, and 1983–1984; low values appear in 1984–1985 and 1986–1987.
Structural change as a source for job turnover, therefore, gained importance in
the mid-1980s. From Table 4.5, it is known that indicators for structural change
showed a decrease, or at least no increase, in the pace of structural change in
the 1980s. Therefore, the explanation for low inter-industry job turnover values
must be determined by a decrease in intra-industry job turnover more than by
restructuring. Indeed, the time dummies in the explorative regressions displayed in Table 6.5 show negative values; that is, job turnover not caused by
restructuring was lower in the 1980s than in the late 1970s.

Most job turnover is caused by intra-industry gross job growth and decline
and not by a changing structure of the economy. The job-substitution rate,
however, correlates negatively (r = −.78) with average establishment size.

6.4 MISMATCH

6.4.1 Measurement Issues

The two axes of the Beveridge curve—vacancies and unemployment—are
both problematic when it comes to real-world data. Both variables are subject
to several qualifications in Germany. It is known that the reporting of unemployment has been problematic and that there are still theoretical controversies
about what defines unemployment. The same is true for vacancy data; it is not
clear what a vacancy stands for and how it should be measured.

The German data on vacancies is the outcome of employers' requests for
labor at employment agencies. Employment agencies are, of course, not the
only means that firms can use to search for workers. Some alternatives include
advertisements in newspapers, headhunters, and the "extended internal labor
market" (Hohn and Windolf 1984). Moreover, not every vacancy has to be
registered with employment agencies; in fact, many are not. Nor is it necessarily the case that a vacancy represents an actual unfilled job. A vacant position
may become available at a later date, or not at all, but it should be filled for at
least 7 days (see Rudolph 1984, 168). A vacancy may be an additional job or
just the outcome of job or labor substitution. Certainly, vacancies cannot be
equated with additional labor demand; some of the demand for workers is sim-

ply substituting for other employees who have left the firm. Therefore, there is a basic rate of vacancies that will never disappear so long as there is labor turnover. Jürgen Kühl (1970, 252–53) has noted that even in the recessions of the 1960s, the vacancy data showed positive values even in declining sectors. The same applies to later recessions. This finding is to be expected on the basis of the arguments made in section 3.5.

A vacancy disappears from the statistics if the vacant job is filled, is redrawn, or is not extended (Kühl 1970, 256). Still, vacancy data give some indication of labor demand developments. In expanding industries, vacancies have increased, whereas vacancies have decreased in shrinking industries (Kühl 1970), and vacancies vary over the business cycle. The available vacancy statistics in Germany provide information on flows as well as on stocks.

By definition, unemployment statistics measure the labor supply available for work immediately. Vacancies in Germany cover a time span of 3 months in advance, however, and it is not clear at all when jobs are to become available or whether they will ever become available. At the very extreme, one can therefore end up in a situation in which both actual unemployment—which represents the labor available immediately for work—and vacancies are high but in which only a few, if any, jobs are actually available. This is, of course, a stylized theoretical possibility. Such a situation might occur at the beginning of an upswing, when employers feel optimistic but do not recruit immediately. This would be a short-term phenomenon that is not important if use is made of annual data, for example. A survey conducted in 1989 showed that about 40 percent of the vacant positions were substitutions for employees who had already left the firm (IAB 1990, 3). That is, these vacant positions represented available jobs.

As mentioned, the German vacancy data reflect vacancies reported to employment agencies. Thus, published vacancy data are only part of the picture of overall vacancies. Furthermore, the share of reported vacancies in overall vacancies can change over time. Indeed, the ratio of reported vacancies to new hires is sensitive to the business cycle and is low in periods of low labor demand (Rudolph 1984, 173). Job placements arranged through employment agencies have decreased in both absolute terms and as a ratio to all hirings. The ratio of vanishing vacancies to overall hiring (including short-term hiring) dropped from about 45 percent in the late 1960s and early 1970s to 20 percent in the mid-1980s (Rudolph 1984, 172). This, however, is only a rough indicator of the participation of employment agencies in the hiring process, since vacancies can disappear because of successful hiring or for other reasons.

Another important indicator is the ratio of the job placements arranged by employment agencies to the vanishing vacancies. This ratio varied slightly around 58 percent from the 1960s until the mid-1970s, increased to 79 percent in 1983–1984, and remained at the 70 percent level in 1986–1987 (Rudolph 1984, 172; Ermann 1987, 183). According to the calculations of Helmut Rudolph (1984), the decrease in the number of job placements from the 1960s to the

1980s was caused mainly by a shrinking share of vacancies reported to employment agencies and by the decreasing number of placements (see section 6.2.2).

Important to the analysis of mismatch, therefore, is the influence of the decreasing share of reported vacancies on the structure of vacancies registered at employment agencies. A priori, the direction of the impact is not clear. It may be that only less qualified, "easy-to-fill" vacant jobs are reported to employment agencies, but it may also be that more difficult vacancies are reported because the other ones can be filled easily, without any assistance.

The IAB survey has concluded that vacancies reported to employment agencies account for about 40 percent of all vacant jobs (Brinkmann and Spitznagel 1990). This ratio is higher for skilled blue-collar workers ("Facharbeiter," 44 percent) than for white-collar workers (35 percent), and it increases with the size of the firm (Brinkmann and Spitznagel 1990; Kühl 1970, 432). A recent survey found that about 50 percent of establishments contact employment agencies if personnel are to be recruited. Perhaps surprisingly, employment agencies are the most-used consulting institutions, including private consultants (Semlinger 1989).

Another statistical problem arises from the fact that the vacancies filled through the mediation of employment agencies are not necessarily filled with unemployed job seekers. They can be filled with job seekers who are not registered as unemployed and who could be nonparticipants or even employees. Less than 50 percent of the new job seekers who reported to employment agencies were unemployed during the period from 1964 to 1973, whereas this share was above 75 percent after 1975 (Rudolph 1984, 173). In other words, recruiting from the unemployment pool has gained importance (see also Section 6.2.1).

In his analysis of mismatch in Germany, Wolfgang Franz (1987a and b, 1990) has used corrected vacancy and unemployment data. His argument is that the vacancies reported to employment agencies are only a fraction of overall vacancies, and he has suggested that reported vacancies should be divided by the new hires managed by employment agencies. Franz has mentioned that his corrections for vacancies and unemployment are only rough approximations (Franz 1987b, 4) and are based on the assumption that reported and nonreported vacancies are of equal duration. With the corrected data, Franz has arrived at a more pronounced outward shift of the Beveridge curve (see Figure 6.7). His corrected vacancy-rate series correlates with a coefficient of .96 with the uncorrected series, and he has noted "that the u/v curve based on official data exhibits shifts, too" (Franz 1990, 4). Since the same picture can be identified in the original data as well, I make use of the uncorrected series as published by the Federal Employment Agency (Bundesanstalt für Arbeit). Because vacancy rates are computed as a ratio of vacancies to employment, the unemployment rate in the following is also computed as a ratio of unemployment to employment instead of as the share of unemployment in the labor force.

6.4.2 The German Beveridge Curve

Figure 6.7 shows the German Beveridge curve based on published data (upper diagram), as well as curves based on corrected vacancy data. Both curves display outward shifts after 1976 and 1983, indicating an increase in the equilibrium rate of unemployment. It is important to look behind these indicators to discover what has caused the outshifts (Figure 6.8).

As displayed in Part I of Figure 6.8, the changes in unemployment and in its duration show the expected business cycle loop during the 1967 recession (see also section 3.5.1). As unemployment grew, the duration increased, and vice versa. During the 1974–1975 recession, the duration increased and remained at a high level; unemployment decreased only slightly. The next increase in unemployment started from this longer duration and drove the duration further out, to more than 30 weeks on average. After both recessions, unemployment did not drop back to former levels, certainly a sign for serious labor market problems.

On the demand side of the labor market, one expects vacancies to be difficult to fill as mismatch increases, so average durations ought to increase as well. Part II in Figure 6.8 shows the relation between changes in vacancies and the average duration of those vacancies. For the 1967 recession, one sees the expected clockwise loop. Increases in vacancies lead to a longer duration of vacancies. In the following recessions of 1974–1975 and 1982, the clockwise developments occur again but at much shorter durations. Recruiting problems were obviously no serious obstacle for production, a result found in the ifo-institute's employer surveys as well (Vogler-Ludwig 1983, 30). For the late 1980s, in another survey with questions similar to those in the ifo survey, Christian Brinkmann and Eugen Spitznagel (1990) found that the number of establishments that regard actual labor scarcity as an impediment to the expansion of production has increased slightly. Nevertheless, this group counts for only 12 percent of all (employee-weighted) establishments. This picture clearly contradicts what one would expect in situations of increasing mismatch.

The developments in the unemployment diagram (Part I in Figure 6.8) would support claims of rising levels of equilibrium unemployment, and persistent, long durations of unemployment can be an indication of hysteresis. At the same time, the vacancy diagram shows that it has obviously not been very difficult to fill vacant jobs. The trend of the average duration of vacancies points in a direction of a labor market that operates in a relatively effective way. The divergent trends between the vacancy and unemployment curves seem to contradict demand deficiency as well as the mismatch explanation of persistent unemployment. In the first case, one would expect unemployment to shrink with increasing labor demand; in the second case, vacancies should not be that easily filled.

Both explanations have to be seen differently, however, if one relaxes the implicit assumption that there is a fixed labor force (see section 3.4.2). It may

Figure 6.7
The German Beveridge Curve, Unadjusted and Adjusted

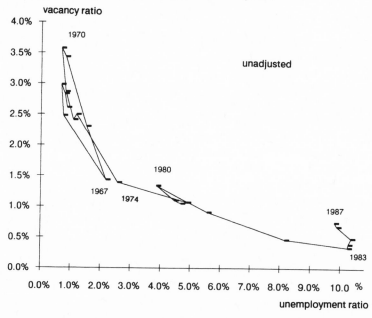

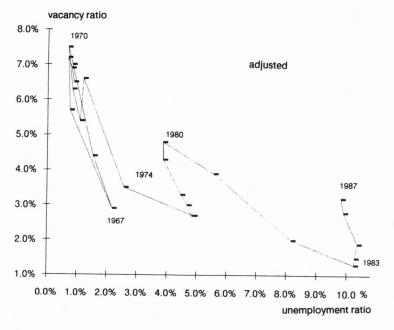

Source: Computations are based on data of the Bundesanstalt fuer Arbeit for unadjusted data; Franz 1990 for the adjusted vacancy data.

Note: The unemployment ratio and the vacancy ratio are computed with employment covered by the social security insurance as denominator.

Figure 6.8
Change-Duration Curves for Unemployment and Vacancies in Germany

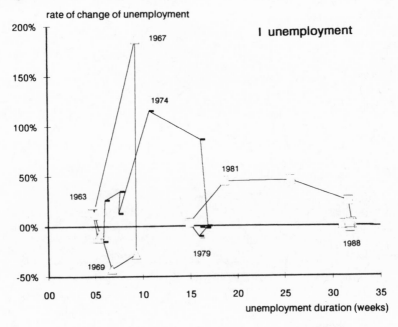

rate of change of unemployment

I unemployment

1967

1974

1981

1963

1979

1969

1988

unemployment duration (weeks)

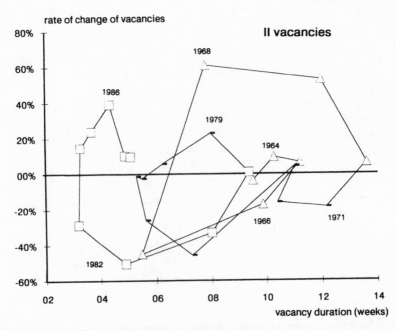

rate of change of vacancies

II vacancies

1968

1986

1979

1964

1971

1966

1982

vacancy duration (weeks)

Source: Computations are based on data of the Bundesanstalt fuer Arbeit.
Note: The durations are computed with the steady-state assumption.

well be that there is a mismatch between the unemployed and jobs but that the vacancies are being filled by "outsiders," that is, by persons newly entering or reentering the labor market. Furthermore, mismatch may be industry-specific, or structural change may lead to vacancies in expanding industries and to unemployment in other sectors. It is, therefore, important to investigate the sectoral composition of unemployment and vacancies.

If mismatch is caused by industry-specific skills (or the lack of them) and by the immobility of labor, then one can expect different industry-specific patterns of change and duration of unemployment and vacancies to occur. The patterns shown in Figures 6.9 and 6.10, which refer to industries starting in 1975, are similar to those in Figure 6.8.

Although the duration of unemployment (Figure 6.9) and the duration of vacancies (Figure 6.10) are at different levels, the patterns for both curves within the industries are very similar. For vacancies, one observes the clockwise business-cycle movement in every single industry. Again, these patterns support the view that recruiting must have become easier in Germany since the mid-1970s. The trends of unemployment point in the opposite direction, however. Unemployment duration has shifted outwards in every single industry, but the levels of duration vary from one industry to another.

6.4.3 Mismatch Indicators

In section 3.5.2, different mismatch indicators were discussed. If they all reveal the same phenomena, they should produce similar values; that is, they should all point in the same direction. All three mismatch indicators discussed earlier are used with the German data, and the results for 10 industries and 32 occupational groups are shown in Table 6.6. The traditional mismatch indicator (mm1) shows decreasing maladjustment for industries and occupations. The same tendency, for both industries and occupations, is shown by the other mismatch indicator (mm3), which gives the lower value of either the vacancy rate or the unemployment rate. This indicator is determined by the vacancy rate only, meaning that the vacancy rate was below the unemployment rate in all years and that the declining trend was thus the result of decreasing vacancies. Reverse trends in mismatch are shown by the indicator composed of the variance of unemployment rates (mm2). This indicator shows a clearly upward trend in the 1980s, which was stronger for industries than for occupations. The correlation coefficients at the bottom of Table 6.6 summarize the contradictory results.

In general, the two indicators (mm1 and mm3), which are influenced by unemployment and vacancy rates, have lower correlation coefficients between industry mismatch and occupational mismatch than mm2, which is computed by unemployment rates alone. Assuming correct measurement, one expects the unemployment and the vacancy rates to develop in the same direction with increasing mismatch. In other words, both rates and both indicators (mm1 and

Figure 6.9
Industry-Specific Change-Duration Curves for Unemployment in Germany

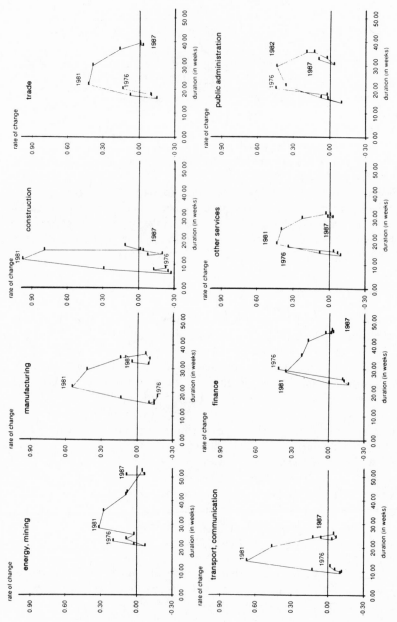

Source: Computations are based on data of the Bundesanstalt fuer Arbeit.
Note: The durations are computed with the steady-state assumption.

Figure 6.10
Industry-Specific Change-Duration Curves for Vacancies in Germany

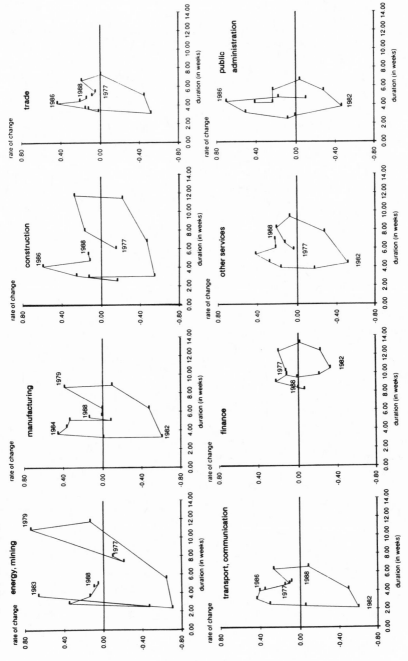

Source: Computations are based on data of the Bundesanstalt fuer Arbeit.
Note: The durations are computed with the steady-state assumption.

167

mm3) should increase. If, however, measurement errors are important and the vacancy rate is downward biased (see section 6.4.1), then mm3 would indicate decreasing mismatch; the same would happen with mm1 if mismeasurement is evenly distributed across industries and occupations, respectively. Surprisingly, indicators mm1 and mm2 do not correlate highly but are connected only in a loose way. At least the correlation between industry and occupational mismatch trends is positive; that is, industry and occupation data point in the same direction for every indicator. But how can one explain the opposite results obtained with different indicators? What has happened in the German labor market? Has it suffered increasing maladjustment, or are its unemployment problems the result of demand deficiency only?

Since mm2 is based on unemployment only and is, hence, less subject to possible measurement errors, it is best to concentrate on this indicator, comparing the trends of indicator mm2 for industries and occupations. It is surprising to see that it increased less for occupations than for industries. From the proposed general trend toward indirect production work (see section 3.5.2), one would expect the opposite in a labor market that adjusts too slowly. Occupational mismatch should have increased within every industry, while the variation of industry-specific unemployment rates should have decreased.

Unrealistically assuming an equal distribution of occupational skill requirements across industries and immobility of labor between industries (for example, because of wage differentials or employers' preferences for workers with industry-specific know-how), one may end up in a situation in which unemployment rate differentials would grow between industries while occupational unemployment rate differentials decrease. In a situation of overall demand deficiency and equal skill requirements across industries, the mobility of workers would reduce mismatch as measured by indicator mm2. But immobility between industries would not be the actual cause of unemployment, only of measured maladjustment. Mobility of workers across industries would change the distribution of unemployment but not its level. The main cause of unemployment in the situation being discussed can hardly be structural, and is more likely demand deficiency. To this extent, the difference in the trends for industries and occupations of mismatch indicator mm2 suggests that Germany's unemployment is explained more by the industry link than by occupational requirements.

The mismatch indicator mm2 for industries has been influenced mainly by the trend of unemployment rather than employment. The dispersion of unemployment (measured by the variance) across the 10 industries in 1987 was 319 percent of its value in 1977. The coefficient of variation, however, was only 92 percent of its 1977 value. Dispersion had decreased relative to the level of unemployment. In other words, unemployment had become a general, industry-wide phenomenon. Employment, on the other hand, showed a decrease in the coefficient of variation and a decrease in the variance as well. As mm2 indicates, however, the dispersion of the unemployment rate was higher than the

Table 6.6
Mismatch Indicators for Germany

years	industries			occupations		
	mm1	mm2 (*1000)	mm3 (*100)	mm1	mm2 (*1000)	mm3 (*100)
1975	5.28	0.24	1.15			
1976	4.11	0.16	1.16			
1977	3.55	0.12	1.17	22.74	1.73	1.17
1978	3.36	0.11	1.23	22.36	1.51	1.22
1979	3.23	0.06	1.47	23.08	0.97	1.42
1980	2.34	0.08	1.41	22.72	1.05	1.40
1981	3.05	0.20	0.84	22.64	2.21	0.84
1982	4.32	0.59	0.39	21.83	3.56	0.39
1983	3.28	0.70	0.38	17.06	3.37	0.38
1984	2.46	0.73	0.44	16.79	2.72	0.44
1985	2.39	0.75	0.56	17.10	2.64	0.56
1986	2.07	0.60	0.78	17.10	2.34	0.78
1987	2.44	0.59	0.84	17.31	2.39	0.84
1988		1.30		16.99	2.18	0.95
			1977 = 100			
1975	148.57	201.66	97.87			
1976	115.84	133.92	98.69			
1977	100.00	100.00	100.00	100.00	100.00	100.00
1978	94.68	88.89	104.80	98.35	87.26	104.30
1979	90.84	53.78	125.28	101.47	55.96	120.63
1980	65.76	69.51	120.20	99.93	60.55	119.26
1981	86.00	171.09	71.70	99.58	127.35	71.83
1982	121.73	499.13	33.11	96.00	205.51	33.42
1983	92.42	587.07	32.34	75.02	194.65	32.65
1984	69.34	613.16	37.30	73.85	156.95	37.66
1985	67.30	630.79	47.65	75.22	152.38	48.04
1986	58.40	508.79	66.54	75.21	135.10	66.58
1987	68.66	497.56	71.52	76.13	138.26	71.76
1988		1094.90		74.73	125.90	80.55

Coefficients of Correlation

	industries			occupations		
industries	mm1	mm2	mm3	mm1	mm2	mm3
mm1	1.00	-0.34	0.15	0.50		
mm2		1.00	-0.91		0.85	
mm3			1.00			0.51
occupations						
mm1				1.00	-0.63	0.06
mm2					1.00	-0.48
mm3						1.00

Source: Computations are based on data of the Bundesanstalt fuer Arbeit.

Note: For the definitions of the indicators, see text.

two components, unemployment and employment. One would expect this fact to be the result of a more than proportional increase in unemployment in industries in which employment is shrinking as compared to those industries in which employment is increasing. The data do not confirm this view. Unemployment grew more in the expanding industries than in the shrinking ones. If industries are an appropriate unit for investigating the mismatch in the labor market, then one must conclude that mismatch in Germany is caused not by insufficient or misdirected labor mobility but by disproportionately great increases in the labor supply in expanding industries. This problem is the inverse of what is usually meant by the term "mismatch."

The same results are obtained when occupations are used. The only occupational group (out of 32) in which the unemployment rate was not higher in 1987 than in 1977 was unskilled workers. All other occupational groups had higher unemployment rates in 1987 than in 1977. Even in expanding occupational groups, unemployment grew at a disproportionately high rate compared to employment. Again, there is thus no support for the view that the German labor force is characterized by a high degree of skill inflexibility. Labor seems to move in the proper direction, but labor demand is not growing quickly enough to absorb the supply.

The trend toward a shorter average duration of vacancies in the late 1970s and especially in the 1980s may simply have been the effect of the structure of vacancies, if, for example, it was changing to less qualified jobs that are easier to fill. This could be especially true for the share of vacancies which are reported to employment agencies. Since this trend occurred in every industry, the trend toward a shorter duration of vacancies cannot be just an effect of a changing industrial structure. Nevertheless, reporting easy-to-hire vacancies to employment agencies may be only an economy-wide phenomenon, so occupational groups should be investigated as well.

From 1977 to 1987, the shares of occupational groups in overall vacancies were very stable. The groups in which the share changed more than 1 percentage point were agricultural (+1.8 percentage points), producers of metal (−1.6 percentage points), electricians (+2.0 percentage points), mechanics (−2.2 percentage points), construction (−5.2 percentage points), engineers (+4.3 percentage points), technicians (+1.8 percentage points), social occupations (+3.4 percentage points), and other service occupations (−1.6 percentage points). The occupational groups that lost importance were those whose members are expected to be more easily hired. Conversely, the occupations that gained in importance were those whose members were most likely to be more difficult to hire. Empirical evidence, therefore, points more to an increasing duration of unemployment. A similar result is reached if the skill structure of vacancies is investigated. The share of unskilled vacancies dropped from 44 percent in 1977 to 27.7 percent in 1987.

6.5 RISING EQUILIBRIUM RATES OF UNEMPLOYMENT IN GERMANY?

The analysis for Germany so far has shown a clear outward shift of the change-duration curve for unemployment, but the duration of unemployment is influenced by the labor market situation itself and by various other factors (see section 3.4.2). Because vacancies were filled quickly and the change-duration curves for vacancies showed improvements rather than deteriorations of the hiring process, it is very likely that Germany's unemployment and its long duration have been caused by demand deficiency in the labor market. Using formula 3.22, one can answer the question of whether the flow-equilibrium rate of unemployment has changed and what factors have contributed to this variation. As mentioned earlier, the factors that may have contributed to the rise in the unemployment rate are—in addition to the duration of unemployment—the separation rate, the share of hirings from unemployment in overall hiring, and the share of separations into unemployment in all separations. If the focus is on changing labor market dynamics as a function of variations in the employment system, other than changes of level, then one might take the substitution rate of employment as an approximation of separation and hiring rates that is less influenced by changes in the level of employment.

Table 6.7 shows the estimates for the flow-equilibrium rate of unemployment arrived at under the assumption that unemployment is caused solely by the dynamics of the employment system. The computations are based on data of the Arbeitskräftegesamtrechnung (Reyher and Bach 1988) and take into account only mobility between the employment system and nonemployment. All intra-employment mobility is hidden. The rates are artificial, of course, because they reflect only a part of the overall labor market. The only inflow into unemployment comes from employment, and the only outflow out of unemployment goes into employment. Furthermore, only the flows caused by the lower value of either the separation or the hiring rate are taken into account. Still, the values do give estimates for unemployment related to employment dynamics, which is an undisputed source of unemployment.

Different equilibrium rates were computed. The rate in column 8 of Table 6.7 is a rate given the values of the variables for each year. In other words, a steady-state process is assumed for these particular years. The next columns (9 to 11) display rates in which one of the variables of formula 3.22 always varies and the others are held constant. The values chosen as constants are averages for the years 1970 to 1973, when the actual unemployment trend was close to a steady-state process. That is, the values did not change very much. The exact values for the constants in the computations of columns 9 to 11 are given in the top line of the left part of Table 6.7.

As can be seen from the trend in column 9, the ratio y/z^2 increased the unemployment rate up to the end of the 1970s, but in the middle of the 1980s, when unemployment was high, this ratio tended to lower the unemployment

Table 6.7
Labor Market Flow Ratios and Estimations for Flow-Equilibrium Rates of Unemployment in Germany

years	separation rate of employment (EX/E)	hiring rate of employment (XE/E)	ratios (in %) substitution rate (1 or 2)	y (UE/XE)	z (EU/EX)	y/z²	duration of unempl. (weeks) (U/XU)	estimates for flow-equilibrium rates of unemployment (in %) all	y/z²	varying variables substitution rate	duration of unempl.	none	unemployment rate OECD data (in %)
	1	2	3	4	5	6	7	8	9	10	11	12	13
average 1970-1973	13.6	14.2	13.6	26.0	38.7	1.7	7.4						
1970	12.8	13.7	12.8	22.9	34.7	1.9	7.7	0.5	0.5	0.6	0.6	0.6	0.6
1971	13.8	13.8	13.8	25.5	37.9	1.8	5.8	0.4	0.6	0.6	0.5	0.6	0.7
1972	13.7	14.6	13.7	27.6	39.8	1.7	8.4	0.7	0.6	0.6	0.7	0.6	0.9
1973	14.2	14.6	14.2	28.1	42.4	1.6	7.7	0.7	0.6	0.6	0.6	0.6	1.0
1974	17.4	14.9	14.9	39.1	50.7	1.5	9.0	0.9	0.7	0.7	0.7	0.6	2.1
1975	18.5	16.6	16.6	45.3	58.3	1.3	14.3	1.7	0.8	0.7	1.1	0.6	4.0
1976	17.3	17.6	17.3	49.9	57.0	1.5	19.5	2.2	0.7	0.8	1.5	0.6	4.0
1977	17.5	18.0	17.5	48.2	57.4	1.5	17.1	2.0	0.7	0.8	1.3	0.6	3.9
1978	16.7	17.8	16.7	44.4	53.8	1.5	18.4	2.0	0.7	0.7	1.4	0.6	3.7
1979	16.4	18.5	16.4	39.7	49.9	1.6	18.4	1.9	0.6	0.7	1.4	0.6	3.3
1980	17.4	17/9	17.4	37.2	50.4	1.5	14.6	1.7	0.7	0.8	1.1	0.6	3.3
1981	18.5	17.6	17.6	41.0	54.7	1.4	16.5	2.1	0.7	0.8	1.3	0.6	4.6
1982	19.7	18.2	18.2	44.0	55.4	1.4	23.9	2.9	0.7	0.8	1.8	0.6	6.7
1983	19.8	19.4	19.4	47.8	53.9	1.6	31.2	3.6	0.6	0.8	2.4	0.6	8.2
1984	19.4	20.0	19.4	46.3	54.0	1.6	33.3	3.9	0.6	0.8	2.5	0.6	8.2
1985	19.5	20.6	19.5	49.8	54.3	1.7	32.2	3.6	0.6	0.9	2.5	0.6	8.3
1986	19.3	20.5	19.3	49.9	52.5	1.8	33.6	3.4	0.6	0.8	2.6	0.6	8.0
1987	18.7	19.2	18.7	48.6	54.7	1.6	31.0	3.4	0.6	0.8	2.4	0.6	7.6
1988	18.2	19.2	18.2	49.1	51.8	1.8	32.7	3.2	0.6	0.8	2.5	0.6	7.6
1989	16.9	18.8	16.9	48.4	50.1	1.9	29.9	2.6	0.5	0.7	2.3	0.6	7.6

Source: Computations are based on data of the Arbeitskraeftegesamtrechnung (Reyher and Bach 1988).

Note: The flow-equilibrium rates of unemployment are computed with formula (3.22) $u^* = 1/(1+y/z^2 \cdot 1/(\text{subr} \cdot \text{avdur}))$. The average duration of unemployment is computed with the steady-state assumption. For abbreviations, see text.

rate. Hiring from the ranks of the unemployed gained importance. From Figure 6.1, one would expect the substitution rate to be higher than it had been before the mid-1970s; it reached its highest values in the early 1980s. This has tended to increase the unemployment rate, but again, the increase caused by a higher substitution rate is very small. The most important factor in the increase in the unemployment rate has been the duration of unemployment. Even with enormous increases in the average duration, the unemployment rate in the 1980s was below the 5 percent level if, as was assumed, only the employment dynamics were taken into account.

One can conclude that employment dynamics and the ratio y/z^2 did not change enough to explain a substantial rise in unemployment. As mentioned above, the increasing duration of unemployment has to be analyzed in the macroeconomic context and in terms of changes in political measures (see section 7.2).

7

Conclusions for Labor Market
Theories and Employment Policies

7.1 THEORETICAL EXPLANATIONS FOR CHANGING
UNEMPLOYMENT RATES IN THE LIGHT OF LABOR
MARKET DYNAMICS

The analysis of labor market dynamics as presented in foregoing sections provides answers to the theoretical explanations raised in section 3.6. In the following section, these findings are summarized and linked to the theoretical hypotheses.

The wage structure has destroyed incentives for mobility. Arguments that assert that a less flexible wage structure can explain high unemployment rates were discussed in section 2.3. It turned out that empirical findings so far do not support the view that the wage structure either in the United States or in Germany has become more inflexible or narrower than in earlier periods. Germany experienced low and high unemployment with no observable changes in the wage structure. Wage variations are higher in the United States than in Germany, but the view that Germany is a country with one fixed wage rate is certainly wrong. Wage differentials exist between industries and between regions.

Although the variation of wages is higher in the United States, recent research on the U.S. wage structure has shown that persistent industry-specific wage patterns exist. This means that the characteristics of individuals and, hence, assumed individual productivity differentials cannot be the main cause of wage differentials. Wages seem to depend substantially on the characteristics of industries. This is a surprising result, because the United States has been regarded as the less regulated economy and as the economy in which institutional arrangements are closest to the competitive labor market model. These results can be taken as support for Akerlof's "fair wage" hypothesis and as a contradiction of models that try to explain wage distribution in terms of the individual's marginal productivity or market-clearing mechanisms.

Making use of the wage differentials computed by Alan Krueger and Lawrence Summers (1987) for manufacturing industries in the United States, this study found that wage differentials do not compensate for high job instability as implicit contract models would suggest. Wage differentials are not simply premiums for the higher risks of dismissal caused by job instability, a result one would certainly not expect if positive (high wage) and negative (instability) job characteristics compensated. Instead, negative and positive characteristics cumulate, as dual labor market theories predict. It has also been found that voluntary labor turnover (quits) is negatively correlated to the wage differentials ($r = -0.7$) in the United States. That is, the higher the relative wage, the lower the quit ratio. Employees in high-wage industries tend to stay there, a behavior one would not expect if wage differentials just compensate for disadvantages.

Although there is no empirical evidence for narrowing wage differentials and increasing wage inflexibility in Germany, it may well be that the pace of structural change has increased and that this has caused adjustment problems in connection with the old, unchanged flexibility standards of wages.

The pace of structural change has increased. Different indicators for the pace of structural change in the U.S. and German economies were presented in section 4.3. In general, there was no known evidence that the pace of structural change has increased, thereby causing high levels of unemployment in both the United States and Germany, although the share of service industries has increased in both economies. Measured with conventional indicators, the United States has experienced a slightly higher pace of structural change than has Germany in the 1980s. The two economies differ in one important aspect, however. In the early 1980s as well as in the 1960s, U.S. employment grew substantially, whereas employment in the German economy stagnated. Using a structural change indicator that takes overall employment trends into account shows overall higher values for Germany than for the United States in the 1980s. That is, Germany has experienced restructuring along with stagnating or slowly growing employment. This pattern may have caused greater adjustment problems and higher mismatch in the German labor market.

In addition, the German economy has experienced much higher productivity growth, which may have been caused partly by increasing skill standards for labor. An analysis of innovative activity and skill changes offers some empirical support for this view. The more innovative German manufacturing industries employed more highly skilled labor to a greater extent than did the less innovative ones (Warnken and Ronning 1989). Technological change seems to complement highly skilled labor, rather than be used for labor saving as is the case with unskilled labor (Kugler, Müller and Sheldon 1989). Other empirical evidence can be found in the fact that the labor force participation rates in the upper age groups have declined substantially. Measured as GDP per hour worked, productivity growth was much higher in Germany than in the United States, but the difference was much less dramatic if GDP per person in the age range of 15 to 65 years is instead taken as an efficiency indicator. This latter ratio, however, is also influenced by the duration of education and the organization of vocational education. The different ratios for the effectiveness of the societal division of labor presented in chapter 4 suggest that Germany's high productivity growth was at least partly paid for by a concentration of the work force in the core age groups. By the same token, the price that the United States paid for high employment growth might be its low productivity growth (Freeman 1988b). In the case that positive rather than negative feedback effects are determining economic development, however, the choice of the economic development path may not be just a zero-sum game but can produce extra gains (see section 4.1.4).

The insider-outsider hypothesis, the reluctance-to-hire hypothesis, and the hysteresis hypothesis are not mutually exclusive but rather interlinked and compatible in general. Blanchard and Summers (1986), for example, have explained hysteresis in terms of wage setting that is dominated by membership groups (insiders) that do not allow outsiders to price themselves into employment. The three hypotheses focus on different phenomena, however, so the hysteresis hypothesis will be discussed separately in the following paragraphs.

Insiders exclude outsiders from employment and *employers are reluctant to hire.* The insider-outsider and reluctance-to-hire hypotheses both suggest that the exchange between employment and nonemployment is low. According to the first hypothesis, insiders take advantage of their position and exclude outsiders. According to the second hypothesis, it is assumed that fixed labor costs, high costs of firing, and other factors make employers reluctant to hire. According to both hypotheses, however, one would expect low flow ratios into the employment system, and if these explanations have gained importance over the last decade or so, one would expect the ratios to decline further.

The ratio of overall hires in the German economy seems to support insider-outsider considerations or the reluctance-to-hire hypothesis. Overall hiring, which takes hiring from outside employment as well as intra-employment hiring into account, declined substantially from the 1960s to the 1980s. This drop, however, is the result of reduced intra-employment mobility. Hiring ratios from outside the employment system have increased since the 1970s. Direct mobility from one job to another can be assumed to be largely voluntary mobility. Recent research has shown that voluntary labor mobility is a function of opportunities and therefore more likely to appear in tight rather than in slack labor markets. In addition, much new recruitment has to be made directly from other employment in a tight labor market. Hiring employees of other organizations produces a vacancy immediately and, most likely, new hiring. The decreasing rate of the overall hiring ratio in Germany is, therefore, most likely the result of the slack labor market itself than of other factors. If hiring is made from unemployment or nonparticipation, it fills a vacancy but does not produce a new one simultaneously.

What is important with respect to the insider-outsider hypothesis is that real outsiders, those who are unemployed or not in the labor force at all, have been increasingly hired. As shown by the various flow ratios, the composition of overall hirings has shifted from hiring other firms' employees to the hiring of the unemployed, while hiring of nonparticipants has remained fairly constant. Insiders thus seem to have let outsiders in to a substantial degree.

In the United States, hiring from nonparticipation and separations into nonparticipation have declined, but the exchange between employment and unemployment has increased in both directions from the early 1980s on. The U.S. data must be regarded with caution, however, because flow data and cross-sectional data, although both computed with the CPS, produce divergent results, even after corrections. Still, the shift to a higher share of recruitments from unemployment instead of from nonparticipation seems to be plausible in view of the now-integrated "baby-boomer" generation and the higher integration of women into the labor force. Unemployment has become more important in the United States in cases of separation as well as in cases of recruitment.

The argument that an excessively high minimum wage protects insiders and places the burden for their well-being on outsiders relies, of course, on the assumption that a downward flexibility of wages is an effective, and indeed the only, means to increase employment or, more precisely, the number of employees. A comparative analysis of economic developments in the United States and Germany in the 1980s suggests that flexible wages in the United States were not the only cause for its employment expansion; aggregate demand was also important (Appelbaum and Schettkat 1990a).

Since the importance of membership groups (Blanchard and Summers 1986)—that is, unions—is stressed in insider-outsider models, it may be important to mention that German unions did not use insider power to keep outsiders out of employment. In the metal workers union (IG-Metal) strike in 1984, perhaps the most severe strike in Germany since World War II, the stated goal of the metal workers was a reduction of the standard work week from 40 hours to 35 hours. The request for shorter working time was based on the understanding that shorter working hours must be paid for by reduced income growth. The central argument put forward by the unions was that, by implementing this policy, the number of employees could be increased substantially and that unemployment could thus be reduced. This was the official reasoning for the strike, and it was certainly not compatible with the idea of strengthening the insiders' position at the expense of outsiders. Still, an important factor in the decision to call a strike for these reasons may have been the comparatively high degree of centralization in the German unions which allows for more general policy formulations. In this respect, German unions differ substantially from U.S. unions, which are more involved in firm-specific negotiations (Flanagan 1990), although some firm-specific contracts exist in Germany as well.

With respect to hiring, there is some indication that it is less the quantitative risk of how many employees can be employed than the qualitative uncertainty concerning future skill requirements that may have increased the reluctance to hire. If anything, the employment elasticity of economic growth in Germany has increased rather than decreased (see chapter 4). It may well be that the reluctance is rooted more in qualitative factors. If the production mode has shifted to higher flexibility and higher quality, it is quite possible that uncertainties about future skill requirements have increased. This situation may have led to a greater choosiness on the part of employers in order to find flexible, highly skilled employees. For example, it has been reported that German banks, which used to hire personnel with middle-ranking educations, now require the "Abitur," a level that qualifies for university study, for new recruitments (Bertrand and Noyelle 1988).

The argument can also be made that newly hired outsiders do not really threaten the position of insiders since they are in unstable jobs and are likely to leave firms sooner. Whatever the mechanisms that put the newly hired in the least secure jobs, this relation could be labeled in terms of insider-outsider relations, but it is really the classical dual labor market argument. Many arguments have been put forward to explain the interest that employers have in stable employment. These range from hiring costs (the early efficiency wage model; see Schlicht 1978) and human capital considerations (Pencavel 1972) to explanations that include social processes, such as employment stability as a precondition for employees to cooperate with newcomers (Thurow 1983). In this sense, flexibility within firms requires a certain degree of employment stability. The importance of this relation may have increased in more innovative economies, where internal flexibility (Sengenberger 1984) has become increasingly important.

Mismatch and bottlenecks have occurred. Whatever the underlying mechanism for adjustment may be, the economy can be prevented from growing if mismatch or bottlenecks in the labor market occur. Mismatch has recently become one of the most discussed explanations for persistently high unemployment in industrialized countries. As with explanations of wage-setting, economists nowadays seek to explain persistently high levels of unemployment in a way that does not put all the burden on the unemployed individual but instead takes more structural reasons into account. In this sense, mismatch explanations have superseded models that try to explain high unemployment in terms of the individual's search behavior or characteristics.

The conventional analysis of mismatch in the labor market is based on the Beveridge curve or numerical mismatch indicators. As always in empirical research, the available data do not fit the ideal requirements but data in this area nevertheless allow for some in-depth analysis. Beveridge curves for both countries have shown an outward shift—or increasing mismatch in the labor market—that seemed to be more pronounced in the United States than in Germany. The disadvantage of the Beveridge curve analysis is that the underlying causes of such an outshift cannot be identified. Both the rate of unemployment and the rate of vacancies can be broken down into one component showing the duration and another showing changes of inflows or levels. Using these relations provides additional insights into labor market dynamics.

Data on the duration of vacancies are not available for the United States, but the change-duration curves for unemployment showed an outward shift for every business cycle; this was experienced in every industry. Nevertheless, the average duration of unemployment in the United States was much lower than in Germany, a fact that can be at least partly explained by the different institutional settings. In Germany, labor market dynamics have shifted in different directions. The change-duration curves for unemployment showed an outward shift with every business cycle, but the curves for vacancies showed an inward shift. Obviously, with every business cycle it has become more difficult on average for the unemployed to be hired, but at the same time it has become easier to fill vacant jobs.

This pattern is universal; that is, it cannot be explained in terms of shifting industry structure, since it appeared in every industry. The analysis of mismatch indicators shows that Germany cannot be classified as suffering from the insufficient adaptability of the labor market. The mismatch indicators rose not because labor is scarce in the expanding industries and affluent in the declining ones but because labor has grown faster than demand in growing sectors—a phenomenon that can hardly be classified as mismatch.

No empirical evidence was found in this study to indicate that vacancies could not be filled in Germany. The opposite is suggested by the data. Vacancy duration was shorter in the business cycles of the 1980s than in those of the 1960s and 1970s. This finding is not an indication that bottlenecks or mismatch have prevented employment from growing. At the same time, the duration of unemployment shifted outward in Germany. Although the expansion of the German economy does not seem to have been restricted by bottlenecks, unemployment has risen to record levels and the duration of unemployment has increased substantially.

Unemployment is self-sustaining (hysteresis). In every business cycle, the duration of unemployment increased and did not return to the preceding levels in Germany. This pattern is certainly an indication of hysteresis.

But how can the increasing duration of unemployment in Germany be explained? One interpretation, of course, would be that the long-term unemployed are not interested in work but prefer to receive unemployment benefits and to maximize their utility in this way. The share of beneficiaries among the unemployed has decreased, however. With the above argument, the question is thus why long-term unemployment is concentrated in the upper age groups and why they have additional so-called negative attributes, like disability and fewer skills (see Schettkat and Semlinger 1982; ANBA 1989), in a system in which benefits are linked to former incomes?

The answer could be that these individuals were formerly employed at fairly high wages and could only find new jobs at wages lower than their previous ones; unemployment benefits have freed them from the pressure to accept these jobs. Another interpretation, which does not discount or preclude the former one, would be that an older person who becomes unemployed has only a small chance of finding a job again, especially if there are only a few jobs available and younger persons are competing with them. From a study by Lena Gonäs (1990) in Sweden, we know that persons who have lost their jobs because of closures are more likely to find new jobs than those who have been dismissed from surviving firms independently of age. In the case of normal dismissals, preselection of those who are dismissed signals a "lemon," whereas, in the case of closures, unemployment is not preselected and not regarded as the personal failure of the dismissed employee. This is also the logic underlying attempts at prenotification in the United States.

The analysis of the duration of unemployment by age groups (ANBA 1989, 660) clearly shows that the duration of unemployment is a function of age. Furthermore, unemployed persons aged 50 years or older even have shown increasing unemployment duration after 1986, whereas unemployed persons of younger age groups declined slightly in number. About 50 percent of the unemployed aged 55 to 60 years entered nonparticipation if they left unemployment; for those 60 to 65 years old, this share was about 90 percent (ANBA 1989, 661). For those who went from unemployment into nonparticipation, the duration of unemployment was almost twice as high as for those who went from unemployment into employment.

Still, the analysis of job turnover in Germany shows that closures contribute little to overall job turnover. Most of the job turnover is caused by employment variations in existing and surviving establishments. Why then are the elderly becoming unemployed at all in a system that provides so much employment stability? Contrary to all rumors in the community of economists, German labor law does allow for dismissals (see Büchtemann and Höland 1989), but in some cases these have to be negotiated with the works council and a "Sozialplan" (severance payment) has to be offered. A "Sozialplan" can also be an instrument to make unemployment more attractive, and it is often agreed that the older colleagues have to leave because a pension offers them an alternative to work. German pension legislation allows for early retirement at the age of 60 years after at least 12 months of unemployment. Distinguishing the unemployed by one-year age groups shows that leaving unemployment into nonparticipation peaks at the age of 60 years, accounting for more than 93 percent of those who leave unemployment. In the older and younger age groups, this share is much lower (ANBA 1989, 661). By this means, unemployment has become the first step into early retirement and thus has caused long durations of unemployment.

Early retirement has been a widely used measure in Germany to reduce a company's labor force (Kühlewind 1988). This is an instrument for companies to reduce both the size and the age of their work force and to improve their skill structure (Schusser 1987). Although measures to prevent firms from using unemployment as an entry into early retirement have been taken (Maier and Schettkat 1990), it still is important.

The outcome of this trend to early retirement is that the older unemployed are not regarded as candidates for vacant jobs by employers, and most of them do not expect to find new jobs. In this sense, they are not part of the actual labor supply, either in the employers' view or in their own. It is hard to express this process in insider-outsider terms, since it is a core group of insiders who become unemployed. It is also difficult to label this process as hysteresis because preselection has already been made, with the understanding that the dismissed older workers are early pensioners, although they have to suffer unemployment for some time. This process, however, might not occur in times of tight labor markets or without political measures that at least support it.

Another source for hysteresis might be access to training. If training on the job is important or if only employment offers access to training and retraining, this situation may produce a further disadvantage for the unemployed. They cannot keep up with skill requirements; conversely, employers may not be willing to invest in their training because a "lemon" is signaled. Empirical evidence has been found that access to jobs with new technology is given to insiders first (Schettkat 1989), that technological progress replaces unskilled labor but complements skilled labor (Kugler, Müller, and Sheldon 1989), and that training and retraining are a positive function of initial skills (Ewers, Becker, and Fritsch 1989). All these factors produce positive feedback effects and segmented labor markets (Vietorisz and Harrison 1973), excluding some of the unemployed from the effective labor supply as long as there is a slack labor market.

Recession (or slow employment expansion) in connection with a restructuring process gives a double disadvantage to the unemployed, who become older and remain unemployed for ever longer periods. Older employees do not have the chance to reenter employment after becoming unemployed because they are regarded as less flexible and preselected. Moreover, long-term unemployment leads to a deterioration of human capital and limits access to skill development. In a situation in which there is a growing supply of young labor, firms recruit younger people whose skills are already likely to be modern or whose periods of employment seem to be long enough to repay investments in training. In this sense, "normal" unemployment ends up as structured unemployment (Schmid 1980).

Changes in the dynamics of the employment system have contributed little to the increase in the unemployment rate in the United States and Germany. Computed with the corrected flow data for the United States, the substitution rate of employment has remained roughly constant since the end of the 1960s and has not contributed to a rising flow-equilibrium rate of unemployment. The share of unemployment in the inflow into and outflow out of employment has contributed most to a rise of the flow-equilibrium rate of unemployment in the

United States, but this still leaves the rate at a level of about 2.5 percent. In Germany by contrast, the substitution rate of employment increased, but the main contribution to the rising flow-equilibrium rate of unemployment was the duration of unemployment. Without the longer duration of unemployment, the flow-equilibrium rate of unemployment would still be at the 1 percent level, which was the actual level in the early 1970s. As mentioned above, the duration of unemployment is strongly influenced by labor demand and institutional arrangements. Overall, there is little empirical evidence that changes in employment dynamics have caused a rising flow-equilibrium rate of unemployment in both countries. Normal rates of unemployment would be substantially lower than the actual rates in the United States and Germany.

7.2 LABOR MARKET DYNAMICS AGAINST THE BACKGROUND OF MACROECONOMIC DEVELOPMENTS

Labor market dynamics in Germany have shifted in different directions. Vacant jobs have become easier to fill while it has become more and more difficult for the unemployed to find jobs. Since the 1960s, interfirm mobility has largely declined, whereas separations into and hirings from unemployment have gained importance. In the United States, on the other hand, the characteristics of the labor market process have seemed to be more stable, although unemployment as a source of recruitments and as a destination for separations gained importance here as well in the 1980s. The two countries are obviously following different developmental paths with respect to economic growth and employment expansion. The United States has achieved its growth in GDP partly by additional labor input, whereas Germany has reduced its labor input continuously despite GDP growth similar to that of the United States. These trends have appeared since the 1960s and were not unique to the 1980s. In both countries, they occurred with both high and low unemployment.

During the German "economic miracle" of the 1960s, unemployment was low and labor markets were tight, despite more or less constant employment, because the shrinking domestic labor force kept unemployment low and even allowed for immigration (Schettkat 1987). Given the tight labor market, it can be assumed that labor mobility was mainly voluntary. Furthermore, the economic miracle made possible for a short time (Lutz 1984) what otherwise can be experienced only in growing countries with continuous immigration. Everybody could move up the positional ladder, and the lower-level jobs were filled with foreign labor.

This trend, however, changed in Germany in the middle of the 1970s when the economy was stagnating. Measured in persons employed, employment did not decrease substantially from the mid-1970s on, but the domestic labor force grew in that period. Upgrading became difficult from then on, and the stagnation of employment together with a growing labor force (the German baby-boom generation) has led to increasing reintegration problems for the unemployed. This does not mean that unemployment should be labeled as demographic, but ignoring demographic trends is acceptable only if a frictionless adjustment model is assumed.

In an economy that has continued to achieve comparatively high levels of productivity growth even after 1975 and that has been forced by its strong integration in the world market to keep quality standards high, firms look for highly skilled and young labor when recruiting in the external labor market. This approach allows the firms to achieve high functional flexibility, which seems to be of increasing importance. This shift in the organization of work, together with the implementation of modern computerized technology, has given an advantage to the younger workers, who are more likely to have broader, more theoretical skills and who are—or at least have the image of being—more flexible.

Would an expansionary policy have prevented the increase and the structuring of unemployment in Germany? Higher economic growth might have reduced dismissals and prevented especially the dismissal of older workers, but, to the extent that job and labor turnover are caused by structural changes, these workers would have been affected by unemployment anyway. True, in a faster growing economy, mobility would probably have been higher and reintegration easier, but it is unlikely that unemployment would have been prevented totally. In any case, what is regarded as "normal" would certainly have been substantially lower, as the estimates for the flow-equilibrium rates of unemployment in sections 5.5 and 6.5 suggest.

To the extent that productivity growth in Germany has been caused by the segregation of older workers, the German economy would have paid for an expansionary policy (and thus higher employment and lower unemployment) by lower productivity growth. As Richard Freeman (1988b) has argued that the United States pays for its low unemployment with low productivity growth, one can argue that part of social security expenditures, unemployment benefits, and the like are payments for Germany's high productivity growth. Two different, although not mutually exclusive, links between productivity growth and the segregation of older workers can be distinguished. The first is the question of skills and the second is the labor supply effect of early retirement. The latter allows for high productivity growth and stagnating employment despite a growing working-age population and might be a necessary social policy to make high productivity growth rates socially acceptable. Still, with a different measure for the efficiency of the production process—GDP per capita aged 15 to 65 years old—the situation would have improved more in Germany than in the United States. This fact suggests that high productivity is not simply a zero-sum game, in which the gains have been paid into transfer programs, but that instead real gains have occurred; the winners can compensate the losers. Furthermore, positive feedback effects may drive a high-productivity economy on a different development path, as compared with an economy that allows for low-productivity trends.

The analysis shows clearly that Germany's unemployment cannot be classified as entirely structural. The German unification process has plunged the conservative German government into enormous deficit spending, which in 1990 reached levels that no one would have proposed as a stimulating program for the economy. The effect of this enormous demand potential on the German economy has been that of a conventional expansionary policy. The same politicians who implemented the program and argued that an expansionary policy would be short-lived and would ultimately fail have to face the fact that their deficit spending has shown clearly that employment in Germany can be increased. In 1990, it rose by roughly 700,000 persons, showing how realistic the conclusion of this study is that a more expansionary policy in Germany was possible and could have increased employment. At the same time, this trend should have shown that "Eurosclerosis" or other modern economic diseases are not as important as they have been taken to be in economic theory and policy. This trend can be taken as empirical support for the findings of this study.

Labor market dynamics as they actually appear have to be seen in the context of overall economic trends. It is important, therefore, to take the macroeconomic context into account. It makes a difference, for example, whether economic restructuring takes place with overall growing or stagnating employment; the labor market situation itself influences voluntary labor mobility and causes different mobility chains. Adjustments are easier in a growing economy than in a stagnating one, or, as James Galbraith (1989) has formulated it, it is easier to balance on a rope at high speed. The functioning of the labor market depends considerably on the labor market situation. In this sense, demand in the economy matters, and a major part of the German labor market seems to be produced by demand deficiency rather than by structural problems of the labor market.

Although job and labor turnover have shown variations over time in both countries, it has been surprising to find very stable industry-specific patterns. Explanations for this finding may include the dominance of product markets, as argued in some versions of dual labor market theory. Together with similar technologies, that dominance produces similar labor outcomes. Still, job turnover patterns across industries are surprisingly similar in the United States and Germany, although Germany's job turnover is lower. This is surprising as well, since the German economy is much better integrated into the world market, so one would expect competition (and hence gross job growth and decline) to be higher in Germany (Leonard and Schettkat 1991). In general, the German economy seems to experience a higher degree of coordination than the U.S. economy. It is beyond the scope of this study to analyze the complex coordination mechanisms, but contributing factors surely include the higher degree of organization of both employees and employers, bipartied and tripartied coordination of the social security insurance system, the involvement of banks in the strategic, long-term decisions of firms, and the orientation toward long-run rather than short-run profits.

Not enough is known about the complex interaction of technology, society, and the economy, but it has become clear that all variables interact and that a policy focusing only on the improvement of an isolated variable will most likely fail. The educational and training-retraining system, industrial relations, work organization, investments, and infrastructure have been identified as important subsystems for economically progressive technological developments (Freeman 1989). It is not that economies can switch easily from one mode of development to another; today's choice depends on past developments (David 1975). In this sense, economic development is path dependent, although not completely determined.

The analysis of gross flow data has provided additional insights into the labor market process, but one has to admit that this line of analysis is still rudimentary. It is far from being sophisticated enough to answer all questions related to labor market dynamics. This analysis, as well as the work of others, shows that some lines of thinking seem to be implausible in light of the flow data. What has seemed to be a plausible explanation of the underlying dynamics of trends in stock data can be questioned in light of flow-analysis results. Although analysis along the theoretical and empirical lines described above falls far short of giving definite answers, it does open new ways of thinking about the labor market and draws a different map of where answers must be sought.

If labor market analysis based on gross changes and flows, rather than on net changes and stocks, is still in its very early stages, it already shows that these methods can produce findings that allow economists to look more deeply into processes and that leave less room for speculation about the dynamics of economies. Dynamic analysis will substantially contribute to a richer view of labor markets and to a better understanding of the functioning of the economy in general and the labor market in particular.

The optimal situation for management would of course be to run a production with a highly flexible, highly skilled work force and to have no restraints with respect to numerical adjustments (Piore 1986). This would be the situation of the perfect market model, but the real world has more restraints, and highly flexible production requires at least some degree of employment stability, not only because insiders use power but also because every production process relies on tacit knowledge and "voice" that are not available on the external labor market. These "imperfections" are universal, and it seems time to follow the recent suggestion of Robert Gordon (1990, 1163) in his article on new-Keynesian economics; that is, to recognize "that these features are part of the way that markets function." In addition, it has to be recognized (again) that the functioning of the economy cannot be analyzed from the micro perspective only. The macroeconomic situation sets the conditions for individual decisions, as the flow analysis in this study has shown. These are the facts of normal economic life and not just deviations from the otherwise valid perfect market model.

Bibliography

Abowd, J. M., and A. Zellner. 1984. Application of Adjustment Techniques to U.S. Gross Flow Data, in *Proceedings of the Conference on Gross Flows in Labor Statistics,* ed. BLS, 45–61.

Abowd, J. M., and A. Zellner. 1985. Estimating Gross Labor-Force Flows. *Journal of Business & Economic Statistics* 3: 254–83.

Abraham, K. 1983. Structural/Frictional vs. Deficient Demand Unemployment. *American Economic Review* 73: 708–24.

Abraham, K. 1986. Structural/Frictional vs. Deficient Demand Unemployment: Reply. *American Economic Review* 76: 273–76.

Abraham, K. 1987. Help-Wanted Advertising, Job Vacancies, and Unemployment. *Brookings Papers on Economic Activity* 1: 207–43.

Abraham, K. G., and S. N. Houseman. 1988. *Employment and Hours Adjustment: A U.S./German Comparison.* Washington, D.C.: University of Maryland and Brookings Institution.

Abraham, K., and L. F. Katz. 1986. Cyclical Unemployment: Sectoral Shifts or Aggregate Disturbances? *Journal of Political Economy* 94: 507–22.

Adams, F. G. 1987. Increasing the Minimum Wage: The Macroeconomic Impacts. *Economic Policy Institute Briefing Paper,* July.

Akerlof, G. A. 1982. Labor Contracts as Partial Gift Exchange. *Quarterly Journal of Economics* 97: 543–69.

Akerlof, G. A., and B. G. M. Main. 1981. An Experience-Weighted Measure of Employment and Unemployment Durations. *American Economic Review* 71: 1003–11.

Akerlof, G. A., A. Rose, and J. L. Yellen. 1988. *Job Switching and Job Satisfaction in the U.S. Labor Market.* Berkeley: University of California.

Akerlof, G. A., and J. L. Yellen. 1986a. Introduction. In *Efficiency Wage Models of the Labor Market,* ed. G. Akerlof and J. Yellen.

Akerlof, G. A., and J. L. Yellen, eds. 1986b. *Efficiency Wage Models of the Labor Market*. Cambridge: Cambridge University Press.

Akerlof, G. A., and J. L. Yellen. 1988. Fairness and Unemployment. *American Economic Review* 78: 44–49.

Akerlof, G., and J. L. Yellen. 1990. The Fair Wage-Effort Hypothesis and Unemployment. *Quarterly Journal of Economics* 105: 255–83.

Alchian, A. A. 1970. Information Costs, Pricing, and Resource Unemployment. In *Microeconomic Foundations of Employment and Inflation Theory*, ed. E. S. Phelps et al., 27–52.

ANBA (Amtliche Nachtrichten der Bundesanstalt für Arbeit). Various years.

Appelbaum, E. 1982. Der Arbeitsmarkt. In *Über Keynes Hinaus*, ed. A. S. Eichner, 115–33.

Appelbaum, E. 1990. Unbalanced Growth and the U.S. Employment Expansion. *Structural Change and Economic Dynamics* 1: 91–101.

Appelbaum, E., and P. Albin. 1990. Differential Characteristics of Employment Growth in Service Industries. In *The Impact of Structural Change and Technological Progress on the Labor Market*, ed. E. Appelbaum and R. Schettkat, 36–53.

Appelbaum, E., and R. Schettkat. 1990a. Determinants of Employment Developments: A Comparison of the United States and the Federal German Economies. *Labour and Society* 15: 13–31.

Appelbaum, E., and R. Schettkat, eds. 1990b. *The Impact of Structural Change and Technological Progress on the Labor Market*. New York: Praeger.

Appelbaum, E., and R. Schettkat. 1991. Employment and Industrial Restructuring: A Comparison of the US and West Germany. In *Beyond Keynesianism: The Socio-Economics of Production and Full Employment*, ed. E. Matzner and W. Streeck.

Archibald, G. C. 1970. The Structure of Excess Demand for Labor. In *Microeconomic Foundations of Employment and Inflation Theory*, ed. E. S. Phelps et al., 212–23.

Ashenfelter, O., and R. Layard, eds. 1986. *Handbook of Labor Economics*. Amsterdam and New York: North-Holland.

Auer, P., and C. Riegler. 1990. *Post-Taylorism: The Enterprise as a Place of Learning Organizational Change*. Stockholm: Arbetsmiljoefonden.

Azaridis, C. 1979. Implicit Contracts and Related Topics: A Survey. Conference paper presented at "The Economics of the Labour Market," September, Magdalen College, Oxford.

Baethge, M. 1988. Neue Technologien, berufliche Perspektiven und kulturelles Selbstverständnis: Herausforderungen an die Bildung. *Gewerkschaftliche Monatshefte* 1: 15–23.

Bailar, B. A. 1975. The Effects of Rotation Group Bias from Panel Studies. *Journal of the American Statistical Association*. Pp. 22–30.

Bakke, E. W., ed. 1954. *Labor Mobility and Economic Opportunity*. Cambridge, Mass.: MIT Press.

Bangel, B. 1990. Vorzeitiger Rentenübergang und Arbeitsmarkt. (manuscript). Berlin: Wissenschaftszentrum Berlin.

Barro, R. J. 1988. The Persistence of Unemployment. *American Economic Review* 78: 32–36.

Baumol, W. 1967. Macroeconomics of Unbalanced Growth: The Anatomy of the Urban Crisis. *American Economic Review* 57: 415–26.

Baumol, W., S. Blackman, and E. Wolff. 1989. *Productivity and American Leadership: The Long View.* Cambridge, Mass.: MIT Press.

Becker, A. 1983. Berufschancen nach der Ausbildung zum Baecker, Konditor, Fleischer. *WSI-Mitteilungen* 9: 543–552.

Bednarzik, R. W., and J. E. Sabelhaus. 1985. Earning Losses of Displaced Workers. *Economic Discussion Paper,* No. 16. Washington: Department of Labor.

Bell, L. A. 1986. Wage Rigidity in West Germany: A Comparison with the U.S. Experience. *Federal Reserve Bank N.Y. Quarterly Review.* Autumn: 11–21.

Bell, L. A., and R. Freeman. 1985. Does a Flexible Wage Structure Increase Employment?: The U.S. Experience. *NBER Working Paper,* No. 1604. Cambridge, Mass.: National Bureau of Economic Research.

Bell, L. A., and R. Freeman. 1987. The Facts About Rising Industrial Wage Dispersion in the U.S. *Industrial Relations/Research Association, Proceedings.*

Berman, B. R. 1965. An Approach to an Absolute Measure of Structural Unemployment. In *Employment Policy and the Labor Market,* ed. A. R. Ross, 256–68.

Bertrand, O., and T. Noyelle. 1988. *Human Resources and Corporate Strategy.* Paris: OECD.

BIBB and IAB. 1981. Qualifikation und Berufsverlauf, *Sonderveröffentlichung.* Berlin/Nürnberg.

BIBB and IAB. 1987. Neue Technologien: Verbreitungsgrad, Qualifikation und Arbeitsbedingungen; Analysen aus der BIBB/IAB-Erhebung 1985/1986 (manuscript). Berlin and Nürnberg.

Blackburn, P., R. Coombs, and K. Green. 1985. *Technology, Economy and the Labour Process.* London: Macmillan.

Blanchard, O. J., and P. Diamond. 1989. The Beveridge Curve. *Brookings Papers on Economic Activity* 1: 1–60.

Blanchard, O. J., and L. Summers. 1986. Hysteresis and the European Unemployment Problem. In *NBER Macroeconomic Annual 1986,* ed. S. Fisher, 15–78.

Blazejczak, J. 1989. Perspektiven der gesamtwirtschaftlichen Entwicklung bei verstärkten und bei unterlassenen Innovationsanstrengungen. In *Technologischer Wandel und Beschäftigung,* ed. R. Schettkat and M. Wagner, 375–94.

BLS, ed. 1984. *Proceedings of the Conference on Gross Flows in Labor Statistics,* Washington, D.C.

Blüchel, F., and G. Weißhuhn. 1989. Zur Stabilität der Wiederbeschäftigung nach Arbeitslosigkeit. (manuscript) Berlin: Technische Universität.

Bluestone, B., and B. Harrison. 1982. *The Deindustrialization of America.* New York: Basic Books.

Bombach, G., B. Gahlen, and A. E. Ott, eds. 1987. *Arbeitsmärkte und Beschäftigung: Fakten, Analysen, Perspektiven.* Tübingen: Mohr.

Boyer, R. 1987. Schaffung oder Zerstörung von Beschäftigungsmöglichkeiten durch neue Techniken hängt vom Ensemble der institutionellen Arrangements. In *Arbeit für alle ist möglich,* ed. E. Matzner, J. Kregel, and A. Roncaglia, 247–85.

Boyer, R., ed. 1988. *The Search for Labour Market Flexibility.* Oxford: Clarendon Press.

Boyer, R. 1989. New Directions in Management Practices and Work Organisation: General Principles and National Trajectories. Paper presented at the International Conference on Technological Change as a Social Process. OECD and Government of Finland, Helsinki, December.

Braverman, H. 1977. *Die Arbeit im modernen Produktionsprozeß,* Frankfurt/New York: Campus.

Brinkmann, C., and E. Spitznagel. 1990. Ausgewählte Ergebnisse der IAB-Erhebung über Personalbedarf und offene Stellen. Paper presented at the SAMF conference, "Matching-Probleme am Arbeitsmarkt." Frankfurt, November.

Brödner, P. 1986. *Fabrik 2000: Alternative Entwicklungspfade in die Zukunft der Fabrik.* Berlin: Edition Sigma.

Brown, C. 1983. Unemployment Theory and Policy, 1964–1980. *Industrial Relations* 22: 164–85.

Bruni, M. 1988. A Stock-Flow Model to Analyse and Forecast Labor Market Variables. Department of Economic Sciences, University of Bologna, Italy. Paper presented at the Second Annual ESPE Congress, Mannheim, June 23–25.

Brunner, K., A. Cuikerman, and A. H. Meltzer. 1980. Stagflation, Persistent Unemployment and the Permanence of Economic Shocks. *Journal of Monetary Economics* 6: 467–92.

Büchtemann, C. F., and A. Höland. 1989. Befristete Arbeitsverträge nach dem Beschäftigungsförderungsgesetz 1985. *Forschungsberichte* Band 183. Bonn: Bundesminister für Arbeit und Sozialordnung.

Burda, M., and C. Wyplosz. 1990. Gross Labour Market Flows in Europe: Some Stylized Facts. *Working Papers,* No. 90/511EP: INSEAD.

Burkhauser, R. V., and T. A. Finegan. 1989. The Minimum Wage and the Poor: The End of a Relation. *Journal of Policy Analysis and Management.* 8: 53–71.

Burtless, G. 1983. Why Is Insured Unemployment So Low? *Brookings Papers on Economic Activity* 1: 225–49.

Burtless, G., ed. 1990. *A Future of Lousy Jobs?* Washington, D.C.: Brookings Institution.

Buttler, F. 1987. Labour market flexibility by deregulation? The case of the Federal Republic of Germany. *Labour and Society* 12: 29–35.

Carlin, W., and D. Soskice. 1990. *The Macroeconomics of Wage Bargain.* Oxford: Oxford University Press.

CEPR (Centre for Economic Policy Research). 1990. Unemployment: Mismatch and labour mobility. *CEPR Bulletin* 37: 11–14.

Clark, K. B., and L. H. Summers. 1979. Labour Market Dynamics and Unemployment: A Reconsideration. *Brookings Papers on Economic Activity,* 13–61.

Cohen, S. S., and J. Zysman. 1987. *Manufacturing Matters: The Myth of the Post-Industrial Society.* New York: Basic Books.

Cottman-Job, B. 1979. How Likely Are Individuals to Enter the Labor Force? *Monthly Labor Review* 102: 28–34.

Council of Economic Advisers. 1962. *Annual Report 1962.* U.S. G.A.O.

Cramer, U. 1976. Zur durchschnittlichen Dauer der Arbeitslosigkeit. *Mitteilungen aus der Arbeitsmarkt- und Berufsforschung,* April.

Cramer, U. 1986a. Wieviel Arbeitslose erhalten noch Lohnersatzleistungen? *Mitteilungen aus der Arbeitsmarkt- und Berufsforschung* 2: 203–08.

Cramer, U. 1986b. Zur Stabilität von Beschäftigung. *Mitteilungen aus der Arbeitsmarkt- und Berufsforschung,* February, 243–56.

Cramer, U., and F. Egle. 1976. Zur durchschnittlichen Dauer der Arbeitslosigkeit. *Mitteilungen aus der Arbeitsmarkt- und Berufsforschung,* 482–95.

Cramer, U., and M. Koller. 1988. Gewinne und Verluste von Arbeitsplätzen in Betrieben—der "Job-Turnover"—Ansatz. *Mitteilungen aus der Arbeitsmarkt- und Berufsforschung* 3: 361–77.

Curvie, D., D. Peel, and W. Peters, eds. 1981. *Microeconomic Analysis*. London.

Cyert, R. M., and D. C. Mowery, eds. 1988. *The Impact of Technological Change on Employment and Economic Growth*. Cambridge, Mass.: Ballinger.

Danziger, S., P. Gottschalk, and E. Smolensky. 1989. How the Rich Have Fared, 1973–87. *American Economic Review* 79: 310–14.

David, P. 1975. *Technical Choice and Economic Growth*. London/New York: Cambridge University Press.

Davidson, C., and M. Reich. 1989. Income Inequality: An Inter-Industry Analysis. *Industrial Relations* 27: 263–86.

Davidson, P. 1983. The marginal product curve is not the demand curve for labor and Lucas's labor supply curve is not the supply curve for labor in the real world. *Journal of Post-Keynesian Economics* 6: 105–16.

Davidson, P., and E. Smolensky. 1964. *Aggregate Demand and Supply Analysis*. New York: Harper & Row.

Davis, S., and J. Haltiwanger. 1989. Gross Job Creation, Gross Job Destruction and Employment Reallocation (manuscript). Stanford University and University of Maryland.

Dickens, W. T., and L. F. Katz. 1987. Inter-Industry Wage Differences and Industry Characteristics. In *Unemployment and the Structure of Labor Markets*, ed. K. Lang and J. S. Leonard, 48–89.

Dickens, W. T., and K. Lang. 1987. Where Have All the Good Jobs Gone? Deindustrialization and Labor Market Segmentation. In *Unemployment and the Structure of Labor Markets*, ed. K. Lang and J. S. Leonard, 90–102.

Dickens, W. T., and K. Lang. 1988. The Reemergence of Segmented Labor Market Theory. *American Economic Review* 78: 129–34.

Doeringer, P., and M. Piore. 1971. *Internal Labor Markets and Manpower Analysis*. Lexington, Mass.: Heath Lexington Books.

Dow, J. C. R., and L. A. Dicks-Mireaux. 1958. The Excess Demand for Labour: A Study of Conditions in Great Britain, 1946–56. *Oxford Economic Papers* 10: 1–33.

Duesenberry, J. S. 1949. *Income, Saving, and the Theory of Consumer Behavior*. Cambridge, Mass.: Harvard University Press.

Dunlop, J. G. 1938. The Movement of Real and Money Wages. *Economic Journal* 48: 413–33.

Dunne, T., M. Roberts, and L. Samuelson. 1989. Plant Turnover and Gross Employment Flows in the U.S. Manufacturing Sector. *Journal of Labor Economics* 7: 48–71.

Dutt, A. K. 1986. Wage rigidity and unemployment: the simple diagrammatics of two views. *Journal of Post-Keynesian Economics* 9: 279–90.

Eatwell, J., J. Milgate, and P. Newman, eds. 1987. *The New Palgrave: A Dictionary of Economics*. London and Basingstoke: Macmillan Press.

Eichner, A. S., ed. 1982. *Über Keynes Hinaus*. Köln: Bund Verlag.

Emmerich, K., H.-D. Hardes, D. Sadowski, and E. Spitznagel, eds. Einzel- und Gesamtwirtschaftliche Aspekte des Lohnes. *Beiträge zur Arbeitsmarkt- und Berufsforschung* 128.

Employment and Earnings. Various Years.

Erber, G., and G. A. Horn. 1989. Wirkungen von Forschung und Entwicklung auf Beschäftigung, Preise und Außenhandel. In *Technologischer Wandel und Beschäftigung,* ed. R. Schettkat and M. Wagner, 185–206.

Erdmann, E.-G. 1985. Die Verbindlichkeit der Tarifnormen ist unverzichtbar. *Wirtschaftsdienst* 5: 222–24.

Ermann, K. 1987. Arbeitsmarktstatistische Zahlen in Zeitreihenform. *Beiträge zur Arbeitsmarkt- und Berufsforschung* 31.

Evans, J. M., W. Franz, and J. P. Martin. 1984. Youth Labour Market Dynamics and Unemployment: An Overview. In *The Nature of Youth Unemployment,* ed. OECD, 7–28.

Ewers, H.-J., C. Becker, and M. Fritsch. 1989. Effekte des Einsatzes Computergestützter Technologie in Industriebetrieben. Der Kontext ist Entscheidend. In *Technologischer Wandel und Beschäftigung,* ed. R. Schettkat and M. Wagner, 27–71.

Feldstein, M. S. 1976. Temporary Layoffs in the Theory of Unemployment. *Journal of Political Economy* 84: 937–57.

Fisher, S., ed. 1986. *NBER Macroeconomic Annual 1986.* Cambridge, Mass.: MIT Press.

Flaim, P. O., and C. R. Hogue. 1985. Measuring Labor Force Flows: A Special Conference Examines the Problems. *Monthly Labor Review* (July): 7–17.

Flaim, P. O., and E. Seghal. 1985. Displaced Workers of 1979–1983: How Have They Fared? *Monthly Labor Review* 108: 3–16.

Flanagan, R. J. 1973. The U.S. Phillips Curve and International Unemployment Rate Differentials. *American Economic Review* 63: 114–31.

Flanagan, R. J. 1984. Implicit Contracts, Explicit Contracts, and Wages. *American Economic Review* 74: 345–49.

Flanagan, R. J. 1987. Labor Market Behavior and European Economic Growth. In *Barriers to European Growth,* ed. R. Z. Lawrence and C. L. Schultze, 175–211.

Flanagan, R. J. 1989. Unemployment as a Hiring Problem. *Revue Economique.* OECD.

Flanagan, R. J. 1990. Employment Arrangements in the United States (manuscript).

Flanagan, R. J., D. Soskice, and L. Ulman. 1983. *Unionism, Economic Stability and Incomes Policy: European Experience.* Washington, D.C.: Brookings Institution.

Franz, W. 1987a. Hysteresis, Persistence, and the NAIRU: An Empirical Analysis for the Federal Republic of Germany. In *The Fight Against Unemployment,* ed. R. Layard and L. Calmfors, 93–122.

Franz, W. 1987b. Beschäftigungsprobleme auf Grund von Inflexibilitäten auf Arbeitsmärkten? *Discussion Paper,* No. 340–87. Universität Stuttgart.

Franz, W. 1987c. Strukturelle und Friktionelle Arbeitslosigkeit in der Bundesrepublik Deutschland. In *Arbeitsmärkte und Beschäftigung: Fakten, Analysen, Perspektiven,* ed. G. Bombach, B. Gahlen, and A. Ott, 301–27.

Franz, W. 1990. Match and Mismatch in the German Labor Market. *Diskussionsbeiträge Sonderforschungsbereich Internationalisierung der Wirtschaft.* Universität Konstanz.

Franz, W., and H. König. 1986. The Nature and Causes of Unemployment in the Federal Republic of Germany since the 1970s: An Empirical Investigation. *Economica* 53: S219–S244.

Freeman, C. 1989. National and Regional Capabilities for Innovation and the Role of Government. Paper presented at the Government of Finland and OECD Conference on Technological Change as a Social Process. Helsinki, December.

Freeman, R. B. 1988a. Labor Market Institutions and Economic Performance. *Economic Policy* 6: 63–80.

Freeman, R. B. 1988b. Evaluating the European View that the United States Has No Unemployment Problem. *American Economic Review* 78: 294–99.

Freiburghaus, D. 1978. *Dynamik der Arbeitslosigkeit*. Meisenheim am Glan: Anton Hain.

Friderichs, H. 1985. Lohnstrukturdifferenzierung—ein Rezept zur Lösung des Beschäftigungsproblems? *Wirtschaftsdienst* 7: 426–27.

Friedman, M. 1968. The Role of Monetary Policy. *American Economic Review* 58: 1–17.

Galbraith, James K. 1989. *Balancing Acts: Technology, Finance and the American Future*. New York: Basic Books.

Galbraith, John K. 1978. On post-Keynesian economics. *Journal of Post-Keynesian Economics* 1: 8–11.

Galbraith, John K. 1987. *Economics in Perspective: A Critical History*. Boston: Houghton Mifflin.

Gerlach, K., and O. Hübler, eds. 1989. *Effizienzlohntheorie, Individualeinkommen und Arbeitsplatzwechsel*. Frankfurt: Campus.

Gerlach, K., and O. Hübler. 1989a. Effizienzlöhne und individuelles Einkommen—Einige einführende Aspekte. In *Effizienzlohntheorie, Individualeinkommen und Arbeitsplatzwechsel*, ed. K. Gerlach and O. Hübler, 8–26.

Gerlach, K., and O. Hübler. 1989b. Berufliche Lohndifferentiale. *Effizienzlohntheorie, Individualeinkommen und Arbeitsplatzwechsel*. Frankfurt and New York: Campus.

Gerlach, K., and O. Hübler, eds. 1990. Betreibszugehörigkeitsdauer und Mobilität-Theoretische und Empirische Analysen. *Arbeitspapier* 1990–4. Arbeitskreis Sozialwissenschaftliche Arbeitsmarkforschung.

Gerlach, K., and U. Schasse. 1990. Arbeitsmarktwirkungen von Kündigungen und Entlassungen. In *Effizienzlohntheorie, Individualeinkommen und Arbeitsplatzwechsel*, ed. K. Gerlach and O. Hübler, 121–42.

Giersch, H. 1983. Arbeit, Lohn und Produktivität. In *Weltwirtschaftliches Archiv* 119: 3–19.

Giersch, H., ed. 1987. *Macro and Micro Policies or More Growth and Employment: Symposium 1987*. Tübingen: Mohr.

Ginzberg, E. 1976. *The Human Economy: A Theory of Manpower Development and Utilization*. New York: McGraw-Hill.

Ginzberg, E. 1979. *Good Jobs, Bad Jobs, No Jobs*. Cambridge, Mass.: Harvard University Press.

Gonäs, L. 1990. Labor Market Adjustments to Structural Change in Sweden. In *The Impact of Structural Change and Technological Progress on the Labor Market*, ed. E. Appelbaum and R. Schettkat, 180–205.

Gordon, R. J. 1987a. Wage Gaps versus Output Gaps: Is There a Common Story for All Europe? In *Macro and Micro Policies or More Growth and Employment: Symposium 1987*, ed. H. Giersch, 97–151.

Gordon, R. J. 1987b. Productivity, Wages, and Prices inside and outside of Manufacturing in the U.S., Japan, and Europe. *European Economic Review* 31: 685–739.

Gordon, R. J. 1988. Back to the Future: European Unemployment Today Viewed from America in 1939. *Brookings Papers on Economic Activity*, 271–312.

Gordon, R. J. 1990. What is New-Keynesian Economics? *Journal of Economic Literature* 28: 1115–71.

Green, G. P. 1969. Comparing Employment Estimates From Household and Payroll Surveys. *Monthly Labor Review* 92: December.

Hagemann, H. 1988. Lohnhöhe und Beschäftigung in Keynesianischer Sicht. In *Keynes' General Theory nach fünfzig Jahren,* ed. H. Hagemann and O. Steiger, 183–210.

Hagemann, H., and P. Kalmbach, eds. 1983. *Technischer Fortschritt und Arbeitslosigkiet*. Frankfurt: Campus.

Hagemann, H., and O. Steiger, ed. 1988. *Keynes' General Theory nach fünfzig Jahren*. Berlin: Duncker & Humblot.

Hall, R. E. 1970. Why Is the Unemployment Rate So High at Full Employment? *Brookings Papers on Economic Activity*, 369–402.

Hall, R. E. 1972a. Turnover in the Labor Force. *Brookings Papers on Economic Activity* 3: 709–64.

Hall, R. E. 1972b. The Rigidity of Wages and the Persistence of Unemployment. *Brookings Papers on Economic Activity* 2: 301–335.

Hall, R. E. 1979. A Theory of the Natural Unemployment Rate and the Duration of Employment. *Journal of Monetary Economics* 5: 153–69.

Hall, R. E. 1980. Employment Fluctuations and Wage Rigidity. *Brookings Papers on Economic Activity* 1: 91–141.

Hall, R. E. 1982. The Importance of Lifetime Jobs in the U.S. Economy. *American Economic Review* 72: 716–24.

Hansen, B. 1970. Excess Demand, Unemployment, Vacancies, and Wages. *Quarterly Journal of Economics* 84: 1–23.

Haveman, R. 1988. *Starting Even*. New York: Simon & Schuster.

Harrison, B., and B. Bluestone. 1988. *The Great U-Turn: Corporate Restructuring and the Polarizing of America*. New York: Basic Books.

Helberger, C. 1980. Die Entwicklung der bildungssopezifischen Einkommenschancen in der BRD zwischen 1969/71 and 1978 (manuscript). Technische Universität Berlin.

Hicks, J. R. 1937. Mr. Keynes and the "Classics." *Econometrica* 5: 147–58.

Hilaski, H. J. 1968. The Status of Research on Gross Changes in the Labor Force. *Employment and Earnings*.

Hirschman, A. O. 1970. *Exit, Voice, and Loyalty*. Cambridge, Mass.: Harvard University Press.

Hogue, C. R., and P. O. Flaim. 1986. Measuring Gross Flows in the Labor Force: An Overview of a Special Conference. *Journal of Business & Economic Statistics* 4: 111–21.

Hohn, H. W., and P. Windolf. 1984. *Arbeitsmarktchancen in der Krise: Betriebliche Restrukturierung und sozial Schliessung*. Frankfurt: Campus.

Holt, C. C. 1970a. Job Search, Phillips' Wage Relation, and Union Influence: Theory and Evidence. In *Microeconomic Foundations of Employment and Inflation Theory,* ed. E. S. Phelps et al., 53–123.

Holt, C. C. 1970b. How Can the Phillips Curve Be Moved to Reduce Both Inflation and Unemployment? In *Microeconomic Foundations of Employment and Inflation Theory,* ed. E. S. Phelps et al., 224–255.

Holt, C. C., and M. H. David. 1966. The Concept of Job Vacancies in a Dynamic Theory of the Labor Market. In *The Measurement and Interpretation of Job Vacancies,* ed. NBER, 73–110.

Horvath, F. W. 1982. Forgotten Unemployment: Recall Bias in Retrospective Data. *Monthly Labor Review* 105: 40–44.

Horvath, F. W. 1984. Comment on Poterba and Summers (1984). In *Proceedings of the Conference on Gross Flows in Labor Statistics,* ed. BLS, 96–97.

IAB (Institut für Arbeitsmarkt- und Berufsforschung). 1990. 630000 sofort zu besetzende offene Stellen Vakanzen im September 1989. *IAB-Kurzbericht,* VII/2.

Jablonsky, M., K. Kunze, and P. F. Otto. 1990. Hours at Work: A New Base of BLS Productivity Statistics. *Monthly Labor Review* 113: 17–24.

Jackman, R., and B. Kan. 1988. Structural Unemployment: A Reply. *Oxford Bulletin of Economics and Statistics* 50: 83–87.

Jackman, R., R. Layard, S. Nickell, and S. Wadhwani. 1990. *Unemployment.* (book manuscript, forthcoming).

Jackman, R., R. Layard, and C. Pissarides. 1989. On Vacancies. *Oxford Bulletin of Economics and Statistics* 51: 377–94.

Jackman, R., R. Layard, and S. Savoury. 1990. Mismatch: A Framework of Thought. Conference Paper, CEPR/CLE/STEP Conference in Venice.

Jessen, T., and D. Winkler. 1979. Tempo des Strukturwandels bei Produktion und Beschäftigung. *Wirtschaftsdienst* 6: 304–8.

Johnson, G. E., and P. R. G. Layard. 1986. The Natural Rate of Unemployment: Explanation and Policy. In *Handbook of Labor Economics,* ed. O. Ashenfelter and R. Layard, 919–99.

Kahn, R. 1976. Unemployment as seen by the Keynesians. In *The Concept and Measurement of Involuntary Unemployment,* ed. G. D. N. Worswick, 19–34.

Kalecki, M. 1954. Kosten und Preise, Englisches Original. In *Krise und Prosperität im Kapitalismus,* ed. M. Kalecki, 100–17.

Kalecki, M. 1987. *Krise und Prosperität im Kapitalismus.* Marburg: Metropolis.

Kalmbach, P. 1983. Die Berechnung der Freisetzung und Einsparung von Arbeitskräften: Einige Überlegungen anläßlich der ex-post-Betrachtung einer Prognose. In *Technischer Fortschritt und Arbeitslosigkeit,* ed. H. Hagemann and P. Kalmbach, 296–311.

Kalmbach, P. 1985. Lohnhöhe und Beschäftigung: Ein Evergreen der wirtschaftspolitischen Debatte. *Wirtschaftsdienst* 7: 370–76.

Kalmbach, P. 1988. Der Dienstleistungssektor: Noch immer die große Hoffnung des 20. Jahrhunderts? In *Technik und Zukunft,* ed. W. Seuss and K. Schroeder, 166–81.

Kalmbach, P. 1989a. Lohnleitlinien, Preisniveaustabiltät und Beschäftigung. *Discussion Paper FSI,* No. 89–9. Berlin: Wissenschaftszentrum Berlin.

Kalmbach, P. 1989b. Reallohnsatz und Beschäftigung, Zur Theorie und Empirie eines umstrittenen Zusammenhanges. In *Einzel- und Gesamtwirtschaftliche Aspekte des Lohnes,* ed. K. Emmerich et al., 157–75.

Kern, H., and M. Schumann. 1984. *Das Ende der Arbeitsteilung? Rationalisierung in der industriellen Produktion,* 2d ed. München: C. H. Beck.

Kerr, C. 1954. The Balkanization of Labor Markets. In *Labor Mobility and Economic Opportunity,* ed. E. W. Bakke, 305–11.

Keynes, J. M. 1936. *The General Theory of Employment, Interest and Money* (new edition, 1973). Cambridge: Macmillan.

Keynes, J. M. 1939. Relative Movement of Real Wages and Output. *Economic Journal* 49. Here in Keynes, J. M. 1981. *The General Theory of Employment, Interest and Money.* London/Basingstoke: Macmillan Press.

Killingsworth, C. 1963. The Nation's Manpower Reaction. Washington D.C.: U.S. Senate, Committee on Labor and Public Welfare, Part 5.

Killingsworth, M. R. 1983. *Labor Supply.* Cambridge/London: Cambridge University Press.

Knepel, H., and R. Hujer, eds. 1985. *Mobilitätsprozesse auf dem Arbeitsmarkt.* Frankfurt/New York: Campus.

Knight, F. H. 1921. *Risk, Uncertainty and Profit.* Boston: Houghton Mifflin.

König, A., and G. Weißhuhn. 1989. Betriebsgrößenentwicklungen, Beschäftigungsgewinne und -verluste in den Wirtschaftsbereichen der Bundesrepublik Deutschland 1980–1986. In *Technologischer Wandel und Beschaftigung,* ed. R. Schettkat and M. Wagner, 121–46.

König, H., and K. F. Zimmermann. 1986. Determinants of Employment Policy of German Manufacturing Firms: A Survey-Based Evaluation. In *Business Cycle Surveys in the Assessment of Economic Activity,* ed. K. H. Oppenlaender and G. Poser,

Kösters, W. 1986. Das Vollbeschaftigungsziel—eine konzeptionelle Kritik. *Wirtschaftsdienst* 5: 259–64.

Kohler, H., and L. Reyher. 1985. Jahresarbeitszeit und Arbeitsvolumen. *Mitteilungen aus der Arbeitsmarkt- und Berufsforschung* 1: 14–19.

Krelle, W. 1987. Bericht über die Diskussion zum Referat von Wolfgang Franz. In *Arbeitsmärkte und Beschäftigung: Fakten, Analysen, Perspektiven,* ed. G. Bombach, B. Gahlen, and A. E. Ott, 329–30.

Kromphardt, J. 1987. *Arbeitslosigkeit und Inflation: Eine Einführung in die makroökonomischen Kontroversen.* Göttingen/Zürich: Vandenhoeck und Ruprecht.

Krueger, A. B., and L. H. Summers. 1987. Reflections on the Inter-Industry Wage Structure. In *Unemployment and the Structure of Labor Markets,* ed. K. Lang and J. S. Leonard, 17–47.

Kugler, P., U. Müller, and G. Sheldon. 1989. Arbeitsmarktwirkungen moderner Technologien—eine ökonometrische Analyse für die Bundesrepublik Deutschland. In *Technologischer Wandel und Beschäftigung,* ed. R. Schettkat and M. Wagner, 207–34. 1990. The Labor Market Effects of New Technologies—An Econometric Study for the FRG. Schettkat, R., and M. Wagner eds. 191–214.

Kühl, J. 1970. Zum Aussagewert der Statistik der Offenen Stellen. *Mitteilungen aus der Arbeitsmarkt und Berufsforschung* 3: 250–76.

Kühl, J. 1976. Bereitstellung und Besetzung von Arbeitsplätzen. *Mitteilungen aus der Arbeitsmarkt und Berufsforschung* 4: 414–49.

Kühlewind, G. 1988. Erfahrungen mit dem Vorruhestand aus beschäftigungspolitischer Sicht. In *Vorkürzung oder Verlängerung der Erwerbsphase,* ed. W. Schmähl, 54–63.

Kuhn, T. S. 1970. *The Structure of Scientific Revolutions.* Chicago: University of Chicago Press.

Kutscher, R. 1990. Structural Change in the United States, Past and Prospective: Its Implication for Skill and Educational Requirements. In *The Impact of Structural Change and Technological Progress on the Labor Market,* ed. E. Appelbaum and R. Schettkat, 54–74.

Landenberger, M. 1990. *Beschäftigung und Arbeitsmarktpolitik aus der Perspektive der gesetzlichen Rentenversicherung.* Berlin: Sigma.

Lang, K., and J. S. Leonard, eds. 1987. *Unemployment and the Structure of Labor Markets.* New York: Basil Blackwell.

Lawrence, R. Z., and C. L. Schultze, eds. 1987. *Barriers to European Growth.* Washington, D.C.: Brookings.

Layard, R., and L. Calmfors, eds. 1987. *The Fight Against Unemployment.* Cambridge, Mass.: MIT Press.

Leijonhufvud, A. 1967. Keynes and the Keynesians: a suggested interpretation. *American Economic Review* 57: 401–10.

Leipert, C. 1975. *Unzulänglichkeiten des Sozial-roduktes in seiner Eigenschaft als Wohlstandsmass.* Tübingen.

Leithäuser, G. 1988. Crisis Despite Flexibility: The Case of West Germany. In *Labour Flexibility and Employment: Market or Cooperation?* ed. R. Boyer, 171–88.

Leonard, J. S. 1987a. Carrots and Sticks: Pay, Supervision, and Turnover. *Journal of Labor Economics* 5: S136-S152.

Leonard, J. S. 1987b. In the Wrong Place at the Wrong Time. In *Unemployment and the Structure of Labor Markets,* ed. K. Lang and J. S. Leonard, 141–63.

Leonard, J. S., and R. Schettkat. 1991. A Comparison of Job Stability in Germany and the U.S.A. *Labour* 5: 111–23.

Levy, F. 1987. *Dollars and Dreams.* New York: W. W. Norton.

Lilien, D. M. 1982. Sectoral Shifts and Cyclical Unemployment. *Journal of Political Economy* 90: 777–92.

Lilien, D. M., and R. Hall. 1986. Cyclical Fluctuations in the Labor Market. In *Handbook of Labor Economics,* ed. O. Ashenfelter and R. Layard, II: 1001–35.

Lindbeck, A., and D. Snower. 1984. Labour Turnover, Insider Morale and Involuntary Unemployment (Seminar Paper No. 310). Stockholm: Institute for International Economics.

Lindbeck, A., and D. J. Snower. 1985. Explanations of Unemployment. *Oxford Review of Economic Policy* 1: 34–59.

Lindbeck, A., and D. J. Snower. 1986. Changes in Wage Norms: Wage Setting, Unemployment, and Insider-Outsider Relations. *American Economic Review* 76: 235–39.

Lipsey, R. G. 1965. Structural and Deficient-Demand Unemployment Reconsidered. In *Employment Policy and the Labor Market,* ed. R. A. Ross, 210–55.

Lucas, R. E., and E. C. Prescott. 1974. Equilibrium Search and Unemployment. *Journal of Economic Theory* 7: 188–209.

Lutz, B. 1976. Bildungssystem und Beschäftigungsstruktur in Deutschland und Frankreich. Zum Einfluß des Bildungssystems auf die Gestaltung betrieblicher Arbeitskräftestrukturen. In *Betrieb-Arbeitsmarkt-Qualifikation* 1, ed. G. Mendius et al., 83–151.

Lutz, B. 1984. *Der kurze Traum immerwährender Prosperität.* Frankfurt: Campus.

Mahoney, T. 1961. Factors Determining the Labor Force Participation of Married Women. *Industrial Labor Relation Review* 14: 563–77.

Maier, F., and R. Schettkat. 1990. Beschäftigungspotentiale der Arbeitszeitpolitik. *Aus Politik und Zeitgeschichte,* January, 37–51.

Markmann, H., and D. Simmert, eds. 1978. *Krise der Wirtschaftspolitik.* Köln: Bund Verlag.

Marshall, A. 1890. *Principles of Economics*. Reprinted eighth edition, 1979. London/ Basingstoke: Macmillan Press.

Marshall, R. F., and V. M. Briggs. 1989. *Labor Economics: Theory, Institutions, Policy*. 6th ed. Boston: Irwin.

Marston, S. T. 1976. Employment Instability and High Unemployment Rates. *Brookings Papers on Economic Activity* 1: 169–210.

Matzner, E., J. Kregel, and A. Roncaglia, eds. 1987. *Arbeit für alle ist möglich*. Berlin: Sigma.

Matzner, E., and W. Streeck, eds. 1991. *Beyond Keynesianism: The Socio-Economics of Production and Full Employment*. Aldershot: Edward Elgar.

Mayer, H.-L., and H. Wolny. 1980. Amtliches statistisches Grundlagenmaterial für Erwerbspersonenprognosen. *Beiträge zur Arbeitsmarkt- und Berufsforschung* (Nürnberg) 44: 162.

McIntire, R. J. 1984. Comment on Abowd and Zellner (1984). In *Proceedings of the Conference on Gross Flows in Labor Statistics*, ed. BLS, 64–65.

Medoff, J. 1983. U.S. Labor Markets: Imbalance, Wage Growth, and Productivity in the 1970s. *Brookings Papers on Economic Activity* 1: 87–128.

Meidner, R., and A. Hedborg. 1984. *Modell Schweden: Erfahrungen einer Wohlfahrtsgesellschaft*. Frankfurt/New York: Campus.

Mendius, G., et al., eds. 1976. *Betrieb-Arbeitsmarkt-Qualifikation I*. Frankfurt: Aspekte.

Miles, I. 1983. Adaptation to Unemployment? *SPRU Occasional Paper Series*, No. 20, University of Sussex.

Mortensen, D. T. 1986. Job Search and Labor Market Analysis. In *Handbook of Labor Economics*, ed. O. Ashenfelter and R. Layard, 849–919.

Murphy, K. M., and R. Topel. 1986. The Evolution of Unemployment in the United States: 1968–1985. In *NBER Macroeconomic Annual 1986*, ed. S. Fisher, 12–68.

Murphy, K. M., and R. Topel. 1987. Unemployment Risk and Earnings: Testing for Equalizing Wage Differentials in the Labor Market. In *Unemployment and the Structure of Labor Markets*, ed. K. Lang and J. S. Leonard, 103–40.

National Commission on Employment and Unemployment Statistics. 1979. *Counting the Labor Force*. Washington, D.C.: U.S. Government Printing Office.

National Commission on Employment and Unemployment Statistics. 1980. *Data Collection, Processing and Presentation: National and Local*. Washington, D.C.: U.S. Government Printing Office.

NBER, ed. 1966. *The Measurement and Interpretation of Job Vacancies*. New York/ London: Columbia University Press.

Nelson, R. R., and S. G. Winter. 1982. *An Evolutionary Theory of Economic Change*. Cambridge, Mass.: Harvard University Press.

Neubourg, C. de. 1987. *Unemployment, Labour Slack and Labour Market Accounting: Theory, Measurement and Policy*. Groningen: Proefschrift, Rijksuniversiteit te Groningen.

Nevile, J. W. 1979. How Voluntary is Unemployment? Two Views of the Phillips Curve. *Journal of Post-Keynesian Economics* 2: 110–19.

Noll, H.-H. 1984. Arbeitsplatzsuche und Stellenfindung. In R. Hujer, and Knepel H. eds., *Mobilätsprozesse auf den Arberbmarkt*. Frankfurt/New York: Campus.

Obey, D., and P. Sarbanes, eds. 1986. *The Changing American Economy*. New York: Basil Blackwell.

OECD, ed. 1984. *The Nature of Youth Unemployment*. Paris: OECD.

OECD. 1987 and 1989. *Employment Outlook*. Paris: OECD.

OECD. various years. *Labor Force Statistics*. Paris: OECD.

OECD. various years. *National Accounts Statistics*. Paris: OECD.

Oi, W. 1962. Labor as a Quasi Fixed Factor of Production. *Journal of Political Economy* 76: 538–55.

Oppenlander, K. H., and G. Poser, eds. 1986. *Business Cycle Surveys in the Assessment of Economic Activity*. Aldershot: Gower Publishing Co.

Ostermann, P., ed. 1984. *Internal Labor Markets*. Cambridge, Mass.: MIT Press.

Ostleitner, H. 1978. Keynesianische und Keynes'sche Wirtschaftspolitik. In *Krise der Wirtschaftspolitik*, ed. H. Markmann and D. Simmert, 87–96.

OTA (Office of Technology Assessment). 1986. *Technology and Structural Unemployment*. Washington, D.C.: U.S. Government Printing Office.

Parnes, H. S., and R. S. Spitz. 1969. A Conceptual Framework for Studying Labor Mobility. *Monthly Labor Review* 92 (November): 55–58.

Pasinetti, L. 1981. *Structural Change and Economic Growth: A Theoretical Essay on the Dynamics of the Wealth of Nations*. Cambridge: Cambridge University Press.

Pasinetti, L., and R. Scazzieri. 1987. Structural Economic Dynamics. In *The New Palgrave*, ed. J. Eatwell, J. Milgate, and P. Newman, 525–28.

Pencavel, J. H. 1972. Wages, Specific Training, and Labor Turnover in U.S. Manufacturing Industries. *International Economic Review* 13: 53–64.

Perry, G. L. 1972. Unemployment Flows in the U.S. Labor Market. *Brookings Papers on Economic Activity* 2: 245–92.

Peters, A. B., and G. Schmid. 1982. Aggregierte Wirkungsanalyse des arbeitsmarktpolitischen Programms der Bundesregierung für Regionen mit besonderen Beschäftigungsproblemen: Analyse der Beschäftigungswirkungen. *Discussion paper IIM/ LMP 82–32*. Berlin: Wissenschaftszentrum Berlin.

Petit, P. 1990. Structural Change, Information Technology, and Employment: The Case of France. In *The Impact of Structural Change and Technological Progress on the Labor Market*, ed. E. Appelbaum and R. Schettkat, 75–92.

Phelps, E. S. 1970a. Introduction: The New Microeconomics in Employment and Inflation Theory. In *Microeconomic Foundations of Employment and Inflation Theory*, ed. E. S. Phelps et al., 1–23.

Phelps, E. S. 1970b, Money Wage Dynamics and Labor Market Equilibrium. In *Microeconomics Foundations of Employment and Inflation Theory*. ed. E. S. Phelps. 124–66.

Phelps, E. S. et al., eds. 1970. *Microeconomic Foundations of Employment and Inflation Theory*, New York: Norton.

Phillips, A. W. 1958. The Relation between Unemployment and the Rate of Change of Money Wage Rates in the UK, 1861–1957. *Economica* 22: 283–99.

Piore, M. J. 1973. Fragments of a "Sociological" Theory of Wages. *American Economic Review* 63: 377–84.

Piore, M. J. 1979a. Introduction. In *Unemployment and Inflation*, ed. M. J. Piore, xi–xxx.

Piore, M. J., ed. 1979b. *Unemployment and Inflation*. Armonk, N.Y.: Sharpe.

Piore, M. J. 1986. Beyond Social Anarchy. In *The Changing American Economy*, ed. D. Obey and P. Sarbanes, 156–66.

Piore, M. J., and C. Sabel. 1984. *The Second Industrial Divide*. New York: Basic Books.

Pissarides, C. A. 1976. *Labour Market Adjustment*. Cambridge: Cambridge University Press.

Pissarides, C. A. 1978. The Role of Relative Wages and Excess Demand in the Sectoral Flow of Labour. *Review of Economic Studies* 45: 453–67.

Pissarides, C. A. 1981. Contract Theory, Temporary Layoffs and Unemployment: A Critical Assessment. In *Microeconomic Analysis*, ed. D. Curvie, D. Peel, and W. Peters.

Podgursky, M. 1988. Job Displacement and Labor Market Adjustment. In *The Impact of Technological Change on Employment and Economic Growth*, ed. R. M. Cyert and D. C. Mowrey.

Podgursky, M., and P. Swaim. 1987a. Job Displacement and Earnings Loss: Evidence from the Displaced Worker Survey. *Industrial and Labor Relations Review* 41: 17–29.

Podgursky, M., and P. Swaim. 1987b. Duration of Joblessness Following Displacement. *Industrial Relations* 26: 213–26.

Polanyi, K. 1944. *The Great Transformation*. German trans. 1978. Frankfurt: Suhrkamp.

Poterba, J. M., and L. H. Summers. 1984. Adjusting the Gross Change Data: Implications for Labor Market Dynamics. In *Proceedings of the Conference on Gross Flows in Labor Statistics*, ed. BLS, 81–95.

Poterba, J. M., and L. H. Summers. 1986. Reporting Errors and Labor Market Dynamics. *Econometrica* 54: 1319–38.

Price, J. L. 1977. *The Study of Turnover*. Ames, Iowa: Iowa State University Press.

Raff, D. M. G., and L. H. Summers. 1987. Did Henry Ford Pay Efficiency Wages? *Journal of Economics* 5: S57–S86.

Reder, M. W. 1964. Wage Structure and Structural Unemployment. *Review of Economic Studies* 31: 309–22.

Reyher, L., and H. Kohler. 1988. Arbeitszeit und Arbeitsvolumen. *Beiträge zur Arbeitsmarkt- und Berufsforschung* 70: 245–59.

Reyher, L., and H.-U. Bach. 1988. Arbeitskräfte-Gesamtrechnung: Bestände und Bewegungen am Arbeitsmarkt. *Beiträge zur Arbeitsmarkt- und Berufsforschung*. 70: 127.

Riese, M., M. Hutter, and S. Bruckbauer. 1989. *Bewegungsgroessen der oesterreichischen Arbeistlosigkeit im internationalen Vergleich*. Linz: Oesterreichisches Institut für Arbeitsmarktpolitik.

Robinson, J. 1937. *Essays in the Theory of Employment*. New York, cited according to the 2nd edition of 1947, Oxford: Blackwell.

Robinson, J. 1962. *Economic Philosophy*. London, deutsche Übersetzung, Doktrinen der Wirtschaftswissenschaft, 3. Auflage, München: Beck.

Robinson, J. 1973. *Collected Economic Papers*. Oxford: Blackwell.

Rosen, S. 1986. The Theory of Equalizing Differences. In *Handbook of Labor Economics*, ed. O. Ashenfelter and R. Layard.

Rosenberg, N. 1982. *Inside the Black Box*. Cambridge: Cambridge University Press.

Rosenberg, S. 1989. From Segmentation to Flexibility. *Labour and Society* 14: 363–407.

Ross, A. R. 1965. *Employment Policy and the Labor Market.* Berkeley: University of California Press.

Rotemberg, J., and L. Summers. 1988. Labor Hoarding, Inflexible Prices and Procyclical Productivity. *NBER Working Paper Series,* No. 2591.

Rothschild, K. W. 1963. *Lohntheorie.* Berlin and Frankfurt.

Rothschild, K. W. 1978. Arbeitslose: Gibt's Die? *Kyklos* 31: 21–35.

Rothschild, K. W. 1981. *Einführung in die Ungleichgewichtstheorie.* Berlin and Heidelberg: Springer Verlag.

Rothschild, K. W. 1984. Ökonomische Theorie im Wandel. *Wirtschaftsdienst VI,* 303–08.

Rothschild, K. W. 1988a. Mikroökonomische Fundierung, Ad-Hocery und keynesianische Theorie. In *Keynes aus nachkeynescher Sicht,* ed. K. G. Zinn, 107–25.

Rothschild, K. W. 1988b. *Theorien der Arbeitslosigkeit.* München and Wien: Oldenbourg.

Rudolph, H. 1984. Die Entwicklung der Vermittlung in Arbeit. *Mitteilungen aus der Arbeitsmarkt- und Berufsforschung* 17: 168–82.

Rudolph, H. 1986. Die Fluktuation in sozialversicherungspflichtiger Beschäftigung. *Mitteilungen aus der Arbeitsmarkt- und Berufsforschung* (February): 257–70.

Rürup, B. 1989. Lohnpolitische Flexibilisierungsformen im Lichte der Effizienzlohnhypothesen. *Discussion Papers FSI.* Berlin: Wissenschaftszentrum Berlin für Sozialforschung.

Rumberger, R. W. 1981. The changing skill requirements of jobs in the U.S. economy. *Industrial and Labor Relations Review.* Pp. 578–90.

Sachs, J. D. 1983. Real Wages and Unemployment in the OECD Countries. *Brookings Papers on Economic Activity* 1: 255–304.

Sachverständigenrat. 1988/89. *Jahresgutachten 1988/89: Arbeitsplätze im Wettbewerb.* Stuttgart: Kohlhammer.

Salter, W. 1959. Internal and external balance: The role of price expenditure effects. *Economic Review* 35: 226–36.

Salter, W. E. G. 1960. *Productivity and Technical Change.* Cambridge: Cambridge University Press.

Samuelson, P. A., and R. Solow. 1960. Analytical Aspects of Anti-Inflation Policy. *American Economic Review* 40: 177–94.

Sargent, T. 1973. Rational Expectations, the Real Rate of Interest, and the Natural Rate of Unemployment. *Brookings Papers on Economic Activity* 21: 429–72.

Sawyer, M. 1987. The Political Economy of the Phillips' Curve. *Thames Papers in Political Economy.* Thames Polytechnic.

Scharpf, F. W. 1990. Structures of Post-Industrial Society—or Does Mass-Unemployment Disappear in the Service and Information Economy? In *The Impact of Structural Change and Technological Progress on the Labor Market,* ed. E. Appelbaum and R. Schettkat, 17–35.

Schettkat, R. 1984. Generelle Arbeitszeitverkürzung, Gesamtwirtschaftliche Kostenund Beschäftigungswirkungen. *Discussion paper IIM/LMP* 84-2. Berlin: Wissenschaftszentrum Berlin.

Schettkat, R. 1987. *Erwerbsbeteiligung und Politik.* Berlin: Edition Sigma.

Schettkat, R. 1989a. *Innovation und Arbeitsmarktdynamik*. Berlin and New York: De Gruyter.

Schettkat, R. 1989b. The impact of taxes on female labour supply. *International Review of Applied Economics* 3: 1–24.

Schettkat, R., and K. Semlinger. 1982. Der eigenständige Effekt gesundheitlicher Einschränknugen als Vermittlungshemmnis. *Mitteilungen aus der Arbeitsmarkt- und Berufsforschung* 15: 434–42.

Schettkat, R., and M. Wagner. 1989. *Technologischer Wandel und Beschäftigung*. Berlin and New York: De Gruyter.

———. 1990. *New Technologies and Employment Innovation in the German Economy*. Berlin and New York: De Gruyter.

Schlicht, E. 1978. Labour Turnover, Wage Structure, and Natural Unemployment. *Zeitschrift für die gesamte Staatswissenschaft* 134: 337–46.

Schmähl, W., ed. 1988. *Verkürzung oder Verlängerung der Erwerbsphase*. Tübingen.

Schmid, G. 1980. *Strukturierte Arbeitslosigkeit und Arbeitsmarktpolitik*. Königstein: Athenäum.

Schmid, G. 1990. Institutions Regulating the Labor Market: Support or Impediment for Structural Change? In *The Impact of Structural Change and Technological Progress on the Labor Market*, ed. E. Appelbaum and R. Schettkat, 119–43.

Schmid, G., B. Reissert, and G. Bruche. 1987. *Arbeitslosenversicherung und aktive Arbeitsmarktpolitik*. Berlin: Edition Sigma. (Published in English as *Unemployment Insurance and Active Labor Market Policy: An International Comparison*. Detroit: Wayne State University, 1991.)

Scholz, L. et al. 1989. Innovation, Wachstum und Beschäftigung. In *Technologischer Wandel und Beschäftigung*, ed. R. Schettkat and M. Wagner, 147–84.

Schusser, W. H. 1988. Stufenweiser Übergang in den Ruhestand aus der Sicht der betrieblichen Praxis. In *Verkürzung oder Verlängerung der Erwerbphase*, ed. W. Schmähl, 213–24.

Schwartz, A. R., M. S. Cohen, and D. R. Grimes. 1986. Structural/Frictional vs. Deficient Demand Unemployment: Comment. *American Economic Review* 76: 268–72.

Scitovsky, T. 1976. *The Joyless Economy*. Oxford: Oxford University Press.

Semlinger, K. 1989. Vorausschauende Personalwirtschaft—betriebliche Verbreitung und infrastrukturelle Ausstattung. *Mitteilungen aus der Arbeitsmarkt- und Berufsforschung* 22: 336–47.

Semlinger, K. 1990. Personalanpassung und Personalentwicklung in der Deutschen Stahl- und Automobilindustrie. *SAMF Arbeitspapier* 1990–2.

Sengenberger, W. 1984. Zur Flexiblität im Beschäftigungssystem. In *SAMF Arbeitspapier* 1984–3.

Sengenberger, W. 1987. *Struktur und Funktionsweise von Arbeitsmärkten*. Frankfurt and New York: Campus.

Sengenberger, W. 1990. Flexibility in the Labor Market—Internal versus External Adjustment in International Comparison. In *The Impact of Structural Change and Technological Progress on the Labor Market*, ed. E. Appelbaum and R. Schettkat, 144–62.

Shapiro, C., and J. E. Stiglitz. 1984. Equilibrium Unemployment as a Worker Discipline Device. *American Economic Review* 74: 433–44.

Shapiro, G. 1984. Comment on Poterba/Summers (1984). In *Proceedings of the Conference on Gross Flows in Labor Statistics*, ed. BLS, 98–99.

Shapiro, N. 1990. Firms, Markets, and Innovation. Paper presented at the University of Tennessee International Workshop in Post-Keynesian Economics.

Simon, H. A. 1959. Theories of Decision-Making in Economics and Behavioral Science. *American Economic Review.* 49: 253–83.

Smith, J. E., and R. E. Vanski. 1979. Gross Change Data: The Neglected Data Source. National Commission on Employment and Unemployment Statistics. In *Counting the Labor Force,* 132–50.

Solow, R. M. 1979. Another Possible Source of Wage Stickiness. *Journal of Macroeconomics* 1: 79–82.

Solow, R. M. 1985. Unemployment: Getting the Questions Right. *Economica* 53: S23–S34.

Sorge, A., and W. Streeck. 1987. Industrial Relations and Technical Change: The Case for an Extended Perspective. *Discussion paper IIM/LMP* 87-1. Berlin: Wissenschaftszentrum Berlin für Sozialforschung.

Soskice, D. 1990. Skills Mismatch, Training Systems and Equilibrium Unemployment: A Comparative Institutional Analysis. *Conference Paper,* CEPR/CLE/STEP conference in Venice.

Spahn, H.-P. 1986. Sind "effiziente" Löhne zu hoch für die Vollbeschäftigung? *Discussion paper IIM/LMP,* 82-2. Berlin: Wissenschaftszentrum Berlin.

Standing, G. 1983. The notion of structural unemployment. *International Labour Review* 122: 137–53.

Stigler, G. J. 1962. Information in the Labor Market. *Journal of Political Economy* 70: 94–105.

Stille, F. 1990. Structural Change in the Federal Republic of Germany: The Case of Services. In *The Impact of Structural Change and Technological Progress on the Labor Market,* ed. E. Appelbaum and R. Schettkat, 93–118.

Suess, W., and K. Schroeder, eds. 1988. *Technik und Zukunft.* Opladen: Westdeutscher Verlag.

Summers, L. H. 1986. Why Is the Unemployment Rate so very High near Full Employment? *Brookings Papers on Economic Activity* 2: 339–96.

Tarshis, L. 1939. Changes in Real and Money Wages. *Economic Journal.* 49: 150–54.

Thaler, R. H. 1989. Anomalies: Interindustry Wage Differentials. *Journal of Economic Perspectives* 3: 181–93.

Thurow, L. C. 1983. *Dangerous Currents: The State of Economics.* Oxford: Oxford University Press.

Tobin, J. 1972. Inflation and Unemployment. *American Economic Review* 62: 1–18.

Trevithick, J. A. 1976. Money Wage Inflexibility and the Keynesian Labour Supply Function. *Economic Journal* 86: 327–32.

Ulman, L. 1965. Labor Mobility and the Industrial Wage Structure in the Postwar United States. *Quarterly Journal of Economics* 79: 73–97.

Ulman, L. 1989. Labor Market Analysis and Concerted Behavior. *IIR Working Paper Series,* 15. Berkeley: Institute of Industrial Relations, University of California.

Vietorisz, T., and B. Harrison. 1973. Labor Market Segmentation: Positive Feedback and Divergent Development. *American Economic Review* 63: 366–76.

Vogler-Ludwig, K. 1983. *Auswirkungen des Strukturwandels auf den Arbeitsmarkt.* München: ifo.

Vogler-Ludwig, K. 1985. Flexibilisierung der Lohnstrukturen. *ifo-schnelldienst* 16: 18–31.

Wagner, J. 1985. Mangelnde Faktormobilität eine Ursache für Arbeitslosigkeit? *Wirtschaftsdienst* 65: 297–303.

Warnken, J., and G. Ronning. 1989. Technischer Wandel und Beschäftigungsstrukturen. In *Technologischer Wandel und Beschäftigung,* ed. R. Schettkat and M. Wagner, 235–78.

Weißhuhn, G., A. König, K. Sakkas, and J. Seetzen. 1988. Betriebsgrössenspezifische Analyse der Beschäftigung 1980–1986 in der BRD. Final Report. Berlin: Technical University. Federal Ministry for Science and Technology.

Wermter, W. 1981. Die Beschäftigungsstatistik der Bundesanstalt für Arbeit. *Mitteilungen aus der Arbeitsmarkt- und Berufsforschung* 4: 428–35.

Wermter, W., and U. Cramer. 1988. Wie hoch war der Beschäftigtenanstieg seit 1983? *Mitteilungen aus der Arbeitsmarkt- und Berufsforschung* 4: 468–82.

Wicksell, K. 1934. *Lectures on Political Economy,* ed. by L. Robbins. London.

Williamson, J. G. 1991. Productivity and American Leadership: A Review Article. *Journal of Economic Literature* 29: 51–68.

Wohlers, E., and G. Weinert. 1986. *Unterschiede in der Beschäftigungsentwicklung zwischen den USA, Japan und der EG.* Hamburg: Verlag Weltarchiv.

Wolfbein, S. L. 1960. Gross Change in Unemployment, 1957–59. *Monthly Labour Review* (February): 141–44.

Wood, A. 1988. How Much Unemployment is Structural? *Oxford Bulletin of Economics and Statistics* 50: 71–81.

Worswick, G. D. N. 1976. *The Concept and Measurement of Involuntary Unemployment.* London: Allen and Unwin.

Yellen, J. L. 1984. Efficiency Wage Models of Unemployment. *American Economic Review* 74: 200–05.

Yellen, J. L. 1989. Comment on Blanchard/Diamond: "The Beveridge Curve," *Brookings Papers on Economic Activity* 1: 65–71.

Zapf, W. 1979. Die Wohlfahrtsentwicklung in Deutschland seit der Mitte des 19. Jahrhunderts. *SPES Arbeitspapiere,* No. 6. Universität Frankfurt.

Zinn, K. G., ed. 1988. *Keynes aus nachkeynescher Sicht.* Wiesbaden: Deutscher Universitätsverlag.

Name Index

Subject Index

About the Author

RONALD SCHETTKAT is Senior Research Fellow at the Wissenschaftszentrum Berlin. He is a member of the American Council of Learned Societies and has been a visiting scholar at Stanford University, the University of California at Berkeley, and the Netherlands Institute for Advanced Study. He is the coauthor, with Eileen Appelbaum, of *Labor Market Adjustments to Structural Change and Technological Progress* (Praeger, 1990).